# BOTH YOUR HOUSES

*The Truth About Congress*

WARREN WEAVER, JR.

PRAEGER PUBLISHERS

New York · Washington · London

PRAEGER PUBLISHERS
111 Fourth Avenue, New York, N.Y. 10003, U.S.A.
5, Cromwell Place, London SW7 2JL, England

Published in the United States of America in 1972
by Praeger Publishers, Inc.

© 1972 by Warren Weaver, Jr.

Library of Congress Catalog Card Number: 79-126783

Printed in the United States of America

*For my father and mother*

# Contents

# *Preface*

Any reader who approaches this book in search of a definitive, exhaustive academic treatise on Congress had best break off right here. This is not a work of scholarship but an exercise in contemporary journalism. It touches on the informal as well as the official life of Capitol Hill. It is not sustained by a single footnote. It relies on history—the writings of others and the judgments of the past—only when they seem to illuminate directly the problems of the present.

Much of the research that went into the book has been personal and pragmatic, a product of the author's own observations in covering Congress as a newspaper reporter, watching how it works rather than how it is presumed to work, and talking with its members and other concerned onlookers. (It must be said, however, that there are relatively few members of Congress who have the time or the inclination to think very often or very perceptively about the frailties of their own institution.)

There is no pretense here of covering the subject completely; that would require a series of books that would almost certainly go widely unread by the people with a very real need to know what is right and wrong with their national assembly. Instead, I have attempted to concentrate on the most flagrant inadequacies of the legislative branch, to sketch the outlines of a crisis in government, within a volume of reasonable compass. Its limits should not be interpreted as discounting other Hill problems of legitimate concern to other critics.

x  *Preface*

The author owes compound debts of gratitude to many silent partners in this project: to his colleagues on the congressional staff of the *New York Times,* John Finney, Marjorie Hunter, Richard Madden, and David Rosenbaum, for their cooperation and forbearance; to other congressional correspondents for their generous sharing of illustrative anecdotes, particularly Dan Thomasson of the Scripps-Howard newspapers and John Simonds of the Gannett News Service; to his editors at Praeger Publishers, William Weatherby, who launched the project, and Lois Decker O'Neill, who saw it through nobly; to Shannon Griffin, who typed the manuscript with accuracy and éclat; and to his wife and daughters, who gave him both loving encouragement and generous sanctuary during nearly three years of ongoing travail.

All these share in any credit that may attach to the enterprise. For the rest, all mistakes, oversights, misinterpretations, slights, patent libels, and unjustified mockery are the responsibility of the author alone.

*Alexandria, Virginia*
*July, 1972*

# BOTH YOUR HOUSES

# 1 · The Truth About Congress

On the plan for the city of Washington, laid out in the infancy of the Republic, the Capitol was placed unquestioningly in the center, at the heart of the seat of government. L'Enfant, the French architect and surveyor, reserved the modest eminence of Jenkins Heights for the Congress House and then radiated his network of avenues, circles, and parks from that focal point.

Today, the four quadrants of the city converge as inexorably as ever on the great marble monument, the street numbers diminishing and the letters marching backward down the alphabet toward A until, at precise ground zero, a visitor finds the historic building where the people's representatives, in uneasy congress, write the nation's laws.

But, if Washington is the hub of government, Congress is no longer the hub of Washington. History has left it at the center of the great original plan for citizen self-rule, but power and prestige have moved elsewhere. The Capitol is a hall of illusions, peopled by the myths that the legislative branch remains proudly coequal, that Congress continues to serve the nation well, that the old ways are sufficient to the tasks of the new day.

None of this is true. Congress has been reduced over the years from a vigilant, creative partner of the President to a minor consulting agency that must (a great nuisance, really) be cajoled into concurring as to the course of government. Clumsy, unresponsive,

3

controlled in large part by its most ordinary members, the national legislature blunders on, facing nuclear problems with colonial procedures, insisting all the while that nothing is wrong.

In fact, a great many things are very wrong.

Congress today has lost effective control over its single most basic duty, financing the federal government. Without plan or rationale, it reviews small spending decisions haphazardly and ignores big ones. It raises money almost without reference to spending. Sluggish and uncoordinated, it often fails to furnish funds for key segments of the government until their working year is half over.

The Senate and House of Representatives do not work together to make the laws. Undermined by a false sense of superiority on one hand and petty jealousy on the other, the two houses refuse to cooperate at almost any level. Chairmen of parallel committees are often barely on speaking terms. Socially and professionally, the two houses maintain an adversary relationship that is frequently far more bitter than that between the Democrats and Republicans. Sound lawmaking falls in the crossfire.

Broadly speaking, most members of Congress do not have enough relevant information at hand to reach intelligent decisions on the life-or-death, peace-or-war questions that continuously rise before them. Despite available technology that can produce information, both simple and sophisticated, almost upon call, Congress still, incredibly, relies each day upon word of mouth to learn what is happening on the floor—even the rules that apply there.

The basic sources of congressional power are controlled by men whose sole qualification for leadership is survival, chronological and political. No other ability of any kind is ever required to advance toward this influence. Perversely, the system operates so that those who do rise to power are the least likely to be responsive to their constituents, to the leaders of their house and party, to the President, to anyone. This mindless pattern is obstructive to lawmaking and demoralizing to the men and women who want to do it well.

The most important decisions Congress reaches, those determining the final form of any law, are made by a handful of these dubious elders, whose sole qualification is longevity. They are chosen for this assignment arbitrarily, often even dictatorially, and then commissioned to defend a position that they may have worked and voted against until that moment. Because the entire operation is secret and the published results often confusing, the entire procedure has fallen into serious disrepute.

Outworn methods and secret decisions open the door to venality. Members of Congress have been purchased by private interests in the past. They will be again, and in greater numbers, unless the preponderance of honest men are willing to stop pretending that election to the Senate or House is a form of moral absolution. The way to raise the vaporous ethical reputation of the entire institution, demonstrably, is to subject all of its members, good and bad, to some reasonable standards of public conduct. Instead, Congress goes right ahead, self-destructively protecting its own. Betraying deep and well-founded guilt feelings, it conducts at least half its significant deliberations behind closed doors and discourages public attendance at those it opens. Often, it refuses to disclose vital public decisions reached in private or grudgingly opens the door a crack to tell only the most favorable part of the story.

The American people know very well that the health of their national legislature is not good. But they are allowed to perceive few particulars. Congress flatly prohibits them from getting a real picture—literally—of its lawmaking. It bars television and even still photography from the scene of action. And because, over the years, the pencil press has been so carefully assimilated into the Hill establishment that it rarely reports the deep underlying deficiencies of Congress, limiting its comments instead to the facts of the day, my colleagues and I often convey to the public a sense of over-all congressional well-being that is dangerously inaccurate and misleading.

The resulting ignorance damages everyone. An ill-informed public fails to recognize such achievements as Congress is able to gain, leaving the members who have worked to good purpose anonymous and frustrated. Lacking public recognition and often misunderstood if heeded at all, the lawmakers fall farther and farther behind the President in the continuous competition for federal power. The nation gets bad government—clumsy, costly, unresponsive—and is often too poorly informed to realize it.

The problems of governing a nation today are infinitely more complex than they were when the institution called the Congress of the United States was devised, nearly two hundred years ago. Their complexity, as the futurists nervously remind us, is multiplying geometrically, so rapidly that we sometimes seem to be losing sight of the questions, much less the answers. There are men in Washington who recognize both their own shortcomings and the disturbing consequences, real and potential, of the inadequacy and fragility of the machinery they have to use to make the American system of government work. Not many of them are in Congress. In the legislative branch, with desperately few exceptions, the same old complacent, delusory confidence prevails.

It prevails even though Capitol Hill may be one of the few governmental power centers in history in which the Fourth Estate, fulfilling Thomas Carlyle's fancy, is both more numerous and potentially more powerful than the other three combined.

The Constitution does not recognize the First Estate (lords), although some members of the Senate appear otherwise persuaded from time to time. The Second (clergy) gets scant attention, dismissed out of hand after the daily prayer. The Third (commons) numbers 535 sturdy products of the yeomanry. But the Fourth sends nearly 2,400 of its agents to observe and record the movements, public and occasionally private, of the Third.

Currently accredited to cover Congress are some 1,200 newspaper reporters, 500 radio and television correspondents, 500 magazine writers, and 175 still photographers (who, like the TV cameramen, are not allowed to use their equipment on the floor except on certain circumspectly prescribed occasions.) There are hundreds more in Washington who report from the Hill irregularly on temporary passes. Fortunately, of this great regiment of professional voyeurs, only a hundred or two are likely to be on duty in the Capitol on any given day, else the great stone galleries would sink.

The power of this corps derives, of course, from the fact that it provides the only information the great mass of the public ever receives about how the laws are being made. Large numbers of citizens visit the Capitol every day, but mostly for a courtesy or curiosity call. The glimpse they get of the legislative process is fleeting and generally uninviting. They may learn a little more back in their motel rooms, watching the evening television news, and possibly something more than that from their newspapers the next morning.

For the vast majority of Americans, the House and Senate can only be perceived through what are now loftily called the communications media. If the newspapers, radio, and television fail to report an event that took place in Congress, it hasn't happened as far as the public is concerned. Only through the press can the people learn if their rights are being promoted or trampled on. And, finally, only the press can keep Congress honest, or a reasonable facsimile thereof, by telling the truth about it. This is a big job, and it is not being done as well as it should. The reasons are worth examining, not because the Capitol press corps is part of the lawmaking process—it isn't—but because it holds a mirror up to that process. If the mirror is cracked, spotted, fogged, or simply not there when and where the deals are made, so will everyone's view of Congress be faulty.

Reflecting the dominance of the executive branch in the federal power structure, the reporters who cover the White House regard themselves as the elite corps of Washington journalism. Congressional correspondents are not so presumptuous, preferring to consider themselves merely as "specialists." But this self-limiting self-evaluation has its hazards, too. A sharp focus on the relatively restricted area of the Hill tends to blur the rest of the picture. Close to his own branch, the legislative correspondent too often operates from a position of splendid isolation with respect to the rest of the government. He reports a floor debate over a major new weapon and faithfully records the words of those who defend it, but he rarely tries to seek out the full Pentagon position. His international emphasis is on the challenge that the Senate Foreign Relations Committee is making at the moment, with the State Department's views likely to get secondary attention. (Reporters at Defense and State may write a balancing story the next day, but readers may not see or bother to read the follow-up version.) This problem is natural and sometimes unavoidable for reasons of time alone, but too few reporters in the Capitol press gallery are aware of it and work continuously for balance.

The Hill press corps so emphasizes specialization that it comes complete with an information gap between Senate reporters and House reporters, which accurately mirrors the segregation of the two houses but further distorts the picture for the public. Several papers and both wire services divide their personnel into separate Senate and House staffs, and the communication between them is often less than perfect. In the days when the *New York Times* used such a system, one Senate reporter described in his story events he had witnessed in the chamber and then began a new paragraph: "Meanwhile, there were reports from the House that . . ."—unverified rumors from an unreachable land.

There is a considerable amount of "pack reporting"—joint pursuit of the news source of the moment by a cluster of cooperating reporters—conducted out of the Senate and House press galleries. These expeditions are sometimes promoted by newsmen from lesser-known publications who might not be able single-handed to reach the senator in question but cannot fail in combination with a prestige journal or two; perfectly reasonably, such promoters would rather share their information with other reporters than get none at all.

Individual competitive effort has always produced the best journalism, and it generally does in Congress. Quality congressional reporting is done by the men and women who can interpret a committee chairman's answers rather than merely quote them, who form solid contacts at the staff level where information is anonymous but authoritative, who find unanswered questions in the handout and get the answers. It is even possible to steal an exclusive story from the competition by paying strict attention to Senate debate, which is normally so uneventful that when something *does* happen, say a floor compromise on a spending figure, it occasionally eludes the bemused wire service reporters, who read newspapers and solve puzzles as they sit above the rostrum in the nearly empty press gallery hour after dreary hour. It is only fair to note that John Finney of the *New York Times* can get firsthand access to a newsworthy senator more consistently than can J. D. Scribble of the Smallsville *Clarion-Call*. A good part of the reason is that Finney has worked over the years to establish personal relations with the important men he covers and has won their respect by his reporting. Another part, however, involves the senators' desire to cooperate with a newspaper that is widely and closely read by influential Washington. The cachet of the *Times* or the *Washington Post* cannot save a bad reporter, but it can certainly help a good one.

There is an almost continuous undercurrent of criticism within Congress that press coverage is superficial and too dependent on handouts—mimeographed statements or speech texts that individual members send to the press galleries. (The handout is far from a foolproof guarantee of publicity, but it is less embarrassing than calling a news conference that no one attends or waiting, unasked, for an invitation to comment.) Such criticism usually emanates from a member whose handouts are widely ignored or from his press secretary, who gets blamed for it. But sometimes it is also echoed by serious lawmakers who would like to see broader, better-informed coverage of Congress.

A few years ago, in his book *House Out of Order*, Representative Richard Bolling of Missouri wrote, "A House member whose travels consist of a triangular course between West Wetdrip, Washington, and the Army-Navy game in Philadelphia can make the news with outrageous remarks about our foreign aid program simply by getting a press handout to the gallery early in the morning." There is still more truth in this charge than there should be. When a major subject is on top of the news—a Presidential announcement, a political bombshell, or a catastrophe—and the wire services are hurrying to assemble a reaction story (at any given moment, a paper somewhere is on deadline), any provocative comment from a member of Congress is likely to get scooped up and given a sentence or two. This, in turn, can influence the stories written by the "specials," reporters who write on a more leisurely basis for a single paper. They can and do omit purely publicity-seeking comment from their stories. But the message often comes back from an editor in the home office: "Why don't we have AP's Senator Backbite comment comparing President's statement to Halley's Comet?" Or, worse, "We are inserting Backbite comment in your story." Or, worst of all, the reporter picks up his paper the next morning to find the immortal Backbite quote prominently displayed under his by-line, written in his office without his knowledge, much less permission.

In the days of Senator Joseph McCarthy and Representative

Parnell Thomas of the House Un-American Activities Committee, the congressional press corps was often accused of sensationalism. Its stories reflected the sort of wild-swinging, publicity-hungry
men influential on the Hill during that era, who used as their
weapon the "leak," an unofficial but presumably authoritative
piece of information given privately to one reporter, attributable
only to vague "sources," and usually a prediction of sensational
future developments. Some of these leaks were merely exag-
gerated build-ups for witnesses who later did appear before the
Un-American Committee, but others produced never-to-be-con-
firmed stories that Scientist X was stealing atomic secrets and that
the committee had Mussolini's mistress under surveillance. Finally, for their own protection and that of their readers, the Associated Press, United Press, and International News Service made
an informal compact to confine their stories strictly to the committee's hearings and official reports.

The scarcity of complaints about sensationalism today is a re-
flection of both the decline in the number of demagogues in Congress and the increase in press reluctance to give space to a member whose electrifying charges may or may not turn out to be
true. If anything, the news report from Capitol Hill is now probably too homogenized, with much the same information appearing in all stories from the wire services and newspapers and with
differences largely confined to style and emphasis.

A good deal of this sameness is inescapable. Congress is a highly
structured system—whatever you may think of the structure—
and reporting on its activities is subject to the restrictions of the
system. For example, virtually all the decision-making sessions
that are not public are held at an announced time and place,
political conferences as well as closed committee meetings. Thus,
reporters are on notice and simply show up, usually in some numbers, outside the closed door to await a report on what happened
inside. Once in a great while, a reporter may find himself alone on
the scene when a committee reports an important bill, but others
always pick up the information later. Also, because of the way the
news is breaking, there are usually, on any day, a number of newspapermen looking for the same senator to ask him the same questions on the same subject, then to write roughly the same story.

Given this situation, a man who misses one of the innumerable daily corridor press conferences can always get a "fill" from a colleague—a repetition of the questions and answers. The hand-out system also tends to ensure that all reporters, the least as well as the most enterprising, have much the same information available. This practice promotes the cause of public information as well as congressional publicity but does not tend to encourage aggressive independent coverage.

The most serious problem in congressional reporting today derives not from the sameness of the stories produced, however, but from the tendency of a number of the men and women assigned to the Hill to regard their work and, ultimately, themselves as part of the institution. (This kind of identification may be easier for women journalists to resist, because the female senators and representatives themselves have never really been admitted to full membership in the establishment and also because, below the elective level, Congress is highly unliberated, preferring to confine its women to one of their two traditional roles: sex object or loyal drudge.)

Consciously or not, Congress officially encourages institutional reporting. It provides, at no cost whatsoever to the profit-making companies that benefit, a group of workrooms behind the press gallery in each chamber, equipped with desks, typewriters, banks of telephones, filing cabinets, and couches for relaxing. It employs a gallery staff of a half-dozen for each house to keep a running log of sessions, receive press releases, run a telephone, page, and message service, supply bills and reports, and generally accommodate the press.

Small wonder reporters come to feel themselves adjuncts rather than critical observers of the congressional process. They have daily access to the Senate leaders on the floor and to the Speaker of the House in his office just before each session opens. During the session, they can dispatch a page to get any senator off the floor for an interview in the nearby President's Room. (Senators, of course, may decline to cooperate. Barry Goldwater, back in the Senate after his ordeal of 1964, refused upon occasion to leave the floor to talk with anyone from the *Washington Post*, a journal too liberal for his tastes.) In the House, the entire lobby is open to accredited members of the press, who can similarly summon members off the floor and question them there. The two wire services, the Associated Press and United Press International, have actually been granted "seats" on the floor, which means that each can send one man into the chamber at any time, usually for a quick interview with one of the leaders on the upcoming schedule.

For many years, the weekly rite at which institutional reporters renewed their fealty to the Senate was the gallery news conference held by Everett McKinley Dirksen, the Republican floor leader. Each Tuesday afternoon following the Republican policy meeting, Senator Dirksen entertained in his grandiloquent and sonorous style while newsmen lit his cigarettes, called him "Ev," and roared reflexively at his sallies, but rarely found out much of anything. Jack Germond, the caustic bureau chief of the Gannett News Service, once described these audiences as "casting imitation pearls before real swine."

The institutional Senate reporter probably reached his dubious pinnacle in William White, now a conservative columnist. In his book *Citadel*, written while reporting for the *New York Times*, White refers to the Senate reverently throughout as the "Institution" and clearly implies that his ideal "Senate man," a strong, proud, and careful traditionalist, can in some cases be a newspaperman as well as a member. Understandably, White had few if any suggestions for improving the Senate.

Institutional reporting has its advantages—members are more cooperative with reporters whom they come to sense as acolytes of the establishment—but the pitfalls are deep and dangerous. A reporter who has been admitted into the inner circle, or even allowed to peep in occasionally from the edge, is likely to be protective of the man who admitted him and of those observed there. Protecting in print a source of important information through anonymity is one thing, but withholding important information because it involves a valued source is another.

More serious, if less conspicuous, the institutional reporter tends to accept the whole congressional establishment as it stands and to pass that acceptance on to his readers or viewers. There is rarely even any inference in his copy that there might be a better way to make laws than the closed rule and the filibuster, that an appropriation bill is five months past deadline, that a committee chairman is gently sliding from seniority into senility. Often this kind of correspondent, to quote Representative Bolling again, "regards the House and Senate as hallowed legislative museums rather than as viable organs of government to which major problems are brought for resolution. The emphasis on form rather than content favors the entrenched powers and gives the American people a false sense of security about their national assembly."

It is easy and natural to operate within the system when you share the same professional concerns and working space all day, every day. Even the most independent and cynical reporters can gradually become institutional as the years slip by and one Congress melts into the next. And, to a very real extent, this passive accommodation by the press has permitted Congress to continue its inefficient, outmoded, undemocratic operation right up to the peril point.

Reporters have it in their power to do something to break the pattern. Sometimes, the addition of a single sentence to a news story can lift it out of the class of institutional, all-is-well reporting. "No more than five senators were on the floor during the debate." "The committee spent two months drafting the bill in closed session, but none of its decisions were announced until today." "The three-week filibuster has kept all other business from the Senate floor, including . . ." "Senator Bollweevil became chairman today because he had served on the committee longest; by Senate tradition his colleagues could choose no one else." Sometimes these small gifts of insight are given the reader. Too often, they are not.

Newspapers also can help break the pattern by rotating assignments to Congress and other locations and by sending specialists in areas of knowledge (economics, agriculture, foreign affairs) to the Hill to cover legislation on their specialty. Unfortunately, only larger news organizations have the manpower to employ such specialists, and too many that do don't use them on the Hill enough. But any news organization can limit its congressional correspondent's tour of duty, perhaps to two or three years, as a foreign correspondent's normally is. Readers would thereby enjoy the benefit of a fresh eye and a questioning, critical attitude. True, each new man has to work to build up the contacts his predecessor took away with him, but on balance it is worth it, as it is worth it to send the science or economic writer to the Hill occasionally. Not only does he bring more expertise than the average gallery hand, but he, too, tends to look on the process with the unclouded eye of an outsider, which is generally a good thing (the only danger being that the visitor will accept rather than report curious procedures when told, "This is the way they always do that").

It is interesting and possibly significant that the prestige institution of Washington journalism, the Gridiron Club, has almost the same hierarchical structure as Congress itself. Limited to fifty members, it fills its vacancies by what amounts to the seniority system, electing almost exclusively men who have been in Washington long enough to become bureau chiefs of their respective newspapers, by and large the elders of the tribe. In a one- or two-man bureau, of which there are many, it is easy to build impressive tenure as a bureau chief, and many Gridiron Club members are distinguished more by job-holding tenacity than by reporting ability. The club is an anachronism whose only function, an annual dinner with musical skits, is conducted in white tie and tails. It does not admit women to its dinner—or did not until 1972—or its membership. It does not include any radio or television journalists. It has never had a black member, although one is under consideration as this is written. It does not currently have any members under forty, and the average age is right up there with congressional committee chairmen. As might be expected, the presidency of the Gridiron also follows strict seniority lines, being passed on yearly to the man with the next longest service, without any nonsense about distinction in his trade.

A recently elected member observed, "I'm forty-ninth in seniority, but with a good cold snap I could be twentieth." The Gridiron Club would be harmless enough if it were recognized for what it is: a self-perpetuating body of old newspapermen, based on mutual esteem and survivorship rather than distinguished professional achievement. Unfortunately, too many people in official Washington dimly regard it as important, as representative of the capital press corps at its best, the journalistic component of the establishment. It is not, and appears unlikely ever to be, any of these things. Perhaps a federal city that reveres in its Congress the overriding virtue of longevity deserves just this kind of newspapermen's organization.

There are some first-class reporters in the club, but, like able committee chairmen on the Hill, they were chosen not for excellence but for their position in a rigid and artificial seniority structure.

Television has had a hard time covering Congress, and there is no sign that the situation is about to improve. Television's basic problem is absurdly simple: It is denied physical access to the place where it all ultimately happens, the floor of Congress. The camera is not permitted to do the one thing it does best: observe action. Instead, it must observe people talking about offstage action, like the battles in Shakespearean histories. Sometimes, the person talking is a recent participant in the battle, a member who has withdrawn from the arena long enough to give his version of the heroics to the television audience. Other times, it is a nonparticipant, the television reporter, describing the fierce combat he has seen. Either is a poor substitute for actuality.

The Columbia Broadcasting System rendered a great public service with its nightly accounts of the civil rights filibuster of 1964, with Roger Mudd rampant against the Capitol dome, rain or shine, describing the day's developments. This was enterprising journalism, but it wasn't good television. Mudd's commentary, incisive as it was, could have been delivered on radio, or even printed in the newspapers, without losing much impact. Had CBS been able to fill its screen instead with news film of the Senate in action—or inaction—other media would have been hard pressed to compete. (The long-running story had at least a salutary side effect for Mudd. It produced so much overtime that he was able to build a new wing on his house.)

Under present rules, television is allowed the same access to committee proceedings as the pencil press: It may photograph any or all of the open hearings at which witnesses contribute their views on legislation (the Senate has allowed this for twenty years; the House, only since 1971), but, when the committee goes into executive session to draft the bill, or a bill goes to a conference committee of both houses, the TV newsmen must wait outside in the corridor. The floors of both houses, where the news is ultimately made, are, however, strictly off limits for the television cameras, as they are to any still photographer, amateur or professional. (All tourists are required to leave their cameras at a checking station before being ushered into the galleries.)

"When a man has to run for reelection every two years," Speaker of the House Sam Rayburn observed in the early days of television, "the temptation to make headlines is strong enough without giving him a chance to become an actor on television. The normal processes toward good law are not even dramatic, let alone sensational enough to be aired across the land."

Speaker Rayburn had a point, of course. Moreover, to preserve the scene of lawmaking as a sort of privileged sanctuary is probably not a bad idea in terms of decorum and freedom from distraction. Unfortunately, serious disadvantages outweigh the advantages involved in protecting from the camera's eye the public's elected representatives. Newspaper and magazine writers rarely provide any picture of the Senate or House, as opposed to a summary of events taking place there. If something is happening, they write about it; if little is happening, they ignore the entire scene. The net result, with all photography banned, is that citizens never really get the picture at all. They have no notion of how poorly attended the sessions are, of how dreary debate has become, of how much time is wasted, indeed, of the quality of the men they have elected. And this is precisely the way Congress prefers it.

There could be no greater force for change in the old, outmoded, protected congressional system than the live broadcasting of regular sessions of the Senate and House over educational television. Even with the relatively limited audience that these channels command, it seems almost certain that the public would rise up and inquire if this is any way to run a Congress. School children would ask their parents if this is really how laws are made, and parents would tune in with spreading bewilderment. Squadrons of new congressional candidates would step forward, with the improvement of the system their burning issue.

But such agitation is not the most important reason for admitting television to the Senate and House chambers. The basic reason is that the public is entitled to free and open examination of the lawmaking process it sustains. There is no distinction in principle between admitting a taxpaying voter to the visitors' gallery or an accredited reporter to the press gallery and permitting all the voters in the country to watch from the great gallery that television could so easily provide. No distinction whatsoever.

It is perfectly true that the introduction of a single television camera into the Senate or House would raise a host of practical, political, and even parliamentary problems that do not now exist. But none of these are so large that they should be allowed to interfere with the basic right of the people's access to Congress. All arguments to the contrary ultimately resolve themselves into the contention that Congress would operate better if fewer rather than more of the people who finance the enterprise knew what was going on—a premise that is insupportable on the face of it.

The stock objection to television is that it would turn the deliberations of Congress into a sort of theatrical free-for-all, with members competing for public attention rather than tending to business. A certain amount of this would probably prove inescapable, what with the natural kinship between politics and the stage. But the first few defeats at the polls of men who had obviously been more interested in showboating than legislating would create a natural damper.

Given the sort of searching exposure that television could provide, the voters would have a much sounder basis for discerning judgment in filling Senate and House seats than they do now. And anyone who contends that the voters are not capable of distinguishing between a ham actor and a solid citizen is not questioning the utility of television but denying one of the premises of the entire democratic system.

As a practical matter, it would be very unlikely that all floor sessions would be on continuous electronic display every day. On days when the news warranted, educational television could run substantial segments live, switching from House to Senate and back as events developed. The commercial networks would only want to undertake live coverage on special occasions, when a major debate or a decisive vote was scheduled. But the networks could monitor any or all sessions and record for their regular news shows film clips of floor developments that were not important enough for live coverage. To keep congressional self-consciousness from fluctuating wildly, as well as ensure complete coverage, it would probably be necessary to have cameras running continuously in both chambers, on a pooled basis. There would be no need—and no room—for competitive network camera crews shooting the same scene simultaneously. Three or four cameras could cover each chamber from fixed, concealed locations, and any network could switch from one picture to another—or to a camera in the other house or to its congressional commentator—as it saw fit.

Imagine the possibilities. Midway through Tuesday afternoon's episode of "Secret Storm," a voice interjects, "We interrupt this program to take you to the Senate floor, where debate is closing before the final vote on the consumer protection bill." Will the housewives impatiently switch channels to "Another World"? Well, some of them will, but a portion won't, and that portion may gradually increase. We cannot expect that special events coverage of congressional highlights will ever rival the moon landings, but it cannot help but bring the processes of government closer to millions of Americans and, in turn, compel improvements in those same processes.

There would undoubtedly be some accompanying procedural changes. Both houses would probably want to restructure their debate format somewhat to ensure closing arguments of substance by the major members involved; too often now, the discussion just before the roll call is drab and listless, the least rather than the most significant. But nothing would prevent a network from selective replay of some earlier speeches of merit and color.

The implicit political problems are serious. Before the House admitted television to its committee hearings in 1971, it flatly prohibited the use of any tape or film shot there "as partisan political campaign material to promote or oppose the candidacy of any person for elective public office." Network policy already reflected this concern by barring the gift or sale of any recording to any candidate on the reasonable theory that any such transaction would be open to criticism as either punitive overcharging or favoritism, depending on your political viewpoint.

But this is not a simple question. On one hand, it would not seem too demanding to require that a member of Congress comport himself in public so that no film of his behavior could be used against him in a campaign, and let him take the consequences if he does not. On the other hand, making recordings of Senate and House sessions available politically to the members would almost certainly give birth each election year to the staging of a rash of minidocumentaries on the floor, each a one-minute capsule of The Crusading Congressman in Action by every incumbent, efforts that would clog up the legislative process, even without retakes. But would the political use of segments of hearings or floor debate really be any different in principle from the circulation by a member of reprints of a section of the *Congressional Record* in which he appears favorably, rendering a stirring speech that may never actually have been delivered? Different from circulating reprints of newspaper accounts? Or simply more effective?

Such matters aside, the first thing to do to spread the truth about Congress is let television in. If the members' approval can only be won by limiting the amount of broadcast time and subsequent use of the film, so be it. Once the principle is established, these and other practical and technical problems can be worked out in the light of actual experience. So can a shared-cost formula involving the networks, educational television, and Congress itself. Twenty years of televising Senate committee hearings has produced some good news copy, public enlightenment, and very few circuses. All of the senators have learned to live with television, and some of the brighter ones have learned to use it skillfully to augment their personal publicity. (Senator William Proxmire of Wisconsin has become a master of the catch-all question: "Mr. Secretary, aren't you really telling us that . . ." and then scooping up all the news bits into one very filmable query, to

which the witness can only respond, "That's right, Senator.")
There is precious little evidence that the introduction of the
camera eye into Senate hearings has done any violence to the
parliamentary system or promoted grandstanding to the extent
that it obstructs lawmaking. As a newspaperman, I have come
to believe that my competitors in television are restricted in large
part because Congress is afraid to let the public see it at work.
The safe, comfortable world of Capitol Hill would never be the
same again. And about time.

No discussion of reporting on the Hill can ignore the ultimate
report itself, the *Congressional Record.* Mechanically alone, it is
an impressive project. Early every morning in every member's
office the *Record* arrives from the Government Printing Office, a
complete transcript of every word spoken and every action taken
the day before in each chamber, plus a good many words not
spoken at all, and great, clotted masses of explanatory tables and
texts of supporting documents. On an average day, it will run a
good 250 pages.

Producing the *Record* is very nearly a round-the-clock operation. From the moment the Senate and House convene, a rotating squad of stenographers takes down every word spoken and
transcribes it almost immediately into a typescript. Reporters who
have missed a key speech or want to check an important quote
can ordinarily do so about a half-hour after the speech was made.
Then, before publication, every member who spoke on the floor
has an opportunity to edit what he actually said into what he
wishes he had said.

As a result, for all its speed and comprehensiveness, the *Record*
is not at all what most people believe it to be: a verbatim transcript of Senate and House debate. It is, in fact, another example
of how Congress is reluctant to let the public know what is really
going on in the Capitol, as opposed to what Congress would like
the public to *think* is going on. For a commonplace (but entirely
typical) example, take a floor speech by Representative Carl Perkins, chairman of the House Education and Labor Committee,
during debate on health standards in the 1969 mine safety bill.

Perkins actually said:

We are going to have a greater responsibility. The Secretary of HEW, in arriving at what is a just and fair health standard, is going to consult with all interested parties. He will not be under the political pressure the Secretary of the Interior may be under. He has his own expertise, and it is much better to leave the health standards—that function—with the Secretary of HEW than it is to try to give the final say-so over health standards to the Secretary of the Interior. I say that would be a bad mistake.

But the next morning the Record reported that Perkins had said:

We can expect better results without a diffusion of responsibility. The Secretary of HEW, in arriving at what are just and fair health standards, is certainly going to consult with all interested parties. He will have resources and facilities not now available to the Secretary of the Interior.

This pseudo-quotation is not radically different in meaning from the verbatim one—although it omits the imputation of political influence in the Department of the Interior. What is wrong is that it is not what Perkins said, not at all. And, unless an exceptionally sharp-eared, fast-moving, and accurate newspaper reporter happened to take down the first quote from the gallery, the second version is the only one on record anywhere. If the Secretary of the Interior telephoned the chairman the next day to ask whether he had been accused of susceptibility to political pressure, Perkins could deny everything and point to the *Record*.

During a school desegregation debate in 1971, Senator Abraham Ribicoff of Connecticut accused Senator Jacob Javits of New York of "hypocrisy" and charged that the Republican was "unwilling to accept desegregation for his state, but he is willing to shove it down the throats of the senators from Mississippi." Neither of these statements appeared in the *Record* the next day, as Javits duly noted. What did appear was a sanitized version of what, according to David Rosenbaum's account in the *New York Times*, Ribicoff had told Javits directly: "I don't think you have the guts to face your liberal constituents who have moved to the suburbs to avoid sending their children to school with blacks." The *Record*'s substitution read, "The question is whether northern Senators have the guts to face their liberal white constituents who have fled to the suburbs for the sole purpose of avoiding having their sons and daughters go to school with blacks."

Save for a handful of episodic newspaper clippings, the *Congressional Record* is the only document that historians, political scientists, and other scholars have to work from. Because the members are permitted to rewrite any and all of their floor remarks as extensively as they please, the result is a denatured version of history, synthetic at best and willfully deceptive at worst. The official sanction for this dubious practice of revising the *Record* is a motion, automatically made and approved after passage of every debated bill, that members be allowed a period of time "to revise and extend their remarks." Originally designed only to permit correction of bad grammar, it was soon stretched to cover much more extensive revision, including actual cuts, as well as insertion in the *Record* of the undelivered last half of a long speech and, finally, all of a speech whose total previous public exposure may have involved only the staff aide who wrote it and the secretary who typed it up.

Inserting documents in the *Record* can be hazardous. Senator Ralph Tyler Smith of Illinois, who served almost imperceptibly between the death of Everett McKinley Dirksen and the election of Adlai Stevenson, had a colleague put in the *Record* a whole sheaf of material on agriculture. Among the documents, it was discovered the next morning, when the *Record* appeared, was a private memo calling the Agriculture Committee chairman, Senator Allen Ellender, "obstructionist" and "obstreperous" among other things. Fortunately for Senate good-fellowship, Smith was retired by the voters shortly thereafter.

The insertion in the *Record* of undelivered speeches, along with newspaper and magazine articles and almost anything else reducible to print, gained popularity in the mid 1800's and has proceeded apace ever since. In 1920, Speaker Champ Clark considered barring the printing of speeches that had never been given but finally decided against it. "I concluded," he said, "that it was preferable to let them be printed rather than be compelled to listen to them."

Reforms in this area have been less than sweeping or precipitous. It was not until 1945 that Speaker Rayburn ordered an end to the practice under which members could insert "(Applause)" and "(Laughter)" at appropriate intervals in speeches they had never delivered at all. Aside from such mirthful deception, costly abuse of the insertion privilege does not seem to have slackened. In the first six months of 1969 alone, Representative John Rarick of Louisiana, a sophomore of almost unbelievable presumption, filled 572 pages of the *Congressional Record* with inserted material, at a cost to the taxpayers of over $68,000.

Such an expensive display would scarcely seem worthwhile in terms of circulation, because the *Record* only prints some fifty thousand copies a day, about the same as a small-city daily newspaper. (Beyond Capitol Hill, the subscribers are largely newspapers, libraries, colleges, and universities.) But, having put some words of his own or someone else's into the *Record* at no cost at all, a senator or representative can then have them reprinted for a token fee because the basic cost—setting the type—has already been met at government expense.

Thus, when Senator Jacob Javits wants to issue an annual report to his New York constituents on the accomplishments of Congress and, just incidentally, himself, he writes it all up and inserts it in the *Record*. Then he can buy 1.5 million four-page reprints for about $7,500, a substantial sum of money but less than a fifth of what the job would cost on the commercial market. Such reports are a legitimate service to the voters, and the Javits version contains far more information than promotion. But this remains a very inexpensive communication channel that no Javits opponent will ever be able to tap—unless the laws are changed.

To raise a minor but irritating point, why is the transcript on which the *Congressional Record* is based taken down by hand and then read into dictaphones? In the House, which has had a sound system for more than thirty years, the stenographers can sit at a table below the rostrum, but in the Senate they must scurry about the chamber, pursuing the debate from desk to desk. (The Senate finally acquired a sound system in 1971, but many members have not yet learned to—or won't—don their lapel microphones when they speak.)

Why aren't the proceedings of both houses recorded on tape,

with two or even three machines always running to protect against mechanical failure? One tape watcher and changer could replace at least half of the harried Dickensian stenographers while the rest worked quietly off the floor, transcribing from an incontrovertibly accurate record. Why isn't this the system? The standard congressional answer, "because it's always been done the other way," omits admitting that a change would lop off a few patronage jobs and weaken the editing member's excuse that the stenographer had not actually caught what he said. First-class equipment exists to do this job and has for years, both at the recording and transcribing ends. If the senators learned that the price of inaudibility was losing space in the *Record*, they and their microphones would become inseparable, and the press and public in the gallery would profit accordingly. It is simply one more piece of evidence that Congress stubbornly refuses to vacate the quill-pen-and-snuffbox era, no matter how simple and obvious and beneficial a change may be. In this case, the refusal does not have a serious adverse effect. It is just typically, symbolically discouraging.

The *Congressional Record* itself is a vital and essential document. But think how much more serviceable it could be if it were a really accurate account of the Senate and House proceedings, if extraneous, though valuable, material were separated and clearly identified as such, if each member's reprint material did not have to be included, if the real story were laid out there for all to read. When educational television sends the sessions into every home and taproom, it will no longer be possible to pass off a sanitized, noncontroversial version of what Congress does as the real thing. Why not start printing the real *Record* now?

# 2 · Senate Is a Four-Letter Word

"On entering the House of Representatives at Washington," Alexis de Tocqueville wrote in 1831, "one is struck with the vulgar demeanor of that great assembly. The eye frequently does not discover a man of celebrity within its walls. Its members are almost all obscure individuals, whose names present no associations to the mind; they are mostly village lawyers, men in trade or even persons belonging to the lower classes of society. . . .

"The Senate," the French politician observed by way of contrast, "is composed of eloquent advocates, distinguished generals, wise magistrates and statesmen of note, whose language would at all times do honor to the most remarkable parliamentary debates of Europe."

To listen to the members of both houses nearly a century and a half later, you might think they had all been reading de Tocqueville's pointed review and that most of them, secretly or openly, regarded it as currently accurate. For Congress, along with its other manifold problems, suffers from an immature sort of internal class distinction such as the rest of the country has largely succeeded in outgrowing. If the rest of the country were aware of the ludicrous heights to which this rivalry is taken, it would rightly protest that such childishness seriously interferes with important business.

There are two distinct classes of citizens in Congress, senators and representatives, and neither makes the mistake of regarding them as equal. Even the most open-minded, egalitarian senator is constantly aware that he is a member of the elite, a smaller and thus theoretically more select body. He and his colleagues sustain this view by ignoring the House—its members, its leaders, its views, and its actions—except when absolutely necessary, as at a joint session or in conference.

This separatist policy is relatively easy for senators who never served in the House, who made the long political jump directly from state office or private life. From time to time, these men are approached, usually with some forelock tugging, by representatives from their home state on matters of patronage or co-sponsorship of bills. But the House as a whole is conveniently outside the range of their vision, rather like a slum section of town through which one does not choose to drive.

It is somewhat harder for a former representative to remain aloof. One who has been offered the prize that all secretly covet —a Senate nomination—and then won his race has known the role of peasant, and, for the first few months, the lord's robe hangs uncomfortably about his shoulders. But, in many cases, such a new senator has served fewer than a half-dozen terms in the House, and his loyalty there has not hardened permanently; a representative with more service than that is reluctant to risk his seniority stake, even for the glimmering majesty of a Senate seat.

What makes the arrangement work is a strict system of segregation—separate and more or less equal facilities. The two houses never meet together except for ceremonial functions, at which they provide collective scenery. They do not eat together. They have separate barber shops and gyms. They drink together only when accidentally brushing elbows at cocktail parties.

House members are occasionally brash enough to request the right to testify at Senate hearings but senators never lower themselves to appear at the comparable House functions. "I would never go to the House to testify unless I was specifically requested," one senator said. "We think nothing of a member of Congress coming over here to testify. He is treated very kindly and courteously. But if we go over there, we are viewed with jealousy and suspicion." A handful of the courteous and the jealous serve together on eight joint congressional committees, only half of them of any consequence, but these committees are officially sterile, denied the power to originate legislation. Seemingly whenever possible, the two houses give identical committees different names and call their officials by different titles, proud of their refusal to consult and conform. (Carrying out this stubborn independence to the ultimate, the running gin rummy game in the House press gallery has somewhat different rules from the Senate counterpart; in the House they play a shorter, 100-point game, and the stakes are lower.)

For many years, the Senate itself was believed to have two classes of members: an inner circle known to outsiders but probably no one else as the "club" and the rest of the Senators, who were presumed to be yearning centripetally to move into this select group. The heart of the club was always the hard core of long-term Southerners; as power has slowly sifted from their hands, it has become harder and harder to distinguish any elite squadron among the Senators. An unconscious sort of civil rights movement opened the club to all members, whereupon, having no further function, it vanished.

Most of the occupants of the Capitol's southern chamber suffer from a massive institutional inferiority complex, for which they attempt to compensate by insisting loudly that they are at least as good as the superficial Senate snobs—*better* if you really come down to it. As a class, representatives tend to be political Texans: They are secretly fearful, sometimes incorrectly, that they do not measure up, so they proclaim, frequently and loudly, that they damn well do. Often they are not believed, by their audience or themselves.

Naturally enough, this defensive attitude tends to be strongest in the men and women who have decided to make the House their career. For them, the opportunity to move toward higher office, governor or senator, never opened at the right time. From the high ground of accumulating seniority, they can see ahead the prospect of real influence where they are. They must believe that the House performs serious, significant service. They do believe it. They are right. But they sometimes overstate their case.

House status resentment feeds on the repeated claims of Senate-worshipers, not excluding members, that the more exclusive house is, and of right ought to be, aloof, exalted, perhaps even a little holy. When he covered the Senate as a reporter, William White wrote that its greatest qualities included "its oneness and clannishness, its aloneness before the outer political organisms and the outer world, its instinctual drive for the supremacy of this integrious place." Enough to irritate almost anybody.

One natural result of this congressional love-hate relationship is a history of invective, mostly by House members privately against senators but sometimes, self-consciously, by House members against themselves. Senators generally do not deign to criticize the House, never in public and rarely even in private. Such criticism would be a form of recognition and thus clearly beneath their dignity. In one of the rare exceptions, Senator John Williams of Delaware, his compulsion for probity overwhelming protocol, denounced Representative Adam Clayton Powell on the Senate floor for putting his nonworking wife on the payroll and squandering public funds abroad. A Democrat tried to prevent the Williams speech from appearing in the *Record*, as a breach of Congressional comity, but it turned out that the Senate rules only prohibit members from attributing unworthy motives or conduct to another senator. A House member is fair game.

It should not be surprising then that, in the House, "Senate" is what a four-letter word used to be in polite society, never uttered under any circumstances. It is always the "other body." Woe unto any novice reporter, fresh from a casual state legislature, who refers to the "upper house" or, even more galling, the "lower house." This abhorrence is not merely custom; it is actually written into the rules of the House, with lengthy, detailed, and annotated precedents.

Thus, a representative is not permitted under the rules to criticize the Senate, to refer to any senator by name, to criticize one anonymously, or even to compliment one. He cannot mention procedure, debates, or votes in the Senate. He cannot read from the public record of Senate proceedings or even refer to documents inserted in that record. A House member attacked by a senator on the Senate floor may "explain" his motives and conduct later but may not discuss the controversy or launch any counterattack. All these rules apply to the floor. Off it, if you can get anyone to listen, pretty much anything goes.

The dozen members of the Black Caucus in the House, for example, have made little attempt to conceal their feelings about Senator Edward Brooke of Massachusetts, the first and only Negro in the "other body," for his refusal to join their organization. Brooke is a Republican and all the black men and women in the House are Democrats, but the schism runs deeper than that. The blue-eyed, well-tailored senator is a symbol of the fact that even the cause of black solidarity cannot bridge the gap between the two houses.

One of the most sensitive pressure points on the quivering House psyche is the demonstrable fact that senators are popularly regarded as Presidential candidates and representatives are not. This is no new trend. Only one President, James Garfield, was ever elected directly from the House. Three others, James Polk, Millard Fillmore, and William McKinley, served in the House, but not the Senate, and then subsequently made it to the White House. This is not exactly a distinguished group, but House members express pride in their top alumnus by wearing red carnations each year on January 29, McKinley's birthday.

By contrast, fully armed Presidential candidates seem to spring up in the Senate as though dragons' teeth had been sown beneath the chamber floor. In 1972, no fewer than eight senators were active candidates or distinct possibilities for the Democratic nomination. In the three previous national elections, ten of the twelve major party candidates for President and Vice President were former senators. If you mark the election of Franklin Roosevelt as the opening of the modern political era, four of its six Presidents have come from the Senate.

The superiority posture of the Senate has invited retaliatory comment over the years. Speaker Thomas Reed, with his customary acid perception, observed at the turn of the century that "the Senate is a nice quiet sort of place where good representatives go when they die." William Chapman of the *Washington Post*, an irreverent sometime observer of Congress, was once asked whether he bought the old maxim that the Senate was the world's greatest deliberative body. "It's not a bad body," he replied, "but it's been in the water a little too long."

House members upon occasion burst through their defensive shell and criticize their own organization in terms that no senator would consider. First prize here probably goes to former Representative Dewey Short of Missouri, who, presumably under some stress or other, called the House "that supine, subservient, soporific, supercilious, pusillanimous body of nitwits."

House leaders, while realistic, have tended to be more gentle. Speaker Rayburn was peppered with questions about House efficiency by Representative Joseph Barr, who only survived one term in Congress but went on to become Secretary of the Treasury. "Joe, I'm worried about you," the Speaker replied. "You seem to have an orderly mind, and this is a disorderly body."

The rules against referring to the other chamber or criticizing its actions, which go all the way back to Jefferson's *Manual* of 1797, have been strained upon occasion. In 1903, Senator Benjamin Tillman threatened to block a House-passed appropriation bill unless it was amended to include more money for South Carolina. His stand infuriated House Appropriations Committee Chairman Joseph Cannon, who took the floor and, choosing his words carefully, said, "Another body, under these methods, must change its methods of procedure, or our body, backed by the people, will compel that change. Else this body, close to the people, shall become a mere tender, a mere bender of the pregnant hinges of the knee, to submit to what any member of another body may demand of this body as a price for legislation."

No one in the House rose to criticize Representative Cannon for his attack on Tillman and the Senate or to propose any of the appropriate penalties. Quite the contrary, later that year his colleagues elected him Speaker.

In the area of legislation, each body pretends that the other does not exist, right down to the moment when differences must be resolved in bicameral conference committee and pretense can no longer be sustained. A bill that the House has passed and sent to the Senate retains its numerical title, H.R. 123, because the Senate version can only be admitted to reconciling conference with the House version if it bears the same designation. But, for Senate purposes, most of the rest of its previous history in the House is blotted out. Thus, when the Senate committee reports its version of the measure, there is almost no official reference to the House bill, how it may have been amended on the floor, what vote it passed by and when, or what subsequent changes the Senate committee has made. The committee report on the bill, an explanatory printed booklet that must accompany every measure to the floor, simply deals with the Senate version as if it had sprung into full being without any previous background at all. (The only real exceptions are appropriations bills, which all originate in the House. Senate reports always carry comparative dollar figures—for the Administration's budget request, the House-approved total, and the Senate committee's recommendation.)

This lack of information makes it inconvenient for reporters, who have to dig back in their files for the House report and stories of floor action there. But it is more serious for members, who must vote on amendments and the bill itself and could certainly profit from some knowledge of where the House agreed to move and where it refused. But that, it seems, would violate the principle of legislative independence. Only when two differing bills with the same identifying number are assigned to a conference committee is there official recognition by each house of the other's position. Until that moment, the Senate and House legislate in separate vacuums, each too proud to acknowledge that the other has acted at all.

The social and political rivalry between senators and representatives breaks into the open when a joint congressional committee is formed. For many years, these committees always had a senator as chairman, although membership is equally divided between the two houses, and they thus became the focus for the long-standing contention that senators get control and publicity while House members do the work. Finally, the House scored a break-through with the Joint Atomic Energy Committee. Created in 1946, the group originally had only senators as chairmen, including a Republican during the Eightieth Congress (1947–48). But, after the House went Republican again in the 1952 Eisenhower election, Sam Rayburn, now demoted to minority leader, used the opposite party as a lever for raising House influence. The Democrat succeeded in persuading the new Republican Speaker, Joseph Martin of Massachusetts, to insist that the joint committee's chairmanship be rotated to a House member. Martin, in turn, had to push Representative Sterling Cole of New York, the ranking Republican House member, who was fearful of being presumptuous. At first, naturally, the Republican senators refused to accept such a radical transfer of authority, but, in the end, through a mixture of equity and stubbornness, the House prevailed, and the practice was established. In the Ninety-second Congress (1971–72), representatives headed five of the eight working joint committees.

Rayburn remained convinced that the House got the short end of the stick on joint committees, and he used all his cunning and influence to block creation of new ones. When legislation proposing a joint committee on science and astronautics rocketed out of House committee in 1958, it was amended on the floor to provide for separate standing committees in each house. The Senate, under Lyndon Johnson's leadership, put the joint committee back in the bill, but Rayburn won in conference, and two standing committees—with, of course, different names—were established. An inquiring senator was later told, "That decision was reached at the Texas level."

Another major battle in the House Liberation Movement was fought in 1962 on the right of representatives to preside over a much more important kind of bicameral group, the conference committee. Its significance was largely obscured, however, by reporting that made it seem a comic contest between two doddering and stubborn ancients over petty protocol. It was that, too, but there was substance underneath.

The featured performers were the chairmen of the respective appropriations committees, Senator Carl Hayden, eighty-four, and Representative Clarence Cannon, eighty-three. Although their differences sometimes seemed measured solely by the length of the Capitol—at which end would an appropriations conference meet? —the real stakes involved continued Senate dominance of conference action, the last decisive step in the lawmaking process. For some seven months of the year, no conferences were held on appropriations bills at all, as Cannon demanded that a House member alternate as conference chairman, and in a room at the House end of the Capitol. Hayden agreed, but only if the House would permit the Senate to originate half the appropriations bills, a long-standing House prerogative. When the July 1 deadline for appropriations bills passed with no action, the Senate muffled surrender in much protest but gave in altogether. On July 20, 1962, Senate and House managers of the supplemental appropriations bill flipped a coin, and Representative Albert Thomas of Texas took the conference chair, the first time for a lowly representative in the memory of the oldest living resident.

Hayden may have been overmatched, for his reputation was that of a gentle soul. Senator Guy Cordon of Oregon once said that "Carl Hayden has smiled more money through the Committee on Appropriations than any other senator has gotten by valid argument." But then Cordon may have been soft on old folks; he arrived in the Senate himself at seventy-five.

Woeful lack of communication, much less coordination, between leaders of the Senate and House has contributed to the bitterness with which representatives sometimes view their neighbors to the north. Upon occasion, the House Democratic leadership has laboriously organized a major campaign to push through a highly controversial measure by a narrow margin, only to see the bill die of neglect in the Senate. The result is that individual representatives are put on the spot and forced to commit themselves on a politically sensitive issue without any legislation to show for their discomfiture. It happened in 1965, when the House barely repealed, 221–203, the "right to work" provision in the Taft-Hartley Law that permits states to prohibit the union shop. The Senate never acted on the bill at all, and a number of House Democrats from close, relatively conservative districts were beaten on the issue in 1966, hung for a vote that turned out to have been totally unproductive.

That particular disaster was probably as much the fault of the House as the Senate. Leaders in one house cannot safely proceed on a perilous course without reasonably firm consultation with their colleagues in the other. But proceed they do, every day, even though consultation is almost nonexistent. Not long ago, when

Senator Mike Mansfield, the Democratic floor leader, scheduled a party conference with the House Speaker on the unassailable issue of conservation, he was asked how long it had been since he had met with his Democratic counterpart to harmonize policy. He thought and replied candidly that he could not remember. It had been that long.

A century ago, when senators were presumed aristocrats, chosen by their state legislatures, and representatives were presumed plebeians, elected directly by their ordinary kin, there may have been virtue, or at least some logic, in setting one house against the other, pitting privilege and education directly against commonality, hoping to strike a balance. Surely not today, when the men and women in the two bodies are essentially indistinguishable in background and purpose. When the leaders of the same party in the two houses rarely meet, when the chairmen of parallel committees operate in almost complete ignorance of each other, there can be only one result. Reasoned laws become more difficult to draft and enact. Friction is magnified instead of reduced. The ultimate court of the conference committee is confronted with broad, difficult, undiscussed issues to compromise instead of smaller, more manageable ones. A frail instrument at best, it is strained to the breaking point.

Neil MacNeil, in his definitive portrait of the House, *Forge of Democracy*, develops the thesis that the rivalry between the two bodies is, at least to some extent, a natural outgrowth of their different functions. He sees the Senate, confirming or rejecting Presidential appointees and sharing the President's foreign policy role, as more sympathetic to the Executive, while the House, originating all tax and spending bills, tends to identify more closely with the taxpayers, whose continued approval the members must solicit every two years. MacNeil also concludes that there is always likely to be a liberal-conservative disparity between the two bodies, with the Senate well to the left of the House. He argues that in a number of states the labor, Jewish, and black votes, individually or collectively, can be pivotal for a senator promoting a liberal stance in seeking reelection, while there are relatively few House districts where this kind of constituency holds a balance of power, and thus there are more conservative representatives of both parties.

Repairing historically strained relations between the Senate and House is a long-range project, never fully achievable. However, a four-year term for representatives, discussed in Chapter 13, could reduce some of their sense of insecurity. It is unrealistic to believe that House jealousy of the Senate will ever disappear, but, with some leadership effort, it could be channeled into healthy competition instead of continued hostility.

And, if the two groups of lawmakers are never to become blood brothers, at least they can stop splitting the legislative process into combative camps. Periodic informal conferences between the party leaders in the two houses, now infrequent, and between chairmen of parallel committees, now rare, could go a long way toward bridging this useless gap. No purpose but vanity is served by continuing to pretend that the other half of Congress is not there.

# 3 · A Fine and Private Place

The Senate posed for its first photograph in history on September 24, 1963, just before voting to ratify the nuclear test ban treaty. The House followed suit five months later, seizing on an election-year opportunity to immortalize its members agreeing to reduce taxes. Both panoramic color portraits are remarkable for the way in which they deceive the viewer. Neither resembles any scene ever glimpsed before or since in either chamber. They provide a reasonable, if somewhat distorted, view of the two impressive halls at the ends of the Capitol but those men and women down there—can they really be the members of Congress?

In the Senate, every member is seated precisely behind his desk, with not a single absentee. No one is standing, schmoozing in the aisles, heading for the lobby, nodding, speaking, trying to get recognition, or any of the things real senators do. Each desk is neatly stacked with what seem to be the same three piles of paper. Only Senator Jacob Javits of New York supplies a touch of realism by dropping a copy of the *New York Times* on the otherwise spotless carpet.

The House is just as improbably immaculate. Speaker John McCormack is pounding the gavel, but no other object is in motion. The members are frozen, rank upon rank, in their chairs, lifeless and antiseptic. The only clear sign that this is not a wax museum is the fifty empty seats in the Republican foreground;

the leaders could not even produce a full House for this historic and promotional occasion.

There is a real message in this pair of stiff, ceremonial photographs. First, it took a good hundred years from the time still photography was perfected before Congress permitted this potentially embarrassing medium into its hallowed chambers at all. And, when the magic moment came, the glimpse given the public of its national assembly was completely artificial and contrived, a patent fraud on the people who paid for the building, the salaries of those posing, and, just incidentally, the pictures themselves.

The sorrowful fact is that Congress has never really welcomed any form of public access to its activities, particularly visual, and does not today. Virtually all of its decision-making meetings that precede and follow floor action are closed to the press and public; the open ones tend to be innocuous preliminary airings of pro forma views on legislation that is just getting started. Television, as we have seen, is admitted to these hearings but, like still photography, never to the floor, where the action is. (Senator Estes Kefauver welcomed the electronic eye into his organized crime hearings in 1951; with a foresight denied more timid politicians, he could already see his 1952 Presidential campaign on the horizon. It was in reaction to this display that Speaker Sam Rayburn banned the televising of all House functions in 1952, a ruling that stood for eighteen years, during which the members continued to complain that they got less publicity than senators.)

The ordinary citizen who may be interested in seeing Congress at work, denied photographs or televised glimpses, does not fare much better when he comes to Washington. To make a small but symbolic point, there is almost no parking available for visitors, free or otherwise, within walking distance of the Capitol. All the visible space for blocks, plus two huge new multimillion-dollar garages, is reserved for the 7,500 people who work on the Hill. Maybe Congress didn't plan it that way, but Congress hasn't done anything to correct the situation. Once in the Capitol, a tourist needs permission to visit the Senate and House chambers. He can get a five-minute glimpse of each on the guided tour, but even that may soon be abbreviated; at last report, the Senate was planning to build a plastic soundproof catwalk across one corner of the gallery through which tourists could be herded rather than be seated in the gallery for even a few minutes. Until 1971, the guided tour cost twenty-five cents (fifteen cents for students, children under ten free), giving the majestic Capitol the doubtful distinction of being the only major public building in Washington that charged anything at all.

Visitors who want to see and hear something more than the guided tour offers need two passes, one for each chamber. These are obtainable for the asking at the offices of either of a citizen's senators or at the office of his representative, a block or two away. Some members from the same state exchange passes so that one visit can produce both Senate and House tickets, but many do not. In any event, in return for credentials, every visitor is asked to add his name and address to the member's political mailing list, a ceremony euphemistically referred to as "signing the guest book."

Some elementary system of regulating admission to the galleries is obviously necessary, but the pass procedure is little known to the general public, inconvenient, and clearly reduces the number of people who manage to get into the 600-odd visitors' seats that overlook each chamber. There is no practical reason why passes could not be available at booths in the Capitol—but then the members would not appear to have done their constituents a political favor. Which favor consists of granting them permission to do something they have the right to do anyway: watch in operation the legislature they choose and finance.

Outside of the House and Senate chambers, visitors can catch a glimpse of the lawmaking process in only one place: the committee hearings. These may deal with a specific piece of legislation, such as a gun control or welfare reform bill, or with a broader issue, like foreign aid. Prepared testimony is often routine, unless it reveals a new Administration policy, but cross-examination of witnesses by members can produce lively and informative sessions. A dozen or two of these hearings take place almost every day that Congress is in session, but nowhere in the Capitol or the five massive congressional office buildings around it is there any listing for tourists of place, time, and subject matter. Such a list is distributed to the members and the press and published each morning in the *Washington Post*, but the average Capitol visitor, unlikely to know that, can find no public bulletin anywhere to inform him of the wide variety of congressional inquiries taking place. If he could, more people would go to more hearings and learn how Congress works—or doesn't. (It may be as accidental as the fact that the only hearing list is buried in a newspaper, but it is remarkably difficult to buy that newspaper or any other in the Capitol or the adjoining office buildings. The one Capitol newsstand sells nothing but souvenirs, and there are only a handful of newspaper coin machines anywhere on the Hill, mostly in basements. It just makes it that much harder to find out what's going on.)

For the senators and representatives themselves, inaccessability is a privilege that accompanies length of service. Tucked away in the Capitol are some sixty private, unmarked offices candidly called "hideaways," for the most senior members. Their ostensible virtue is that they are much closer to the floor than the official suites over in the office buildings, enabling a member to keep in close touch while dictating correspondence or making phone calls. Their utility, however, extends to socializing with colleagues, grabbing a quick drink, or otherwise enjoying a higher degree of privacy than is obtained in the staff-filled public offices. One afternoon, a few years ago, a Capitol electrician on a repair mission used a passkey to let himself into the hideaway of one of the most powerful Senate leaders. There he discovered a comely brunette reporter who had prepared for an interview with the senator by removing all of her clothes. Both parties retreated hastily.

Lyndon Johnson, at the peak of his empire, had seven rooms worth of hideaway. The biggest single apartment, with a bathroom, kitchenette, and two crystal chandeliers, goes traditionally as a matter of right to the dean of the Southern bloc, now Senator Allen Ellender of Louisiana, who reached that distinction at eighty. (He once announced in an official Senate report that he neither drinks nor chases women.)

Unscheduled events aside, it is regrettable for many reasons that the public is discouraged from all but a short, nervous glance at the Congress House and its tenants. Not just because a watched government governs better, but because the Capitol is in many ways the embodiment of the heterogeneous American spirit, its architecture, art, and history bespeaking the strengths and weaknesses of the men who have lived and worked there. Seeing Congress without the Capitol is not seeing Congress whole.

The Capitol owes its commanding site to Pierre Charles L'Enfant, the former Revolutionary War major who was commissioned by President Washington to lay out a plan for the proposed seat of government. "I could discover no one [location]," the French-born engineer reported, "so advantageously to greet the congressional building as is that on the west end of Jenkins Heights, which stands as a pedestal waiting for a monument."

Around that spot, L'Enfant drew the conventional grid of streets overlaid with angled avenues, circles, and parks that make Washington the only American city ever deliberately designed handsome. But L'Enfant received little recognition. Congressional critics of the plan forced his dismissal, and he angrily refused their mollifying reward of 500 guineas and a downtown lot. Not until 1889 were L'Enfant's plans pulled back out of the archives and put to use; fortunately, nineteenth-century urban planning being what it was, there was still time. (In 1909, the architect's body was moved to Arlington National Cemetery, an act that may have made some people feel better, but not L'Enfant.)

The building that rose on Jenkins Heights strikes many viewers as so aesthetically coherent that it might have sprung into full being in national prehistory, much as the Constitution did. In fact, it is a patchwork job, begun in 1793, passing through a half-dozen architects and major design changes, and not finally completed in its present form until 1960 (with still another massive alteration currently under debate). The first piece of the building, finished in 1800, is a three-story sandstone box about 150 feet square, now midway between the Senate chamber and the Rotunda and almost completely obscured by later construction. Its only visible outside wall looks west down Constitution Avenue; if you stand well back from the East Front in Capitol Park, you can see the small, windowed cupola that topped the first Capitol and a glimpse of the shallow dome below it.

This tiny Congress House somehow managed to accommodate a Senate of 32 members, a House of 106, the Supreme Court, and the Library of Congress. They slowly began peeling off, the House in 1807 to a matching but separate wing to the south, the Library in 1897 to a replica of the Paris Opera House across the park, and the Court in 1935 to its own marble monument near the Library. Separation of powers had finally been achieved.

In 1814, a British amphibious force stormed Washington and burned the Capitol, gutting the interior of the two stone wings and a connecting wooden walkway. During the Capitol's reconstruction, Congress occupied a nearby brick building, and the 1817 inaugural on its steps set a chilly precedent. Monroe became the first President to be sworn in outdoors, solely because the Senate and House could not agree on which of their chambers to use for the ceremony. Outdoors it has been ever since.

Restoration and expansion of the Capitol continued apace, under architects Benjamin Latrobe, who liked to put corn and tobacco leaves on his pillars instead of the classic acanthus, and Charles Bulfinch, a Harvard man who finally connected the Senate and House wings with the Rotunda and topped it with a squatty, bulbous dome. The two houses held their sessions just off the Rotunda, the House in what is now Statuary Hall and the Senate in a handsome smaller chamber to the north, now closed to the public and rarely used by Congress at all. (A movement is under way to restore this historic room and another just below it and open them for visitors. In one or the other, the Senate sat for 40 years and the Supreme Court for 115, and Samuel F. B. Morse, who may or may not have invented the telegraph, tapped out his first message to Baltimore in a demonstration for curious lawmakers. Surely enough history to warrant preservation, but Congress will not provide the necessary funds.)

Westward expansion produced new states and more members, and in 1850 the 62 senators and 232 representatives, overflowing their semicircular halls, voted to build huge new balancing rectangular wings at each end of the Capitol to house larger and more splendid chambers, where they are today. The expansion was pressed particularly by the House, in whose quarters the acoustics had proved both ineffective and peculiar. John Quincy Adams, who was elected to the House two years after he lost the

Presidency, discovered a spot on the floor from which he could overhear whispers by his political opponents standing fifty feet away. Adams was eavesdropping away on that spot in 1848 when he suffered a stroke, was carried into the Speaker's office, and died on a couch. A bronze marker where he fell enables Statuary Hall visitors to prove that the acoustical quirk still functions. (The couch still stands in the adjoining office, now coyly known as the Congressional Ladies Retiring Room.)

The new House and Senate wings, completed by 1859, nearly doubled the length of the building and made the old, stubby dome look inadequate. So Thomas Walter, a former Philadelphia master bricklayer who was then architect of the Capitol, designed the present one, which soars 260 feet above the Rotunda floor and is intricately assembled of 9 million pounds of cast-iron shell, truss, and girder.

The 20-foot statue of Armed Liberty was bolted atop the dome in 1863. A classically robed figure with sword and shield, she is often mistaken from the ground below for an Indian, because of her feathered helmet. The original design called for a liberty cap, such as freed Roman slaves wore, but the Secretary of War who supervised the dome plans, Jefferson Davis, ordered something less libertarian and more martial—which should have told somebody something.

Work on the porticoes of the new wings dragged on for some years, but the Capitol was now complete except for one latter-day alteration: the rebuilt East Front, completed in 1960, which moved the face of the Capitol's central section forward 30 feet. Among the hundred new rooms created was a handsome paneled reception room just off the Senate floor, used for cocktail parties as well as conferences. (Senator Wayne Morse, otherwise a flaming liberal, used to complain on the floor that liquor defiled the Capitol, but no one raises the issue today, not even the Senate's four resident Mormons and one Christian Scientist.)

A second proposed Capitol expansion, moving the West Front out as much as 90 feet to create still more room, has run into strong opposition from traditionalists, who would prefer to see the crumbling sandstone exterior, which looks down the Mall toward the Washington Monument and the Lincoln Memorial, replaced and strengthened where it stands. This would be a not inconsiderable $15 million job, but less than a third as expensive as the more ambitious project. However, in March, 1972, plans for the West Front were approved. Last-ditch protests included Representative Samuel Stratton's statement that what he termed a "costly and destructive boondoggle" was proceeding "because certain senior members of the House and Senate want secret hideaway offices."

Inside the Capitol, the decoration, painting, and sculpture tend to reflect the congressional membership: a haphazard collection, heavy on tradition and convention, with occasional unmitigated horrors outweighed by a number of genuine high spots. Among the last is the spectacular work of Constantino Brumidi, a Rome-born Greek who did not even arrive in the United States until he was nearly fifty and then devoted twenty-five years to beautifying the interior of its Capitol. Brumidi painted the 62-foot circular fresco in the dome, showing Washington being elevated to heaven, surrounded by allegorical figures representing Liberty, Science, and so on, and the thirteen original states. (For those who cannot distinguish Agriculture from Democracy in such displays, E. W. Kenworthy of the *New York Times* had the best advice: "Remember, if you don't trouble an allegory, it won't trouble you.") Part of the fresco's charm is that the artist saw nothing inconsistent in Minerva advising Robert Fulton about the steamboat, or Neptune garlanded with the Atlantic Cable.

Brumidi decorated two spectacular rooms just off the Senate floor: the reception room, encrusted with color and gilt design, and the President's room, its wall crowded with Washington Cabinet members, cherubs, and allegorical ladies. Perhaps his greatest achievements are the two first-floor corridors in the northwest corner of the Senate wing. Here, walls and ceilings are crowded with rich Venetian design, incorporating flowers, fish, fruit, birds, and musical instruments—a cascade of color and form before which the rest of the Capitol pales.

Only a few of the Capitol's gallery of paintings are worth notice: the Washington portraits by Gilbert Stuart and Charles Wilson Peale, Thomas Sully's paintings of Jefferson and Jackson, and four of the eight historic scenes that ring the Rotunda, those by John Trumbull, who painted many of the figures of the Revolution and early Republic from life.

Seeking some use for the old House chamber, with its curious acoustics, Congress hit upon the idea of inviting each state to submit statues of two outstanding citizens and displaying the collection there. The result, judged generously today, is unimpressive. There are a few memorable statesmen—Webster, Clay, and Calhoun—and some imaginative choices—Charles Russell of Montana, the great Western artist, Will Rogers, the Oklahoma humorist, and the Hawaiian delegation of a priest and a native king. But mostly the hall and adjoining overflow corridors are peopled with long-forgotten politicians and generals of the last century, whose stiff, frock-coated figures fail to arouse even momentary curiosity.

Not all the immortals of Statuary Hall were paragons of virtue. One former member of Congress so honored by his state is remembered for having been discovered by a Capitol guard one night, lying stark naked behind the sparse shrubbery of a Hill hotel whose basement bar still lubricates the legislative process upon occasion. His statue, shifted from the hall to a less conspicuous corridor not long ago, was wheeled through the Rotunda flat on its bronze back, a posture regarded by some observers as entirely appropriate.

Crammed with life, color, and history, the Capitol building could lift the men and women who serve there to new heights of resolution, to heed Daniel Webster's summons carved above the House rostrum: "Let us develope the resources of our land, call forth its powers, build up its institutions, promote all its great interests and see whether we also, in our day and generation, may not perform something worthy to be remembered."

But, as we shall see, the effect these days is often quite the opposite. The Capitol, with its awesome aura of strength and tradition, tends instead to confirm irresolute members in the conviction that the institution is solid, too, that the old ways are still the best, that Congress can survive the nuclear age without rigorous change. For those who accept these questionable notions, the Capitol is a giant security blanket, warm against the chill of doubts and nagging fears.

Suppose, when you opened the drawer of your Senate desk, you found scratched on its bottom panel in schoolboy capitals the last names of these men who had sat there before: Webster, the orator and Secretary of State; Charles Sumner, the abolitionist, so outspoken he was caned in the chamber by a Southerner and needed three years to recover; Henry Cabot Lodge, who kept the country out of the League of Nations; Arthur Vandenberg, who helped bring it into the United Nations one peace and several Republican Parties later. It could not help giving you, as a senator, a sense of the immediacy of past greatness, of the comforting continuity of history, even of self-importance and the power to ignore deepening cracks in the congressional foundation. Presumably, it does precisely that for Norris Cotton of New Hampshire, a tall, testy, seventy-two-year-old lawyer who currently holds that desk. The inspiration of the past has certainly not roused him—or many others of his colleagues—to anything but the most routine, narrow-gauge, time-filling service, the kind that has let Congress drift gradually but inevitably to the brink of futility.

The Capitol and the country deserve better.

# 4 · Swinging on the Hill

Senator Joseph Clark of Pennsylvania summed up the prevailing public perception of Congress when he called it "the sapless branch." Unenlightened by routine press coverage, many Americans tend to regard the members as rather dull, conventional, church-deacon types, rarely given to raising their voices or lowering their standards.

There have been notable exceptions, of course—Huey Long, Joe McCarthy, Adam Clayton Powell—but congressional reporting generally treats most of its subjects protectively, much as sports writers until very recently presented every star athlete as an unblemished model of all-American virtue. The Capitol press corps, as we have seen, often observes Congress through its members' eyes, and the result is a faceless gallery of straight-arrow homebodies, dedicated and desiccated.

It's just not true. One of the few sources of hope for a Congress that is so badly operated as to be effectively ineffectual is the inherent vitality of its members. They are real people, displaying very human flaws and appetites, and all the accounts of Congress that ignore their humanity or skip lightly over it do them, in a real sense, a disservice.

Sometimes it seems as though the elevation of the Capitol above the rest of the city provides a headier, more stimulating social atmosphere, one in which brawling, drinking, and extra-curricular love-making flourish at levels unknown in the careful

civil service company town built on the Potomac marshes below.
Not that anyone should conclude that there are more rakes and
tosspots in Congress, proportionally, than there are among, say,
advertising executives or college professors. Clearly, many senators and representaives—yours if you ask them—are Rotarian
pillars of probity, only dimly aware of the vigorous Hill social life
and content to remain so. But fighting, drinking, and womanizing
have always been inextricably interwoven in the American political process, although less fully advertised than some other aspects.
Sexual prowess and political advancement have often been closely
interrelated over the years, and there seems no reason in our current open society not to recognize the relationship.

It would be withholding a full view of Congress to pretend
that this very real part of many lawmakers' lives did not exist.
Also, it would seem presumptuous to prescribe for the serious
professional ills of Congress without at least some feeling for the
very human side of its concerns. Here, then, are some of the real
residents of Capitol Hill, glimpsed in their off-hours and less
formal pursuits, in an effort to bring out the whole institution and
not just its company-manners image.

Congressional fighting has gone sadly downhill in recent years
and is now a pretty tacky and occasional pastime. The lawmakers are far removed from the early-nineteenth-century days
when duels off the floor were regarded as a natural extension of
quarrels on it.

A half-century of such irregular combat was climaxed in 1839
when Representative William Graves of Kentucky killed Representative Jonathan Cilley of Maine in a duel, and Congress, to
preserve its ranks from further depletion, passed an antidueling
law. But, twenty-five years later, Representative John Potter of
Wisconsin was able to avert a duel only by choosing as his
weapons Bowie knives, not then readily obtainable in the
District of Columbia.

In the old days, floor fights were sometimes literally that. When
Representative Roger Griswold of Connecticut debated personal
cowardice with Matthew Lyon of Vermont in 1798, Lyon climaxed the exchange by spitting in his face, and then, to make

sure Griswold had not missed his point, he hit him with the tongs from the House fireplace. Two motions to censure the combatants failed. The only official corrective for this sort of activity was the Mace, a 4-foot staff of silver-bound ebony rods topped by a globe and eagle, the badge of office of the sergeant at arms and the only physical symbol of the authority of the House. When the full House is in session, the Mace stands on a green marble pedestal to the right of the Speaker. In the days when disturbances erupted on the floor, the Speaker would order the sergeant at arms to break them up by striding into the storm center, carrying the Mace above his head. Apparently, there was a real psychological effect; at any rate, there is no record of anyone having been struck with this awesome weapon.

From contemporary accounts, pistols seem to have been a regular part of the nineteenth-century congressman's haberdashery. In 1835, Vice President Martin Van Buren felt called upon to wear a brace of pistols when presiding over the Senate; forty-five years later, Speaker Warren Keifer of Ohio kept a single weapon in his pocket to repel assaults on the chair. Outside the Capitol, gunfire was even more common. In 1856, Representative Philemon Herbert of California shot and killed a waiter in Willard's Hotel on the grounds that he had not served him promptly —a form of criticism that could produce only a bloodbath in Washington restaurants today. American history very nearly lost a colorful figure when Representative Samuel Houston of Tennessee (not yet migrated to Texas) clashed with a recent floor opponent. Meeting Representative William Stanbery of Ohio later on the street, he hit him with his cane. Stanbery drew his pistol, but it misfired and there were no further casualties.

Senate brawling, on the whole, has been less frequent than the House variety and more rigorously condemned after the fact. In 1850, while Senator Henry Foote of Mississippi was speaking on the floor, Senator Thomas Hart Benton of Missouri made menacing gestures and advanced toward Foote's desk. Foote drew his pistol and ostentatiously cocked it, but cooler heads intervened. An investigating committee recommended censure of both men, but the Senate took no action.

A half-dozen years later, Senator Charles Sumner of Massachusetts was sitting at his desk in the chamber after a session during which he had attacked Senator A. P. Butler of South Carolina for advocating optional slavery in Kansas and Nebraska. Butler's nephew, Representative Preston Brooks of South Carolina, came into the chamber shouting angrily at the abolitionist and beat him over the head with a heavy cane. Sumner fell to the floor bleeding and unconscious and was unable to return to the Senate for the rest of that year. His Massachusetts constitutents re-elected him in the fall, however, and he was finally well enough to reclaim his seat in 1859, more than three years later. After a House motion to expel Brooks failed, he resigned and was re-elected. Two other House members had known of Brooks's intentions but failed to stop him. A censure motion against one of them failed, and the other was censured, resigned, and was re-elected. House members have not felt welcome on the Senate floor since.

In 1902, charges of lying led to a Senate chamber fistfight between the two South Carolina members, John McLaurin and "Pitchfork Ben" Tillman (so known because he had threatened to stick one into Grover Cleveland). The two men were unanimously voted in contempt of the Senate. Five days later, after an inquiry and separate apologies, each was censured for "breach of the privileges and dignity of this body." Tillman was a Populist and, like some other members of that noisy agrarian movement, tended to attract criticism that often bordered on physical attack. Another Populist Senator, Thomas Gore of Oklahoma, was as blunt as the best of them but was sheltered from reprisal by the fact that he was blind. One day, after a particularly bitter debate, an infuriated opponent whispered to Gore, "If you weren't blind, I'd thrash you within an inch of your life." The Oklahoman snapped to an ally, "Blindfold that ruffian and aim him in my direction."

The Senate has maintained a relative calm on the floor since the day in the late 1930's when Senator Kenneth McKellar of Tennessee pulled a Bowie knife and lunged at Senator Royal Copeland of New York, a doctor who fortunately had no need for his own professional services that day. The only recent senatorial bout of any consequence took place in 1964, when Strom Thurmond of South Carolina and Ralph Yarborough of

Texas scuffled and grappled on the floor of the corridor outside a Senate hearing for nearly ten minutes over a civil rights dispute. Both contestants were sixty-one, but Thurmond, a fitness addict, pinned the paunchier Texan at least twice.

The House has been a little livelier. In the 1940's, the chairman of the House Appropriations Committee, Clarence Cannon of Missouri, became so angry at the ranking Republican member, John Taber of New York, that he punched him in the nose and drew blood, which startled members had sworn the niggardly Taber had been operating without. In 1956, Representative Cleveland Bailey of West Virginia knocked Representative Adam Clayton Powell of New York to the floor with a single blow. The best-publicized House bout of recent years took place off the floor, however, at the 1971 Gridiron Club dinner, where Edward Mitchell, a one-term Republican congressman from Indiana, was seated near Representative Hale Boggs of Louisiana, the newly elected Democratic floor leader. Incensed by Boggs's audible running criticism of President Richard Nixon and his Cabinet, the sixty-year-old former member followed him to the men's room and knocked him to the tile floor—white tie, tails, and all. Mitchell, it developed, had been a college boxer some forty years earlier and once went three rounds with Max Schmeling.

A congressman's day can stretch out long and arid. Into the office at 8 or 9 A.M. for reading, staff meetings, and dictation. Hearings from 10 to 12, or longer. Lunch at the desk. The session at noon, often running into the early evening, with interviews, committee work, and politicking sandwiched between visits to the floor. Not surprisingly, by the time the sun slants over Jenkins Heights a low chorus of parched coughing is almost audible in the corridors of Congress, followed shortly by the reassuring rattle of ice in glasses.

Overdrinking does not seem a serious problem in Congress today, despite some unfortunate public appearances by a few leading House Democrats. Of three senators who regularly appeared drunk on the floor in recent years, one is dead, one has had his habits moderated by a new and understanding wife, and one has quit the stuff entirely. (The last man accosted Senator Harold Hughes of Iowa, a reformed alcoholic, at his swearing-in and called him a "goddamned nut." Hughes recognized the symptoms and later was largely responsible for talking the senator onto the wagon.) A fourth current hard-drinking senator does not disturb the proceedings but sits like a stone behind his desk, a faint smile playing over his lips.

In the House, drinking rarely produces floor antics, for a series of reasons. Senators can solve the accessibility problem by ducking out to their hideaways, the unmarked Capitol offices near the floor, but few House members have these convenient special quarters. Most House offices are a brisk two- or three-block walk away, a mildly sobering experience, and the nearest public bar is well beyond that. Generally, a drinking representative doesn't show up on the floor; when he does, it is to vote rather than debate, and the size of the body mercifully clouds him in anonymity.

But there remain moments. Once, in the 1940's, the House Democratic leadership was pushing an important bill dealing with the Tennessee Valley Authority, and the only committee member from Tennessee who could serve as floor manager was Representative Clifford Davis, a notorious lush. Sure enough, on the day the bill was scheduled for floor debate, Davis was drunk by mid-morning. A determined group of colleagues barricaded his office and poured into him great quantities of the House restaurant's soup of the day. Finally more presentable, the congressman agreed to take the floor on one condition: that he be permitted a single drink to steady his nerves. A stiff belt of vodka was poured, but Representative Estes Kefauver said it needed diluting and took the glass into the lavatory where he replaced the liquor with straight water. Davis eagerly grasped the glass, drank it off neat, and passed out cold.

Kefauver probably downed the vodka himself, for he was a prodigious drinker as well as a voracious womanizer, facts that never seemed to influence his political career one way or the other. On tour, reporters were shaken to see an aide wake the Tennessean from an afternoon nap with an undiluted tumbler of

Scotch at the ready. The senator sat up, seized the glass, drained it, and was prepared to face the rest of the day. Acquaintances insist he drove to the Capitol in his limousine each morning with a glassful of straight whisky in his fist.

Other senators have had more controlled habits. A powerful Southwesterner took only sherry for lunch but came on strong and regularly later in the day. One afternoon, a columnist was riding with him at breakneck speed over the plains, when a secretary in the front seat interrupted them by announcing, "It's five o'clock." The senator immediately opened a hidden bar and poured two stiff drinks.

The cup that cheers can also be a political weapon. In 1961, the vote on Speaker Sam Rayburn's proposal to enlarge and thus neutralize the hostile House Rules Committee was expected to be extremely close, and resourceful backers of the plan went to unusual lengths to reduce the size of the opposition vote. On a Sunday, two days before the balloting, they sent a full case of bourbon to the home of a Southern Democrat who, in the past, had disappeared for considerable periods of time once launched on a binge. On Monday, a cooperative lobbyist was assigned to entertain until all hours a Republican who drank heavily but in short bursts. Both maneuvers failed, for the two men managed to make it to the chamber and vote against the Speaker. (Other stratagems must have worked, for Rayburn won 217–212.)

Even so cautious a man as Representative Wilbur Mills can occasionally wander astray. At a late afternoon Hill get-together during the Kennedy years, Representative Eugene Keough of New York began loosening Mills up by secretly pouring him doubles. At the time, the Ways and Means Committee chairman was stubbornly blocking the President's new Medicare program, and after a few drinks he outlined a compromise plan of his own, big news to the partygoers. Riding downtown afterward, a colleague asked Mills when he would bring his Medicare compromise up in committee. "What Medicare compromise?" the sobered chairman inquired.

During the days of his drinking problem, one powerful Senate committee chairman invited a Cabinet officer to drop by his house early the same morning that the Secretary was scheduled to testify before the committee. Appearing for this command performance about 9 A.M., the Administration leader was greeted at the door by a malodorous and disheveled senator in pajamas, who insisted, "Joe, come in and have a drink." The second time the senator proposed such a morning conference, the Secretary was ready. He set his alarm the night before for 3:30 A.M., got up, ate a big breakfast, and worked hard for four hours at his home desk. Then, when he arrived on the senator's doorstep he felt prepared, morally and physiologically, to accept his hospitality.

The fact that Congress swings as almost no other part of the federal establishment does is indisputable. Any halfway attractive female newcomer to the Hill—member, staff aide, or reporter—discovers in short order that invitations from lawmakers for varying degrees of social involvement are rapidly forthcoming. A Southern senator, now in his seventies, is known as the scourge of the elevators because of his fondness for bottom-pinching. In his younger years, the Scourge would sit in the chamber, spot an attractive woman in the gallery, and dispatch a page to invite her to meet him in his office. No one knows how many accepted.

Why do some senators and representatives take a more open and enthusiastic attitude toward extracurricular sex than nonelective civil servants seem to? One answer may be historical. Congress used to be a part-time commuter's job, when the sessions ran six months a year or less and many of the members left their wives and children back in the district. This led to three or four open evenings a week in Washington, on which some members went to the movies and some didn't. Although many members now maintain year-round homes in the capital and apartments back in the district rather than the other way about, there is still a hardy corps of commuters, particularly from the East Coast cities easily reachable by plane. And the unstable, irregular atmosphere of a commuting Congress has never really been dispelled. It is still a hectic, all-hours, catch-as-catch-can sort of existence, never fully domesticated.

Also, Congress is basically campaign-oriented. For the vast majority of people who have never traveled on a political campaign, that special world needs some explaining. As a social experience, campaigning is highly accelerated and intensified, a hothouse process. The candidate, his staff, and the press tend to form a closed, charged-up little world that whirls furiously from place to place, meanwhile observing its own relaxed internal rules. Everyone works harder, sleeps less, drinks more, and moves much more rapidly into close association.

Friendships that might take weeks or months to unfold at home become fast overnight. Love affairs spring up like mushrooms in a wet dirt basement. Heretofore prim secretaries find themselves accepting that invitation for a nightcap in the motel room, offered by a homebody who had never considered such a move before. Over all is a pervasive air of transience: Soon, a new crew of television reporters will replace this one; soon, we will be back in Washington for the weekend; soon, the campaign will be over and life will return to normal. But meanwhile . . .

(Outside Congress, the White House is the only other place in Washington where this campaign atmosphere persists. The staff and reporters there are almost all campaign veterans, and their travels around the country with the President re-create the mood between elections. A high-level example: Not too long ago, the entire White House traveling apparatus—perhaps 150 staff and press members—was uprooted in the midst of a promised quiet weekend and airlifted to New York City for what was advertised as an emergency meeting with the U.N. Ambassador. The Ambassador entered the hotel suite on time all right, but after five minutes of small talk he was whisked out the back door, to be succeeded by an attractive redhead from the West Coast whose visit was reportedly both longer and livelier.)

Besides the commuter tradition and campaign atmosphere, the free-living social standards of Congress partake considerably of Gloria Steinem's theory that power is sexy. From all reports, there is something about sleeping with a senator or even a representative that is different from ordinary mortal cohabitation. Or at least seems to be. It's not that they're any better at it, but the act becomes a form of achievement, even of recognition for some of the women involved, and an avenue to influence for the more determined. (There was a period during which the mistress

of the chairman of one of the Senate's most powerful committees, who also held a ranking position on its staff, literally decided which witnesses would be privileged to testify at its hearings and which would not.)

Not unlike the girls who pursue baseball teams or rock bands,
there is a distinct cultural group that is into politics and governmental power and that takes part of its psychic reward from
obliging the men who wield that power. Some of this attraction
rubs off from time to time on congressional aides and even, God
bless us every one, on reporters covering the scene. For those who
are alive to it—and many are not—this can be a sort of ritual
participation in the congressional establishment. It can also
promote advancement and provide power. It can also be fun.

During the lively Kennedy years, a liberal Republican senator
telephoned a lissome blonde on his staff rather late one evening,
summoning her to his Georgetown quarters. She arrived to find
him proudly wearing a soaking tuxedo; he had been pushed into
the swimming pool during a party at Robert Kennedy's Hickory
Hill estate and wanted to display his new social cachet. Then
they both agreed he ought to get out of those wet clothes.

One of the unwritten laws of sex among the lawmakers demands a high level of discretion, to preserve some balance in the
very small, very close congressional community. A few years ago
a Democratic senator, past his threescore years and ten but dead
game, acquired on his staff a provocative lady of middle years who
claimed a background in show business. One evening, after a
long floor session, the senator decided to stroll over to her Hill
apartment for an unannounced visit. Seeing the light on in her
half-basement flat, he hopped over a hedge and peered into the
window to make sure she was home. She was not only home; she
was on her back on a fur rug on the floor, covered in part by another senator, neither of them overdressed. The onlooker and his
secretary stared goggle-eyed at each other for a moment, and then
he withdrew. When she reported for work the next morning, and
ever after, neither mentioned the incident to the other.

Subtlety does not always prevail. One of the Senate's most
effective leaders had a long-standing affair with his secretary that
he made little effort to conceal. In fact, at a stag party with a

group of newspapermen one night, he absorbed a considerable amount of Scotch and decided to telephone her. "Sally Sue," he bellowed into the phone, "come on over to Bob Black's place. We all want to fuck you." To the relief of his uneasy companions, the lady declined.

Sometimes, conversely, indiscretion can be a matter of breeding. One Eastern senator, later defeated for re-election, provided running entertainment for a whole apartment of neighbors one summer, while he was between wives. Because he never closed his curtains, a prime view of his living room could be had from the balconies of an adjacent apartment. As the news spread, young people lined their railings each afternoon to watch the senator and his current friend perform on the couch. On dull days, only she would be observable, making nude runs for beer from the bedroom to the kitchen. Occasionally, the senator would stroll up to the front window, unaware, and scratch himself. He was not an exhibitionist, just a nearsighted, wealthy man raised in houses so far from the neighbors that it never occurred to him to draw the blinds.

Age has seemed to interfere little with congressional sex, and this is a good thing, considering the average Hill level. Representative Frank Boykin of Alabama, then well into his seventies, used to greet his colleagues in the corridor by proclaiming, "Everything is made for love." Unlike most of us, he lived his ideal. Midweek mornings, Boykin would appear promptly for his committee's 10 A.M. hearing, but about eleven o'clock he would begin to fidget and shortly afterward would exit. (Congressmen are always entering and leaving hearings in their midst, pleading one kind of business or another.) The Alabaman would then repair to the Congressional Hotel, just behind the Cannon House Office Building, and vanish into its upper reaches. Some thirty-five minutes later—his fascinated colleagues took to timing him—he would reappear in the hearing room, relaxed and at peace with the world, a satisfied smile on his face.

Senators like to pretend they're never too old. Carl Hayden of Arizona, who was ninety-one when he finally retired, used to shuffle slowly into the Senate each morning, a tall, gaunt figure, barely in motion. Senator Thomas Kuchel of California, the Republican whip, would regularly call over to him, "Hey, Don Carlos, did you get laid last night?" Hayden would reply with a ponderous wink, so slow and comprehensive that observers swore it put him out of breath for a moment.

Alliances with members of Congress can be advantageous professionally as well as socially, but they sometimes get complicated. A talented, liberal, and attractive woman with good Republican credentials was in line for a relatively high departmental position in the Nixon Administration until the White House learned she was very close to a senator who had been a persistent irritant to the President on Vietnam and other issues. She didn't get the job.

And the sure-footedness a girl needs on the Congressional social trail is not always easy. A national lobbying organization that supports causes and also helps finance candidates discovered that a ranking member of the House committee before which its chief cause bill was pending was also a man whose last political opponent it had helped finance. Clearly a ticklish situation. One of the group's Washington agents, a stylish, long-legged blonde, decided a personal interview might smooth things out. That evening, in his office, the congressman in question plied her with bourbon and then offered to exchange his legislative sympathy for immediate access to her person. Citing precedent, he rattled off a list of House members and their mistresses. Her retreat was prompt but uneasy, and she testified before the committee the next morning with understandable nervousness. At the close of her appearance, her host of the previous evening observed with a leer, "I have other questions, but I will save them for a more personal discussion." The chairman said, "With that, the committee will adjourn."

There is some evidence that the congressional urge can be inherited. One evening, a few years ago, the son of a Southwestern senator asked a Capitol guard to let him and a female companion into his father's office. Five minutes later, the guard discovered he had made a mistake, returned, unlocked the door, and said, "Excuse me, sir, but you're in the wrong room." The senator's son and his friend, on the floor at the time, uncoupled, got up, picked up their respective clothing, and accompanied the guard

58 *Both Your Houses*

a few doors farther down the deserted hall, where he unlocked the proper office for them and then resumed his nightly rounds.

There are many stories told about another member, since voluntarily retired, who managed to convert his broad-ranging Washington social life into an unusual political asset. While his more conventional colleagues cemented alliances by distributing the government publication on child care known as the "baby book," patronage jobs, and legislative favors, he distributed girls. Over an active personal career, he built up a considerable list of lively women who were willing, upon his telephoned recommendation, to go out with other members of Congress, important constituents, and political leaders. Presumably, the same technique stood the senator in good stead in his subsequent activity as a Washington lobbyist.

Politics can be overly preoccupying, of course. The ardent companion of a senator running for President reported later that he became ineffective during the immediate preconvention period when concerned about the ebb and flow of his delegate strength. Another ambitious senator, who shared his political planning with his wife, took time off during the campaign to make love but is reported to have stopped suddenly, looked down at her, and asked, "Do you really think we're doing the right thing in Brown County?" Not surprisingly, that wife later divorced him, and the sequel is not without political significance. Shortly thereafter, she married his campaign manager, leading to the conclusion that there was a heretofore unrecognized advantage in knowing precisely when the candidate was leaving town for a vote-getting tour and when he was returning.

It is a depressing thought, but there are signs that Capitol Hill sex may be going the way of dueling and the unrecorded teller vote. Not very long ago, a pretty young newspaperwoman, newly assigned to Congress, observed wistfully, "I thought I might have to use my body up here, but I find I don't need it with the Democrats, and it doesn't do any good with the Republicans."

Which may or not signal a turnabout. One sure thing is that the arrival of Representative Bella Abzug of New York in the House in 1971 produced acute cultural shock among some congressmen. There had never really been an aggressively liberated female in the body before, and confusion mingled with envy when she dismissed the self-important House doorkeeper, William "Fishbait" Miller, with "Go fuck yourself."

Some of the bolder male House members vied to tempt their outspoken new colleague into even stronger sallies. During the 1971 May Day demonstrations, the *Washington Post* ran a front-page picture of the crowded Capitol steps in which the genitalia of a nude demonstrator were decorously obscured by a small black square. Representative Richard Ichord of Missouri approached Mrs. Abzug with the photo and inquired, "What do you think is under there?" Without a flicker, she replied, "Another Ichord."

But such incisive response is more typical of the private than the public face of Congress. The preceding glimpse of the social ways of Capitol Hill stands for the proposition that senators and representatives, even as you and I, need to project—or at least appear to—the vitality that is inseparable from creative activity. The broader question is whether that demonstrable vitality can be channeled into more serious pursuits, brought to bear if only in part on the deep institutional faults that threaten the very foundations of Congress. If it cannot, then the Hill will no longer be a place to play, because it will not be a place at all.

# 5 · Power to the Survivors

It says something about the books written on Congress over the years that no one since has caught the essence of the Committee system any better than young Woodrow Wilson did in 1885. Six years out of Princeton and still studying for his doctorate, he wrote:

> The House sits, not for serious discussion, but to sanction the conclusions of its committees as rapidly as possible. It legislates in its committee rooms, not by the determination of majorities, but by the resolutions of specially commissioned minorities; so it is not far from the truth to say that Congress in session is Congress on public exhibition, whilst Congress in its committee rooms is Congress at work.

Wilson did not say so, but his observation is far more true of the House than of the Senate. The House, large and ungainly, must rely more heavily on the decisions that presumed specialists have already made in committee. There is simply not enough time for the other 400-odd members to learn through the record and floor debate what a good deal of the complicated material that reaches the floor is all about.

This time problem was institutionalized long ago in the House Rules Committee, whose ostensible function is determining how long floor debate on each bill may last, whether any amendments can be submitted at all, and, sometimes, just what sort of amendment is permissible. (In the Senate, where debate is unlimited as long as one man stands, the Rules Committee is a minor house-keeping body, largely occupied with such concerns as whether girl pages should be required to wear slacks instead of short skirts on the floor. They are.)

The Senate has—or thinks it has—the time to examine in more detail a bill already cleared by committee and to offer a wide range of amendments on the floor and generally do a good deal more rewriting of the committee product than the tightly circumscribed House. Also, senators, who serve on two or three committees to one for most House members, have come to regard themselves, correctly or not, as generalists, more widely expert and thus not required to give as much reverence to a committee draft.

The fact remains, however, that the basic structure of most legislation is laid down in committee and normally stands thereafter as long as the bill does. The burden of proof is always on the member who would alter the committee's considered judgment. Critically important decisions as to a bill's more controversial points will be resolved on the floor more often in the Senate than in the House, but the underlying questions of whether Congress will approach the issue at all and what form its approach will take are decided in committee.

The power of the committee system is nowhere better illustrated than in House Ways and Means, which is charged with originating all tax measures. (The Constitution says they must begin in the House, which for well over a hundred years was Congress's only popularly elected body.) The committee also handles such delicate and complex matters as foreign trade, social security, welfare, Medicare, Medicaid, and revenue sharing. Normally, but not always, Ways and Means first holds public hearings on a major bill, during which the Administration and other interested individuals and groups can present suggestions and criticism. Then the committee goes into executive session, and its highly effective chairman, Representative Wilbur Mills of Arkansas, begins shaping the bill. What emerges from days or weeks of closed-door deliberations is often a long, complicated, technical piece of work, and Mills normally asks the Rules Committee, a screening body, for a "closed rule," a resolution specifying that the measure cannot be amended on the floor but must be voted up or down intact, either ratifying the committee's entire product or rejecting it altogether.

Even under a closed rule, the House actually has two other options available. A rule is nothing more than a resolution from the Rules Committee that must be adopted by the full House before regular debate can begin; if a closed rule is rejected, the Rules Committee must come up with an alternative, presumably one that offers more opportunity for changing the bill on the floor. The second option, always open, is a motion to recommit the bill altogether or to send it back to committee for a specific change, which can be broad or narrow. This motion to recommit is the property of the minority party; if that party's leaders support the bill, they pass the right to make the motion down to one of their colleagues who does not. Ways and Means bills almost always get closed rules and are almost always approved on the floor. Mills has lost only four or five in nearly fifteen years as chairman, and his high batting average is a tribute to the respect, approaching awe, in which his colleagues hold him. "Highly respected, very distinguished" is the sort of language that congressmen use reflexively on the floor in referring to each other; in Mills's case, as in few others, it is seriously meant.

The Senate Finance Committee, the comparable group at the north end of the Capitol, and the Senate itself do not ordinarily change more than about 20 per cent of a given Ways and Means bill, although the changes are often significant. Then the two versions are sent to a conference committee of members of both houses to iron out the differences, because there can be no law unless the Senate and House ultimately pass precisely the same bill. The conference committee, in the way of compromise, normally restores at least half the House language that the Senate has changed; Mills is known to be both persuasive and stubborn in conference. The net result is that about 90 per cent of some of the most important laws that Congress writes are really written in a single committee and are, to a considerable degree, the product of its chairman.

Other legislation may bear less committee imprint in its final form, emerging more as the product of intensive reworking on the floor, but the committee almost always lays down the foundation. And it is the chairman who decides whether or not there will be a foundation at all, what shape it will take, and whose suggestions for the superstructure will be accepted, modified, or rejected. There have been a number of attempts in recent years to reduce chairmen's arbitrary power—mandatory scheduling of meetings, curbs on proxy voting, public announcement of closed committee votes—but many of these men and women still go on running their committees as wholly owned personal subsidiaries.

"Recently, when my chairman announced he planned to proceed in a particular way," a House member said, "I challenged him to indicate under what rules he was operating. 'My rules,' he said. That was it, even though there were no regularly authorized rules permitting him to function in that manner."

When Senator Thomas McIntyre of New Hampshire, a combat infantry officer in World War II, came to the Senate, he won a place on the Armed Services Committee and went diligently to work. With staff assistance, he prepared his first bill, an amendment dealing with the reserves, and presented it forcefully before the committee. The patriarchal chairman, Senator Richard Russell of Georgia, called for a vote, and the amendment was adopted, to the great satisfaction of its freshman sponsor. But the chairman, who had voted no himself, then ordered a second roll call, and, to McIntyre's consternation, his amendment was defeated. Later, a committee aide explained to the still shaken senator, "Sometimes the chairman likes to see how the members feel before they take a real vote."

Representative Mills operates so smoothly and with such solicitude for the views of all his Ways and Means members that he is rarely accused of dictatorial tactics, but he, too, has his methods. Often, he will lead the committee through a discussion of an important and controversial tax provision and, after everyone has had his say, will instruct the staff, "Draft that up." Inasmuch as there has not seemed to have been any resolution of the problem, the unspoken response of a member unaccustomed to the Mills technique is "Draft *what* up?" Subsequently, the staff consults Mills in preparing the language that goes into a preliminary print of the bill, which can be revised later, anytime before the bill is reported, *if* a member wants to propose something different and demand a roll call on his amendment. That doesn't happen too often, probably because amendments without the support of the chairman rarely prevail in Ways and Means.

Chairmanship bestows a new level of social prestige as well as political power on the man who gains it. Representative George Mahon finally scaled one of the major power peaks, chairman of House Appropriations, while his fellow Texan Lyndon Johnson was in the White House, and the President invited the congressman and his wife to Camp David for the weekend. During the visit, Mrs. Mahon observed how much more pleasant Washington social life had become during the Johnson Administration, compared to the doldrums of the Eisenhower and Kennedy years. "My dear," her husband responded gently, "we weren't chairman then."

To reach the chairmanship, a member obviously has to get on the committee in the first place, and the assignment system—if it is systematic enough to deserve that name—has been subjected to criticism over the years, largely by those who found it personally frustrating. Officially, original assignment to a committee and subsequent transfer to a more desirable one are based on a combination of seniority and preference, but there are so many men and women of precisely equal seniority and similar wishes in each entering congressional class and thereafter that other factors inevitably intervene.

In each house, each party has a committee charged with making these assignments. The Republicans use a Committee on Committees in both houses; the Democrats, a Steering Committee in the Senate and the Ways and Means party members in the House. But, when there is competition for a committee vacancy, these units are heavily influenced by the party leaders in the respective house, the chairman or ranking minority member of the committee involved, and the chairman or ranking member of the selection committee. In most but not all cases, it is the top party leader—the Senate majority or minority leader, the Speaker or the House minority leader—who really decides in the long run who shall be put where and for how long.

All kinds of interrelated factors enter into a final decision on committee assignment. Some committees try to maintain a regional balance, with each section of the country represented—or, more accurately, the regions insist on such representation. Thus, a senior man from a mountain state will almost certainly be ignored if he tries to claim a vacancy on Appropriations left by the retirement of a New England man. The preference of the chairman of the committee involved has weight but is not decisive; in 1971, Representative Edward Hebert, the new chairman of House Armed Services, protested bitterly against the assignment to his committee of an outspoken dove, Representative Michael Harrington of Massachusetts, but Hebert failed to block the move, because higher party leaders favored it.

Sometimes issues promote one candidate for a committee assignment over another. For many years, a Democrat could not get onto Ways and Means unless he favored reciprocal trade agreements, and no Republican was named to the committee unless he opposed them. Similarly in the 1940's and 1950's, the test for Democratic membership on the House Public Works Committee was advocacy of the Saint Lawrence Seaway, which Republicans had to oppose. A Republican with ten years of seniority and a professional background as a contractor was turned down for a vacancy after he called the project "inevitable."

Personality enters into committee assignment, as it does in almost all political preferment. When Representative William Fitts Ryan came to the House in 1960 from an intensely liberal Manhattan district, he insisted on trying to rebut almost every conservative argument on the floor, proposing innumerable amendments and speaking over a wider range of issues than most congressmen regard as one man's possible area of competence. Assigned to the Science and Astronautics Committee, a second-rank unit at best, he languished there for eight long years. Finally, in 1969, the Democratic leadership mercifully shifted him to Judiciary, but he wound up five rungs lower on the seniority ladder than he would have been if he had made the better committee in the first place—behind five additional men, all of whose chairmanships he must survive end to end if he is ever to reach a position of real congressional influence.

Quirks are sometimes controlling. In 1955, a Republican freshman, facing stiff competition because his party's share of committee seats had been cut back by losses in the previous election, managed to be named to the committee of his choice over several senior men. The reason: A shrewd adviser discovered that the freshman and the ranking Republican on that committee were both Lincoln buffs and arranged a half-hour chat between the two men, completely confined to the Great Emancipator. The senior man backed his compatible new friend for the vacancy, and he got it.

But, despite its irregularities, the committee assignment system, on balance, ranks fairly low on the list of congressional horrors. Theoretically, it would be possible to computerize the entire process, taking into account seniority, region, party loyalty, leadership estimates of talent, and the background and desires of the individual member, with the machine balancing everything out to several decimal points. Then the man who is still denied the committee he wants could go argue with the programmer. On the whole, however, there are so many human factors inescapably involved that are difficult if not impossible to measure that the present jerry-built, one-case-at-a-time system probably works as well as any. Senators and representatives with a real desire to serve on a particular committee almost always get there, later if not sooner. Entrusting the final decisions to party leaders tends to ensure that more of them will be personal than arbitrary; after all, the leaders must keep the maximum number of their members happy. The system also gives the leaders some measure of control over the committee system. They often have considerable difficulty with strong-minded, autonomous chairmen once such men succeed to power. Explicitly settling in the leadership the right, one way or the other, to balance out a committee through filling its ranks could become a powerful lever if the present seniority rules are recast, as we will see later. It is the seniority rule that is the real problem.

If the committees of Congress are so pivotally important and their chairmen so powerful and prestigious, it becomes important to know how these men and women reach this exalted status. The answer is simplicity itself: They survive. For the Senate and House, unlike almost every other parliamentary body in the world, operate on the seniority system, which allocates its key positions of power on all committees to those who have served on them the longest, independent of any other qualification whatsoever.

One of the most frustrating aspects of the seniority system is the fact that officially it doesn't even exist. The applicable Senate rule, from Jefferson's *Manual*, reads, "In the appointment of the standing committees, the Senate, unless otherwise ordered, shall proceed by ballot to appoint severally the chairmen of each committee." The corresponding House language is just as clear: "At the commencement of each Congress, the House shall elect as chairman of each standing committee one of the members thereof."

The trouble is that this never happens. Or, more precisely, votes of both Senate and House involving the designation of committee chairmen do take place, but they are routine, automatic stamps of approval, not elections at all. There is no competition, there are no speeches, none of the political bargain and maneuver to round up votes that surround every other important congressional decision. In 1971, both parties reacted almost imperceptibly to pressure for change by revising the language but not the effect of the system. The rules now officially include standby machinery under which the party caucus in either house can reject a chairmanship recommendation from the selection committee, a move that had always theoretically been available. As soon as this new provision was on the books, the selection committees proposed all the senior members for chairmanships, and no one in the caucuses said a word.

When the seniority system produces a good chairman, it does so entirely by accident. When it does not, as is far too often the case, the system is so broadly destructive as to offend the entire commonwealth. The elevation to power of men whose only demonstrable qualification is longevity hurts the nation by arbitrarily assigning it the most ordinary leadership, hurts Congress by augmenting its reputation for complacency and disregard of excellence, and, least recognized but most cruel, hurts the men it is designed to serve, often bringing them to high influence well past their prime, however undistinguished that prime may have been.

Such estimates are always arguable, but a rough survey of thirty-eight committees in the Ninety-second Congress (1971–72) indicated that sixteen of them had other members among the top five in seniority who were clearly better qualified—physically, mentally, and professionally—than the sitting chairman. Another eight had senior members who would probably be an improvement, but the margin was closer. Broadly speaking, half the committees in Congress were being directed by men who would almost certainly not qualify if the test were over-all ability rather than length of service.

This is more second-raters than the nation can afford. The seniority system is demonstrably not providing Congress with the best leaders available and, indeed, is denying available first-class men an opportunity to exercise and increase their talent in positions of real responsibility.

"No other free world legislature and no state legislature is bound by the seniority system," Senator Mark Hatfield of Oregon told the Senate in 1971. This statement might have given someone pause if there had been anyone in the chamber to listen. Unfortunately, the alternative proposed by Hatfield, a disillusioned Republican liberal, was not to abolish or modify the seniority system but merely to blunt its effect by restricting all senators and representatives to twelve consecutive years of service. Such a move would not tend to promote qualified committee chairmen; it would only protect the Republic to a modest degree by ensuring that those beneficiaries of the seniority system who were mediocre or worse would hold power more briefly than they now do. (Then, very possibly, to be succeeded by another mediocrity, even less experienced.)

Congressional age figures are not important in an absolute sense —there are wise old members and stupid young ones—but they are illuminating as to one effect of total reliance on seniority. In mid-1971, according to Senator Hatfield, the median age in the country was 27.7, and in Congress it was 52.7. If that gap seems at least ten years too broad, it becomes cavernous where the real power lies, among committee chairmen, for the median age of chairmen in the Senate then was sixty-seven and in the House, sixty-nine.

Of course, there are exceptions—and any proper system would allow for them—but no one can argue that, on the average, men of postretirement age chosen because of longevity, can run the legislative branch of government better than those chosen for ability.

The worst examples of the seniority system are not the outrageous ones but the sad ones. Chet Holifield came to the House from California in 1942, a thirty-eight-year-old Democratic liberal whose strong motivation quickly overcame his lack of formal education. Within a half-dozen years, he had moved into the critical new field of atomic energy, eventually to head (at fifty-eight) the Joint Congressional Committee and advise international conferences. Domestically, when House Democratic liberals occupied an embattled Alamo in the 1950's, seemingly besieged by the Eisenhower Administration on one flank and the Johnson-Rayburn congressional leadership on the other, Holifield was often chosen to make the liberal case to the Speaker. But the luck of the draw made Holifield wait twenty-eight years to become chairman of his standing committee, House Government Operations, and it proved to be too long. Ahead of him in line had been Representative William Dawson of Illinois, Mayor Richard Daley's lone symbolic black envoy in Washington. Dawson's luck proved extraordinary; he made chairman of the committee after only six years and lived to be eighty-four. Never precisely a dynamic leader, Dawson was decreasingly active during his last dozen years, but Holifield never attempted to move into the power vacuum. That was not the way the system worked; you waited until it was your turn, and then you took command.

When Holifield's turn as chairman finally came in 1971, he was simply no longer up to it. He had had almost no experience at running the committee during nearly three decades as a member, denied such background because of rigid application of the seniority system by a chairman whose own chief qualification had been seniority. At sixty-seven, Holifield was just not the leader he would have been at fifty or fifty-five, when his colleagues, given a free choice, might very well have chosen him over Dawson. Apparently anxious to demonstrate authority, he abolished the committee's consumer panel despite its productive record. He merged two active subcommittees to dump one chairman. When the committee finally produced a consumer protection bill in 1971, he collaborated secretly with the Nixon Administration and Republican committee members to emasculate the final product. Challenged by reporters, he would respond with an emotional, incoherent defense of his entire career. Holifield had been forced by the system to wait too long, and it was too bad.

"The seniority system programs men not to get power until they're too old to use it properly," another member of the Government Operations Committee observed bitterly. "What kind of a corporation would pick as its president a sixty-five-year-old man with no proven performance record? No kind. Look at what this means to me: The system says I've got to wait another twenty years before I can be chairman. I'll be just about Holifield's age, and probably no more up to it than he is."

The annals of Congress are littered with the names of men whom the seniority system elevated far above their qualifications. When Republicans seized control of the House in 1946, Representative Fred Hartley of New Jersey, one of the Grand Old Party's dimmer bulbs, automatically moved from ranking minority member to chairman of the House Education and Labor Committee. The chairman thus deposed, Representative Mary Norton of New Jersey, charged that Hartley had attended exactly six committee meetings in the previous ten years. She resigned from the committee rather than serve under him, about as drastic a protest as a member of Congress can make, because it throws away all precious seniority. Brent Spence of Kentucky was already fifty-six when he came to the House and reached seventy-four by the time he survived to the chairmanship of the Banking and Currency Committee. He was deaf and didn't see too well, either. When he served as floor manager of a bill, committee aides had to aim him in the direction of any colleague who was seeking recognition to take part in the debate.

It was a matter of considerable embarrassment to the House generally when Thomas Gordon of Illinois attained the chairmanship of the once-prestigious House Foreign Affairs Committee in 1957. Untutored in international relations and even ungrammatical, he was a complete mismatch for the cosmopolitan State Department officials over whom he was supposed to exercise some measure of informed oversight. Mercifully for Congress, though not for himself, poor health forced his retirement after only one term as chairman.

There have been others who lasted much longer.

Carl Hayden came to Congress when Arizona was admitted to statehood, in 1912, and liked it so much he stayed. After fifteen years in the House, he took up permanent residence in the Senate, and at the time he retired at ninety-two he occupied, at least physically, two key power roles, Appropriations chairman and President pro tempore. As the latter, a stand-in for the usually absent Vice President, he once insisted on presiding over an involved procedural debate during a filibuster. Stubborn and confused when a complicated point arose, he rejected the parliamentarian's ruling, told him audibly, "I want to go with Russell," mumbled some unintelligible decision of his own, and shuffled out of the chamber. It took the Senate the rest of the day to get untangled.

Representative Mendel Rivers was only fifty-nine, a mere stripling, when the seniority system made him chairman of the House Armed Services Committee. His problem was not senility but alcohol. Through many of his thirty years in Congress, he was either drunk periodically during the working day or missing altogether, drying out from the last binge. Not exactly a figure to be entrusted with direction of the defense establishment if the committee had had any choice in the matter, Rivers was a conspicuous success in one regard: He wangled so many military installations for his South Carolina district that colleagues swore that one more base and it would sink into the Atlantic.

At eighty-three, Representative Michael Kirwan of Ohio had not yet made it to a chairmanship, but he directed the politically potent Public Works subcommittee of House Appropriations in a manner that could most charitably be described as eccentric. Pressed by an insecure freshman member of his own party for a bill to make the Chesapeake and Ohio Canal a national monument, Kirwan responded, "I come from an area where we had a canal [the Erie]. Two young boys rode the mules on that canal [Garfield and McKinley]. Both got shot. We don't want any more canal bills."

Speaker John McCormack was a classic example of a good man that the House wore out before it gave him power. Elected from his Boston district at thirty-seven, he became a vigorous floor leader and strong-hearted liberal. But he did not make it to the Speakership until he was seventy, a feeble, confused, and ineffectual old man. Only scandals touching his employees persuaded him into retirement at seventy-eight. Strictly speaking, McCormack's rise was not a product of the seniority system, for he was chosen Speaker in an open, competitive election. But the dead hand of seniority reaches even to such choices, all but dictating the advancement of the next man on the ladder, whatever his qualifications at the time.

Even sadder was the decline of Representative Joseph Martin of Massachusetts, twice Republican Speaker and only replaced as a party floor leader when he was seventy-three. When he finally lost a primary in 1966, at the age of eighty-one, he was very nearly a vegetable, sitting in the chamber hour after hour, staring mindlessly ahead. And yet, had the Republicans recaptured the House, that man would have become a committee chairman, albeit a minor one. The system would have offered no alternative.

Inflexible application of seniority gave the Senate James Eastland of Mississippi as chairman of its Judiciary Committee in 1956, two years after the Supreme Court's school desegregation ruling. An outspoken racist, he had refused to hold a meeting of his civil rights subcommittee for two years and openly attacked the Court as "brainwashed by leftwing pressure groups." Representing an obnoxious minority view in his party, his chairmanship was an intense political embarrassment to Democratic national leaders and an effective blockade against congressional civil rights action for many years. But nothing could be done about it, and he was still there in 1972, presiding less than enthusiastically over the investigation of ITT memos and the relationship, if any, between the Nixon Justice Department and the giant conglomerate.

One practical problem about the seniority system is that it tends to be self-perpetuating and self-justifying. As men and women begin to accumulate service in Congress, they find it more logical that they should be rewarded on the basis of that service, solid and dignified, than that advancement should come to the noisier new arrivals who act pushy in committee. As one congressman observed,

> As you get closer to the top of the hierarchy, the pressures on people who normally would be counted on to aid reformers are enormous, and even people who would be classified as among the good guys rather than the bad guys tend to chicken out. It is the second- and third-termers who really have to lead the rebellion. The new fellows are still in a dream world, and after you get beyond two or three terms, you are part of the team and begin to see some merit in the system.

It is clearly going to take a remarkable assertion of principle over self-interest and indolence for either the House or the Senate to shake up the seniority system, assuming the dividing line between rebel and establishmentarian is the end of six years of service. In the Ninety-first Congress (1969–70), 255 of the 435 House members had served four terms or more, a solid potential majority for the *status quo*. In the Ninety-second Congress (1971–72), as the trend toward re-election of incumbents continued to reduce turnover in the House, the figure rose to 273. In the Senate in the same two congresses, the number of members with more than six years of service was 68 and then 65 out of 100.

If the seniority system rewards the venal and incompetent irregularly, it consistently elevates to power those men in Congress who need have the least regard for the concerns of the electorate It is the inescapable nature of the system. A committee chairman must, by definition, be a man who has survived a series of elections while his colleagues have not. Such survival is naturally a good deal easier if you happen to represent a one-party state or district, one that would cheerfully elect the south end of a northbound moose if it were nominated by the Republican (or, as the case may be, Democratic) Party.

Thus, in the Ninety-second Congress, twelve of the sixteen Senate committee chairmen were from heavily Democratic states, nine of them in the South, and the other four represented states with strong if not overwhelming Democratic voting records: Missouri, New Jersey, New Mexico, and Wyoming. In the House, the picture was even more definite: Twenty of the twenty-one committee chairmen came from districts in which they and their party were utterly unassailable. The sole exception was more statistical than real: Wayne Aspinall of Colorado, the House Interior chairman, gets re-elected by something less than a landslide in a generally Republican district—but it has happened every two years since 1948.

The seniority system does not merely promote but virtually guarantees rule by the unresponsive. It is a proved fact of congressional life that the great majority of committee chairmen need have only the most limited concern for the views of the voters who mechanically return them to office, and even less for national sentiment outside their safe little constituencies. There was no pressure whatsoever on thirty-one of the thirty-six chairmen in the Ninety-second Congress to sensitize themselves to public opinion, to attempt to reflect in their actions what the people feel should be done. It is all very well to point out individual chairmen who go far beyond political necessity in trying to keep their committees and themselves abreast of the latest developments, in information as well as sentiment. But the system automatically produces chairmen who are not under the least compulsion to behave this way.

The counterargument, of course, is that committee chairmen *should* occupy such a position of splendid isolation, that the Republic is better served by lawmakers who feel no burning sense of responsibility to mirror precisely the views of their constituents. There is an element of truth here: Plainly, a congressman should be capable of exercising independent judgment, willing to vote against a poll of the district when principle and intelligence demand. But, sadly, the seniority system places no premium whatsoever on principle and intelligence, does not even recognize their existence. It provides not one crumb of assurance that the men from safe districts it elevates to power will have the qualifications to use wisely that precious independence they so accidentally enjoy.

The basic argument in support of the seniority system holds that it is orderly, dependable, and prevents committee work from being continuously colored by divisive politicking among those pressing for advancement. The key word is "stability," or, if you are a sociologist, "conflict reduction." Under this rationale, a committee will operate with smooth and certain efficiency as long as no member is encouraged to believe he can improve his own standing by learning more, debating more cogently, or organizing a bloc of like-minded colleagues. The committee will remain placid and serene, because there is nothing to be gained by making waves.

But suppose committee members knew that they could improve their position (and advance more rapidly) if they demonstrated capability, could even challenge for leadership one day on the basis of merit. What would follow? It seems inescapable that some congressmen would work harder than they now do, build a better background more rapidly in their committee's area of responsibility, even show up for more meetings. Granted, some bumptious freshmen would talk too much, push foolish amendments, and otherwise clutter up the proceedings. A certain amount of that happens now. But the sensible senator or representative would learn rapidly that building a record within the committee required moderation, common sense, timing, and all the essential political qualities. Only when a chairman had lost control to a challenger but not yet been replaced would smooth committee operation be threatened, and even then a measure of stability would continue.

A long-standing objection to any merit system contends that bitter political factionalism would result, turning brother Democrat against brother and tending to obstruct the constructive work of Congress. In response to that argument, just for openers, it is hard to imagine that the divisions between the liberal and conservative wings of the two parties would grow much deeper than they are now—more apparent, perhaps, but not much deeper. Additionally, if the power to choose a new chairman were restricted to majority-party committee members, factional rivalry could also be held within relatively narrow scope, instead of spilling over into the entire delegation of the party involved.

Actually, in political terms, the seniority system has consistently undermined party regularity and discipline. Under its comforting protection, a congressman can vote against his party's program bills, denounce its platform, ignore its leaders, and openly oppose its national candidates, secure in the knowledge that he will become chairman in God's good time, all the same. Once in a while, in particularly flagrant cases, a party will strip seniority from a member who backed an opposition Presidential candidate, but this is very rare. Generally, any senator or representative can rest assured that he can become an outright party heretic whenever it suits his purpose and still not risk his devoutly wished-for chairmanship.

All right then, what can be done? Surely, there is some better way for Congress to choose the men who really control its efforts. The fact is that there are a lot of better ways—and, generally speaking, the better they are, the harder it will be to get Congress to adopt them. There is no point in pretending here that any modification of the seniority principle is going to find instant favor with the members. It isn't. Although there is more support for change now than there was ten years ago, any real improvement in the present system faces a long, uphill battle.

This has led some members who are anxious for a change to propose solutions that blunt the effect of the seniority system but do not go to the heart of the problem. For example: a limit on the number of terms that a House chairman can serve to four or five. After his eight or ten years, he would step down automatically (to be succeeded by the next senior man), continuing to serve on the committee and holding the next highest rank for all purposes except the chairmanship. This tenure figure could be adjusted up or down; the Senate would probably want to key it to the six-year term. In the Ninety-second Congress, a two-term limit on Senate chairmen would have disqualified only James Eastland of Judiciary, John McClelland of Government Operations, and Warren Magnuson of Commerce. In the House, a five-term, ten-year limit would have affected six chairmen, including Wilbur Mills of Ways and Means, Emanuel Celler of Judiciary, and Thomas Morgan of Foreign Relations.

Another variation of this idea would prohibit any member from becoming chairman after his sixty-fifth birthday and from serving as chairman after seventy—a solution that has the same weaknesses as a term limitation. It reduces rather than prevents the damage an incompetent chairman can do. Because it is just as arbitrary as the seniority system, when it achieves its purpose—good leadership—it also does so accidentally. It would prohibit or limit the service of older men, independent of their quality, benefiting Congress in some instances but depriving it of real talent and experience in others. These palliative remedies tend to appeal to members of Congress: They appear even-handed and less radical than a genuine merit system, and, perhaps most important, they eliminate the necessity for a series of tough individual judgments later on.

Still another replacement for the seniority system involves some form of appointment by party leaders. Representative Richard Bolling of Missouri, the chief advocate of this cause, would give committee assignments indirectly and the selection of chairmen directly to the party leaders. Bolling's goal is not really selection of the ablest men as committee chairmen, but selection of those men who will most faithfully and expeditiously advance the party program through the House. He is chiefly concerned with the operation of the House as a whole and is convinced that it would benefit from a large dose of party regularity.

Bolling should know. He has seen committee chairmen thumb their noses at the leadership. He has seen the nominally Democratic Rules Committee, on which he sits, consistently block Democratic program bills sought by a Democratic President from reaching the floor of a Democratic-controlled Congress. His answer is to arm the Speaker with the power to punish uncooperative chairmen by replacing them at the opening of any new Congress, subject to the condition that a party majority is willing to back him up in the caucus.

While the Bolling plan chips away at the seniority system, it is not really an adequate substitute, either to lift the quality of the entire operation or to meet the objections of junior members toiling in the lower recesses of the committee with little prospect for preferment. Machinery under which chairmen are appointed does not really offer much prospect that an aged, venal, or incompetent man will be nudged off the seniority escalator—only that an uncooperative one will. As long as a sitting chairman sees to it that the party's program bills are processed and delivered to the floor promptly, a Bolling-style Speaker is unlikely to inquire further into his intellectual capacity, diligence, or leadership qualities.

On the occasions, probably fairly infrequent, when the Bolling plan circumvented seniority, the ultimate decision would pass to a large and potentially ill-informed jury: all the members of the majority party in the house involved. Here again, the forum is one likely to sustain the leader's decision to switch chairmen, but not necessarily one disposed to making a reasoned judgment. And, where the leader's decision ran into a serious challenge, the divisive political impact would affect the entire party delegation in the house.

Ultimately, there is only one satisfactory substitute for arbitrary imposition of seniority, and that is biennial election of each committee's chairman and ranking minority member by secret ballot of their party colleagues on the committee. They are, after all, the men and women who must chafe under the rule of an unqualified leader or flourish under a beneficent one. They are the people who know best the limitations of one colleague and the virtues of another, who can render the fairest judgment as between two candidates for leadership, one with longer service than the other.

Parenthetically, this is one area where accommodations for the two parties must be separate but equal. In a Democratic Congress, Republican members of a committee or the whole body cannot be allowed to vote for the chairman, any more than the Democrats should help choose the ranking minority member. The potential for political mischief in allowing such crossovers would certainly prove irresistible upon occasion, with Republican conservatives swinging behind a Southern Democrat who was actually in the minority in his own party, or Democratic liberals doing the same thing for a like-minded Republican. The adversary two-party system is a recognized fact of congressional life, even though it sometimes operates in mysterious ways, and muddling it further by encouraging such a breaking of ranks would only add to the already manifest confusion.

This is not to say that Congress might not operate more constructively some day on something other than the traditional two-party system as we know it. It is just that there are so many other more obvious and more easily remedied deficiencies in the current operation that a wholesale revision of the entire national political system will have to wait its turn.

Some younger members insist that it would never be possible to turn a chairman out if the choice were left to the committee itself. The argument runs that the chairman has so much power—to name subcommittee chairmen, to authorize travel at home and abroad, to promote one member's bill or amendment over another's—that he could bind a more or less permanent majority of his party's members on the committee to his continued chairmanship. Only very rarely, it is said, would a chairman become so objectionable that a majority would scorn the favors he has to dispense and rise up and overturn him. Very likely true, but those are precisely the cases now completely sheltered by the seniority system in which a committee should be free to act in the interest of its own improvement.

A very different situation would arise if, when a chairman dies or retires, a contest developed between the next senior man and a challenger farther down the list. With such a relatively open choice, a merit system would enable the committee to cut off a potentially bad chairman at the pass, to stop him short of leadership when the opening first occurred, with full knowledge that it would be mighty bloody difficult to get rid of him once the initial decision had been made. Obviously, when there are two competitors for a chairmanship, there is going to be a considerable amount of promising future favors in return for votes, but, because both men have exactly the same amount of everything to promise, there is some reasonable assurance that such commitments would balance out, and the decisive factor would be the relative quality of the two contenders. At least, there would be a lot more assurance that excellence would enter into the decision than exists today, when there is none.

In actual practice, any system under which a man with less seniority is promoted over one with more is almost certain to be used sparingly. Seniority would remain the yardstick for more routine congressional decisions, such as filling committee vacancies and assignment of office space. Seniority would be slow to pass as a tradition, and each decision to recognize talent over longevity would be seriously weighed. On any decision to pass over the senior man for a chairmanship, every member voting would be acutely aware that his own future advancement was involved in the result.

"If I vote against seniority now and perhaps again, even with full justification, how will the other members vote when I am the senior man up against a challenge?" That question will be clear in the mind of every functioning senator and representative when the tests come, and often a majority will prefer the conservative answer: stay with the system and protect your own future. Thus, any fears that abolition of the seniority system would produce a political melee—a wild, uncontrollable struggle for preferment—appear to be groundless. At the very least, moving from length of service to quality of service as a test for leadership would be an evolutionary process, gaining acceptability as it rewarded the deserving and raised the standards of the institution.

Another automatic brake on the merit system would be political. It is very likely that passing over a senior congressman for a chairmanship would be a long step toward ending his public career, leading him up to the edge of the cliff, if not actually pushing him over. For example, a bypassed senator—a man so little regarded by his colleagues that they denied him authority commensurate with his experience—would be an obvious target in the next election. In a one-party state or district, rejection for a chairmanship would be an open invitation to a primary challenge; in a closely balanced jurisdiction, it would provide the opposition party candidate with a devastating campaign weapon: "Do you want to be represented in Washington by a man found unfit for leadership by those who know him best?"

The old reliable campaign cry—"Keep Blotch in Congress, He Has the Seniority and Influence To Get Things Done"—would be reversed and handed over to the opposition. It would now read: "Why Keep Blotch in Congress? His Seniority Hasn't Earned Him Any Influence." Again, every member voting to pass over a senior colleague would know he was all but consigning that man to political limbo, and that his own future might hang on just such a vote some day.

Although a little heartless in the eyes of those who treasure congressional palship, this aspect of the merit system has a good deal to recommend it in terms of raising the quality of the Senate and House. Viewed dispassionately, it would tend to weed out of Congress precisely those members who are the least productive: older men who, despite long service, have still not demonstrated enough competence to be entrusted with leadership. There is no reason why Congress itself, with the clearest firsthand view of a member's performance, should not occasionally send just such a signal back to the home state or district, letting the people know that perhaps it was time they retired good old Joe. Not dictating to the voters, mind you, but passing the word that Joe can't hack it any more.

In this way, once the merit system was in operation, the need for unseating chairmen would probably decline markedly. By giving committee members a choice between mediocrity and capability, it would become less and less likely that a chairman would be chosen against whom a challenge would later arise. It would take a while—in Congress everything does—before all the major chairmanships were held by men who represented the best judgment of their colleagues, but that time would come.

The merit system would bring with it a host of collateral advantages. An elected chairman would be continuously conscious of the necessity of making a record, of demonstrating leadership. There is no such pressure on him now. An elected chairman would be much more responsive to sentiment in his own party, right down to the most junior man. Take a typical House committee of twenty Democrats and fifteen Republicans; a conservative Southern chairman might enjoy an ideological majority for legislative purposes, but if one ranking liberal and ten junior Democrats on the committee turned against him, he could be replaced at the opening of the next Congress. A merit system would assure junior members a stronger voice and more respectful treatment than they now enjoy.

There is an old congressional complaint among Democratic liberals: "How can you win with a Union army led by Confederate generals?" It is frequently true that the impressive phalanx of Southern committee chairmen does not reflect the majority views of the party, even of its members in Congress, but this can change. Fear of losing a chairmanship is likely to make the stiffest ideologue considerably more flexible.

Within the merit system, Senate and House leaders can regain an element of control over committee operation and leadership that they now lack almost totally. If chairmen are elected by their committee colleagues and the leaders have the power to fill vacancies on the committee, the Senate majority leader and the Speaker have a new weapon at their disposal. Let us suppose that a revolt is brewing on the Senate Commerce Committee, and five of the eleven Democrats would like to retire Senator Warren Magnuson for a chairman a little less solicitous of the aviation industry. (This is a purely hypothetical example.) One pro-Magnuson Democrat dies, and it is up to the leadership to fill the vacancy. Obviously, in such a situation, the majority leader can determine whether Senator Magnuson continues as chairman, by his choice of a new committee member, one pledged to support the chairman or one with opposite intentions.

As things stand now, Senate and House leaders are very nearly powerless to impose any sort of regularity on a committee chairman once seniority has given him the job. While the kind of delicately balanced situation described here might not arise very often, the continuing possibility would be likely to make chairmen considerably more responsive to the party leadership.

To achieve this merit system, with all its manifest advantages, it will be necessary to overcome the vast congressional reluctance to change, particularly strong where the institution itself is involved. But, in a nation whose whole economic and political structure is grounded in the proposition that competition is the best guarantee of quality, the seniority system simply will not do. A corporation run by the same rules would have gone bankrupt long ago, or had its board overturned by angry stockholders. A Congress that is already fast declining into obsolescence can no longer afford the luxury of this mindless veneration of age over ability.

# 6 · Tiger in Retirement

Representative Philip Campbell of Kansas was a very small meteor in the congressional firmament. Serving briefly as chairman of the House Rules Committee fifty years ago, he left one indelible line traced out against the sky of history, his statement when colleagues asked him to send to the floor bills that he personally opposed. "You can go to hell," he replied. "It makes no difference what a majority of you decide. If it meets with my disapproval, it shall not be done. I am the committee. In me reposes absolute obstructive power."

That power, exercised in varying degree over the years by men more memorable than he, has made the Rules Committee from time to time almost a third house of Congress and its chairman a figure of awesome stature casting a long shadow. As Campbell fully understood, there is no real creative authority in the Rules Committee, but its power to determine what business shall *not* be done has frequently been a major factor in shaping the legislative product of all the rest of Congress.

Basically, the Rules Committee is a power center because the House, its large membership unruly enough under the best circumstances, simply could not tolerate the filibuster. The first curb on debate came early. After a few lengthy performances by Representative John Randolph, a brilliant Virginian intoxicated by his own oratory, the House established in 1811 the motion for the previous question; if approved, it shuts off debate and forces an immediate vote—*if* someone can get the floor to make it.

But debate by members who had the floor remained unlimited, and, as the House grew in size, the luxury became insupportable. Finally, in 1841, to keep the machinery moving, a one-hour limit on any member's speaking in general debate was adopted, followed six years later by a five-minute limit on amendments. But still more restrictions proved necessary.

Established by the first session of the House in 1789, the Rules Committee was originally a select committee, a temporary group with a special purpose, to be dissolved when that purpose had been achieved. Once the basic House rules were developed, and then readopted every two years, the committee did not bother to meet or report in many congresses. But in 1880, it was promoted to standing or permanent status, and three years later it was assigned its present very important function.

What the Rules Committee began then and does today is to hold a hearing of its own on every major controversial bill that is ready for floor action and then recommend a suspension of the regular House rules and substitution of a new temporary set just for that bill. These special ground rules cover how long debate shall last, whether amendments will be permitted, and, sometimes, what sort of amendment. They are spelled out in a resolution that the committee adopts, commonly called a rule, and sends to the floor; if it is adopted there, as is almost always the case, the terms for consideration of the bill are then set. (The same effect could be achieved by a floor motion to suspend the rules, but that would require a two-thirds vote to pass. A rule from the committee only needs a simple majority.)

This practice sometimes results in arbitrary, even unreasonable limits on individual members' right to speak on a particularly controversial issue. In the 1970 House debate on the anti-ballistic-missile system, some speakers were restricted to as little as thirty seconds because so many wanted to speak. The system sometimes presents the House with an unenviable choice, that of accepting a long and highly technical bill intact without any right to amend it, or voting it down altogether. The system frequently leaves opponents of a bill that has reached the floor with only one weapon if they cannot beat the rule: a motion to send the measure back to committee for specific changes or further study. This is a move that the representatives, heavily reliant on their committee system and proud of its strength, are often reluctant to make. But for all its limitations, the practice of tailoring a rule for each bill keeps the lumbering House machine in motion and makes this body, in the end, far more efficient than the Senate, where there are really no effective rules at all.

In the way of such things, the House pays a price for this welcome order and dispatch. For the Rules Committee, which is intended to make only procedural judgments in sending a measure to the floor, winds up making substantive judgments as to whether the bill deserves consideration by the full body at all. The committee is officially limited to determining only the length of debate and the scope of floor amendments, but Representative Richard Bolling, a longtime member, says that "instead, it has taken to itself, without permission, the authority to judge the merits and demerits of the legislation itself."

The Rules Committee cannot amend a bill it finds objectionable. It can deliberately precipitate a free-for-all by sending a controversial bill to the floor under an "open rule," which permits unlimited amendments. But, historically, when the committee— or even its chairman alone—disapproves of a measure that has cleared the standing committee and is ready for floor action, it simply refuses to act. No rule, no floor debate, no passage, no law. Over great stretches of congressional history, most recently for more than twenty years prior to 1961, the Rules Committee has exercised Representative Campbell's "absolute obstructive power" whenever it saw fit, and a dozen or fewer men with no particular qualifications have decided which laws would be enacted by the United States and which would not.

During the iron-fisted regime of Representative Joseph Cannon of Illinois, the Republican leader served simultaneously as Speaker and chairman of the Rules Committee, leaving nothing to chance. His Democratic counterpart, Representative Champ Clark of Missouri, said of one of his bills before Rules, "it might as well be referred to the sleepers in the catacombs. I violate no secret when I tell you the committee is made up of three very distinguished Republicans and two ornamental Democrats." Cannon moved those bills he wanted and blocked the rest, using the committee as a private and wholly controlled arm of his own leadership. Finally, in 1910, a revolt of the members forced Uncle Joe, as he was ironically known, to give up the committee chairmanship and to accept a new method for bypassing a stubborn Rules Committee: the discharge petition, of which we will learn more later.

A different sort of Rules problem erupted in 1937, when a conservative committee under the chairmanship of Representative John O'Connor, Democrat of New York, turned against its own party leaders, Speaker William Bankhead of Alabama and majority leader Sam Rayburn of Texas, and began blocking New Deal legislation. In the 1938 election, President Franklin Roosevelt attempted an unprecedented purge of those Democratic senators and representatives who opposed his programs. The only man he succeeded in defeating was O'Connor, but a conservative coalition of Democrats and Republicans continued to operate the Rules Committee as a largely independent body for more than twenty years.

For much of that time, Representative Adolph Sabath of Illinois was chairman, suffering continuous indignities at the hands of the conservative majority among his members when he tried to advance liberal legislation. An old man—he was seventy-two when he reached the chairmanship—he sometimes sought to extricate himself from a parliamentary corner by staging a fainting spell so that the committee would adjourn. On one such occasion, collapsed in his leather armchair, Sabath waited a few moments, then lifted one eyelid to see a Republican Rules member, Representative Clarence Brown of Ohio, still at the committee table. "Have they all gone, Clarence?" he croaked plaintively.

Only in 1947–48 and 1953–54, when the Republicans somehow managed to win control of the House, did the committee become more responsive to party leadership. Otherwise, Democratic House leaders had almost continuous trouble getting any sort of liberal legislation cleared by Rules. This was not a particularly serious problem during the Eisenhower years when the Johnson-Rayburn leadership set fairly modest legislative goals. But when John Kennedy was elected and launched his New Frontier program, he ran headlong into Representative Howard Smith, a stubborn Virginian whom most voters had never heard of, much less regarded as a Presidential obstacle. Judge Smith, as he was known, was seventy-seven years old and had served as Rules chairman for the previous six of his twenty-six years on the committee. Smith believed firmly that the committee had been entrusted with the duty of passing on the merits of the legislation it cleared, not merely allocating floor time and defining permissable amendments. "My people didn't send me to Congress to be a traffic cop," the chairman would drawl when accused of exceeding his authority. Late in a session when controversial bills that Smith opposed had cleared the Senate and the House standing committees, but not Rules, he had the custom of retiring from Washington to his Loudon County farm "to milk the cows." In his absence, no Rules Committee sessions could be held, and the House was powerless to act on any but the most trivial bills.

Even with its chairman on duty, the twelve-member committee often split down the middle on key votes, with Smith and his confederate, Representative William Colmer of Mississippi, joining the four Republican members to create a deadlock and deny a rule to any bill they opposed. Sometimes Smith chose to avoid the inconvenience of voting at all. Midway in the 1960 session, Democratic leaders pressed him to release some party program bills to help the Presidential election campaign. "The only legislation I will agree to consider," he replied starchily, "is the minimum wage bill. You can tell your liberal friends that they will get that, or nothing. If you try to bring anything else up, I'll adjourn the meeting."

The real crunch came early in 1961, when President Kennedy proposed a federal aid-to-education bill that was almost certain to be blocked in Rules; the year before, the committee had killed an education bill that had passed both houses in different form by refusing to let it go to conference. With the new President's firm support, Speaker Sam Rayburn finally decided to move against Judge Smith. Rather than a frontal attack that the House would never have sustained, Rayburn chose an end run, proposing that the Rules Committee be increased from twelve to fifteen members. Two of the new men would be Democrats chosen by the Speaker, one a Republican; thus, the liberal-conservative balance would shift from 6–6 to 8–7 on key votes, and the Kennedy program would be moved to the floor of the House, if not necessarily beyond it.

Fruitless attempts to negotiate a settlement and then intensive lobbying by the White House and Democratic leaders preceded the vote on Rayburn's expansion plan. (A revealing piece of maneuvering saw Rayburn and Smith each confer privately on the same day with Representative Wilbur Mills, the wily and influential Ways and Means chairman. After their separate audiences, each of the bitter foes emerged with the same message: "Wilbur's all right.") Finally, late in January, the Rayburn proposal carried by the width of a communion wafer, 217–212. A shift of only three votes would have defeated the Speaker and the new Administration in a critical test of strength.

Since that time, as a practical matter, the Rules Committee has generally proved more docile, although its majorities for succeeding Presidential programs bills have rarely been thunderous. In 1966, moderate members took advantage of the departure of Judge Smith to pass new committee rules to circumscribe his successor. They took from the chairman the right to schedule meetings, which had been a powerful blocking weapon, and reduced his ability to control committee decisions with tabling motions and proxy votes.

For the past half-dozen years, the ten Democrats on the committee have included six liberals, two moderates, and two conservatives, while the five Republicans lined up as one liberal, one moderate, and three conservatives. Thus, the narrowest liberal majority had to attract at least one moderate, a perfectly reasonable proposition, but the five hard-rock conservatives were rarely in a position to bottle up legislation, whether it came from Johnson or Nixon.

The current Rules Committee has proved to be no rubber stamp, however, where legitimate procedural questions have been involved. When Representative Mills brought his version of the Nixon Administration's omnibus welfare bill to the committee in 1971, he wanted a closed rule: no floor amendments permitted and a single vote on the 780-page package, which included some politically popular social security benefit increases. But a majority of the Rules members, believing the House was entitled to a separate vote on the controversial plan for a minimum income for poor families, approved a rule authorizing such a vote in spite of Mills. The welfare section carried on the floor, but the vote was much closer than it would have been if the House had been allowed only one decision, on the entire package.

Over the years, the Rules Committee's excesses have not been confined to going beyond its procedural authority and blocking legislation on substantive grounds. On occasion, the group has exercised a startling degree of additional independent enterprise. In 1915, the committee sent to the floor a special order for a shipping purchase bill that had never even been introduced. During one seventeen-year period in the 1940's and 1950's the committee authorized House action on forty-two bills that had not been reported by standing committees. As recently as 1964, under the leadership of Judge Smith, the Rules Committee cleared for floor debate a bill designed to counteract Supreme Court decisions requiring the reapportionment of state legislatures on a one-man, one-vote basis. There was only one problem: the bill was still firmly lodged in the Judiciary Committee, which had not approved it and had no intention of doing so.

(Judge Smith's hostility toward reapportionment proved to be well founded. On the congressional level, it added a good chunk of Virginia's Washington suburbs to his previously rural district, and, in the 1966 Democratic primary, his new constituency voted him into involuntary retirement at the age of eighty-three.)

The Rules Committee startled Congress early in 1972 with a sudden display of positive rather than negative authority, sending President Nixon's dock strike bill to the floor under a closed rule prohibiting amendment, although it had not been reported by the House Education and Labor Committee. It should be confessed that a major motivation for this decision was settling the matter rapidly so that the House could take a one-week recess on schedule. But the action remained an unusual demonstration of audacity by Chairman Colmer in the face of open opposition from Speaker Carl Albert and hostile statements at the Rules hearing by other committee chairmen, who were quick to see their own authority being so undermined. Representative Wayne Hays of Ohio, the House Administration chairman and a peppery sixty, told Colmer to his face that he was reconsidering his support of the seniority system and hoped the next Congress could have "some chairmen who are responsive to the leadership and not a power unto themselves at eighty or ninety years of age." The usually intractable Colmer took the hint and announced two months later that he would not seek re-election.

Until relatively recently, the Rules Committee had another very critical source of power. The House could only go to conference on a bill with a differing Senate-approved version by a unanimous consent motion on the floor, which can be blocked by a single objection or by adopting a resolution previously approved by Rules. Often Rules simply refused to authorize a conference. In 1965, a simple majority of the House was given the right to agree to a conference, pulling down another potential barricade.

Several methods of circumventing a stubborn Rules Committee have been produced over the years, in times of parliamentary crisis. None of them works worth a damn. It has always been theoretically possible, for example, to bring up a bill that has not been cleared by the Rules Committee on a motion requesting "unanimous consent." If a single voice is raised against such a motion, it fails, so the procedure is essentially useless for rescuing any sort of controversial measure from a balky Rules Committee. (Some House members, notably H. R. Gross, an indomitable Iowa Republican, have made a career out of frustrating unanimous consent motions, on the not unreasonable theory that someone may be trying to put something over on a membership that would be better served if there were no exceptions to the rules.)

Two days each month, the House has a suspension calendar, a time when the Speaker can recognize any member he chooses, who then moves to suspend the rules so that his bill can be brought directly to the floor. Since this procedure automatically requires a two-thirds majority, it is almost never used to bypass the Rules Committee; any bill held up there is virtually certain to have more than a third of the House members against it, plus a number who would vote against suspension of the rules as the wrong way to do business on an important issue.

Out of the revolt against Speaker Cannon in 1910 came the discharge petition, which was supposed to cut the Rules Committee down to size. Under this procedure, a bill can be forced out of Rules and brought to the floor for debate and a final vote if an absolute majority of the House membership signs a petition supporting this action. In more than sixty years of trying, only two dozen bills have reached the floor by petition, of which twenty then passed. Only twice has a law resulted: the Roosevelt Administration's minimum wage bill in 1938 (its backers got all their signatures in less than three hours) and a salary increase for federal employees in 1960. Historically, many members have regarded the discharge petition as improper tampering with the committee system, even when they supported the bill to be discharged. Getting 218 signatures under these circumstances is a tough proposition.

Despite its lack of practical effectiveness, the discharge petition has enjoyed a special kind of political popularity, indicated by the fact that some 850 have been filed. Sponsors of bills to authorize prayer in the public schools or to create a new veterans' bonus are forever getting up petitions and collecting 100 or more instant signatures from colleagues anxious to demonstrate public enthusiasm for such causes. If the number of signers gets up over 200, some of the more responsible members—men who were concededly not so responsible as to refuse to sign in the first place— quietly withdraw their names. Everyone understands that this is a show, except those constituents who are thereby persuaded that they have a resolute congressman ready to Stand Up for a Cause.

The only other method of getting around the Rules Committee is Calendar Wednesday, a cumbersome, little-used procedure that is historically interesting because it has provided the few occasions on which the House can engage in its own version of the Senate filibuster. (Calendar Wednesday was instituted by Speaker Cannon in 1909 as a concession to his critics, but it failed to save him. In fact, the first of a series of votes against him that turned into a revolt came on his ruling that the new procedure could be set aside for a privileged bill.)

Each Wednesday, under this special set of rules, the Speaker may call the roll of committees and a chairman may bring to the floor any bill his committee has approved, even if it has not cleared the Rules Committee. The catch is that action must then be completed in one legislative day, or before noon on Thursday. This invites opponents of the bill to delay the proceedings any way they can—and in the House there are plenty of ways.

In 1950, sponsors of the antidiscrimination bill to create a Fair Employment Practices Commission (FEPC) were unable to get it through Rules and brought the measure to the floor by the Calendar Wednesday procedure instead. Southern Democrats and conservative Republicans responded with every stalling device they could muster. They started with a quorum call, a roll call designed to demonstrate upon challenge that there are enough members present to do business legally, 218 if the House is in regular session, or 100 if it is sitting as the Committee of the Whole to process amendments before moving to the final votes.

In the Senate, a quorum call can be begun and then abruptly abandoned after only a few names have been read; it is the accepted method of filling in chinks of unoccupied time while giving the galleries the spurious impression that some sort of constructive activity is under way. But in the House, a quorum call, once launched, must proceed on its inexorable course through two alphabetical runs down the entire 435-name list, and then recognition, one by one, of the remaining members who missed their turn and are standing in the well of the House. On the average, this takes thirty-five minutes each time it happens. A roll call on an amendment, a motion, or a bill takes the same time. During the entire period, the House is in a state of disorganization: members are streaming in and out of the chamber, gathering in conversational knots on the floor. At the end of a roll call, there is at least a result: a vote. At the end of a quorum call, there is nothing; the quorum it sought to achieve has often already vanished through the exits. (In 1970, the House established a new, abbreviated quorum call, under which members could check in on a tally sheet and the call would end as soon as a quorum had done so. But at this writing, a year and a half later, the system has yet to be used.)

Capitalizing on such time-consuming procedures, the 1950

FEPC foes insisted on a roll call on whether to dispense with the reading of the previous day's journal. Then came the reading of Washington's Farewell Address (it happened to be February 22), then a motion to adjourn with a roll call, then a roll call on moving to Calendar Wednesday, then a long series of quorum calls during which the Southerners hid in the cloakroom. Finally, at 11 P.M. Speaker Rayburn ruled that a request for still another quorum call was out of order as dilatory, debate on the bill began, and it was passed at four o'clock the next morning. Small wonder Representative Bolling calls the invocation of Calendar Wednesday "a form of masochism, akin to volunteering for the medieval rack."

This primitive machinery was last used successfully in 1960, when legislation for an Area Redevelopment Administration was brought to the floor without the sanction of the Rules Committee. Twelve roll calls occupied all the afternoon, and the bill was passed at 9:30 P.M. But President Eisenhower proceeded to veto it, further clouding the already poor record of Calendar Wednesday. Once, later in 1960, the system was used to put pressure on the Rules Committee to report a minimum wage bill, but two subsequent attempts to invoke the procedure in the Kennedy years both failed, and no one but dedicated House buffs really talks about Calendar Wednesday any more.

Aside from the Rayburn packing procedure, unlikely to be used soon again, the principal curb against an obstructive Rules Committee has been a rule giving the Speaker and a committee chairman power to call up a bill that Rules has refused to release, a certain amount of time having elapsed after notice. Such rules giving the committee twenty-one days to act were put into effect in the Eighty-first (1949–50) and Eighty-ninth (1965–66) congresses, but dropped each time after the Republicans gained strength in the next off-year election. In each of those two congresses, the procedure was used eight times to circumvent Rules, but it was also effective as a threat, putting pressure on a reluctant committee to clear bills for the floor.

When he became Speaker in 1971, Carl Albert, as one of his first official acts, proposed that he be given the power to take a bill from Rules thirty-one days after notice. The Democratic caucus backed him, but the conservative coalition beat him on the floor, 233–152, not exactly an encouraging portent for the Oklahoman's future influence.

Permanent adoption of such a rule would seem to be a reasonable check on the power of the Rules Committee to set a roadblock in the path of legislative progress, power it was never intended to possess. Perhaps such a proposal would be more palatable to the House if, instead of giving the Speaker arbitrary authority to lift a bill out of Rules, it permitted him to set a deadline within which the committee was required to act. Under such an arrangement, when the committee was laggard, a Speaker could require it to move the measure to the floor within three weeks or a month after notice, but otherwise on its own terms. Thus, the committee would not be forced to surrender its legitimate authority to set the terms and scope of debate, but only to do so within a reasonable time limit.

No one should expect, however, that some masterful reworking of the House rules will restrict the Rules Committee to the procedural considerations that are its nominal assignment. It is unreasonable on the face of it to put a controversial piece of legislation before fifteen politicians and instruct them to ignore the substance of the bill and only determine *how* it can best be handled on the floor. Tailoring a rule to a bill requires an examination of its substance. Determining what sort of amendments, if any, should be permissible cannot be done in a vacuum. All that can reasonably be expected of any Rules Committee is that its members do not allow their collective judgment of the merits of a given bill to obscure their procedural function to the point that they refuse to let the measure reach the floor at all on the basis of its substance.

This screening function could be taken away from the Rules Committee altogether, but the other possible repositories for it do not seem any more promising. If the Speaker were given authority to draft a rule for each bill, even subject to its approval by the full House, we would be back where we were when Uncle Joe Cannon was both Speaker and Rules chairman and was properly regarded as a tyrant. If the chairman of the standing committee had this authority, he would be under considerable pressure from his members to call for a closed rule for every bill, which, in turn, would result either in further restricting the ability of the House to reshape legislation on the floor, or in clogging up still more of the House schedule with debating and defeating closed rules in favor of more flexible substitutes. The theory of entrusting this function to the Rules Committee is not unsound. Only the resulting practice has proved troublesome.

Substitution of a merit system for the seniority system, as discussed earlier, could have a profound effect on the Rules Committee and its level of cooperation with the House leadership. Take the committee in the Ninety-second Congress, headed as it had been for the previous half-dozen years by Representative Colmer of Mississippi, who was located ideologically by one of his colleagues as "perhaps slightly to the left of Ivan the Terrible." It was Colmer who once paused in his hostile questioning of the House Judiciary chairman, Emanuel Celler, during a Rules hearing on civil rights legislation, to observe to a colleague, "I guess I'll have to stop this Jew-baiting."

Of the ten Democrats on the Colmer Rules Committee, a minimum of six could probably be relied on to vote the chairman out of office in favor of a challenger who was more liberal and more loyal to the party leadership, if the system permitted such a choice and Colmer proved unmovable on clearing important legislation. No one would be more aware of this than the chairman himself, who could be expected to adjust his performance accordingly. In addition, the knowledge that the leadership could fill any future Rules vacancy with a member who might deprive the chairman of majority support among his colleagues would go a long way toward keeping that chairman, and thus the committee, in some sort of line.

At that, Colmer has led a charmed life on Rules. Elected with Franklin Roosevelt in 1932, he was a loyal New Dealer at first but then became increasingly uncooperative. When the Republicans won control of the House in 1946 and, with it, a two-thirds share of the Rules Committee, Colmer was among the junior Democrats who were dropped from the committee perforce. When the Democrats regained House control two years later,

Speaker Rayburn was dead set against restoring him to Rules. However, the resourceful Mississippian had already exacted a pledge that he would go back on the committee from Representative John McCormack, then the Democratic floor leader, and Rayburn felt forced to honor it. Eighteen years later, Colmer was chairman.

On the whole, although the Rules Committee has posed a critical problem to House operation in the past, it is not currently a major obstacle. Abolition of the seniority system and establishment of acceptable machinery to impose deadlines on a slow-moving committee should be enough to protect the House and the entire Congress against further recurrence of the committee's notable past excesses.

# 7 · The House: Somehow It Works

Across the congressional stage, passage or defeat of a new law becomes a kind of theatrical event. Only fleeting glimpses of the idea have been caught before—when it was introduced, discussed in open hearing, and reported in revised form after closed committee sessions. But, on the floor, it is all out in the open. The curtain has risen at last, the lights are up, the cast is on display, and the basic script is ready. Often, there is very real suspense in the hall because the last act has not yet been written. It will be improvised there, before your very eyes, as you sit in the gallery or observe secondhand through the press.

Taken as theater, the two houses of Congress are centuries and continents apart. Drama in the House is highly structured and conventional. The principal roles are as stylized and familiar as those of the *commedia dell'arte*: the shrewd manipulator, the pompous savant, the braggart, the buffoon. To keep a cast of 435 close to the lines of the script, there must be rules, and rules to interpret the rules. There must be time limits on every scene, or there would never be a resolution. There must, above all, be order.

The Senate too often approaches the theater of the absurd. Seldom are there more than a few characters on stage—symbolic figures representing vying concepts. There is rarely any script, and what passes for dialogue is often repetitious, pointless, seemingly endless. The only rule is that there shall be free expression. But then come sudden, unpredictable moments of climax and resolution: new figures materialize in the chamber, speeches begin to assume form and order, building to a confluence of new characters and finally to a decision. Then, just as suddenly, order dissolves into emptiness, and all that is left in the chamber are a pair of lonely, slightly seedy figures, debating their own reality and waiting for Senator Godot.

The genius of House floor procedure is that it works. Woodrow Wilson said that the House rules seemed "to have been framed for the deliberate purpose of making usefulness unattainable by individual members," but individual usefulness is not their aim. The rules are directed at collective accomplishment, reaching some joint decision within a reasonable time after a reasonable amount of reasonably free discussion. Arguably, it was regrettable, unfair, and wrong that former Representative Allard Lowenstein of New York, the man who forced Lyndon Johnson out of the White House on the Vietnam issue if anybody did, should have had only one minute of floor time in the 1969 ABM debate. But try to figure a way to conduct debate among 435 politicians that does not restrict the rights of junior members or, alternatively, does not convert the House into another Senate, of which one will do Congress very nicely, thank you.

We have seen how the House Rules Committee sets the ground rules for each major bill: how long it will be debated and what sort of amendments, if any, will be allowed. That rule, once adopted by the House, assures a firm schedule on the floor. It does *not* assure unlimited democratic discussion or freedom to rework a committee draft in all ways that the House might wish. But it does guarantee that the measure will be discussed, approved or defeated, and moved off the calendar to make room for other, equally important bills to follow. This goal may seem pretty limited, but when you are trying to operate the jury-rigged Congress we have today, it isn't. Motion alone is progress.

Beyond the use of a special rule for each bill, the principal efficiency device in the House involves operating as the Committee of the Whole for preliminary processing of amendments. It doesn't look any different from the House itself when it meets, except that someone other than the Speaker is presiding. Its rules, however, are significantly different. In the Committee of the Whole House on the State of the Union—its awesome full title—100 members make up a quorum instead of the 218 out of 435 required at a regular session. This number makes it much easier to do business in the face of chronic absenteeism. In the full House, an amendment apparently approved 110 to 105 would fail for want of a quorum; in the Committee of the Whole, the same amendment could pass on a 60–40 vote.

Now, there is nothing to prevent every House member from coming to the chamber and voting on every amendment proposed in the Committee of the Whole. In theory they should, and those who are really concerned over the issue at hand will. But there are often large numbers of representatives out of Washington, downtown making speeches and socializing, or unable to avoid conflicting professional appointments when votes are taken. The smaller quorum requirement permits House leaders to continue processing legislation on the floor, moving toward a final vote.

A House member who brings up his amendment in the Committee of the Whole, thinking he can round up enough allies to slip it through, is taking a chance. Amendments defeated in this smaller forum cannot be raised again in the full House. But an amendment passed by the Committee of the Whole can be challenged and voted down later, after the committee completes its preliminary work on the bill and passes it over to the full House for the final decisive voting.

There are three types of votes in the Committee of the Whole, all less than a full formal roll call: the voice vote, the division, and the teller vote.

A voice vote, obviously, goes unrecorded as to either numbers or names. (Until very recently, one of the most important aspects of the Committee of the Whole procedure was the fact that *none* of the votes taken while the committee was sitting were recorded. That is, the number of ayes and nays was recorded and the result announced, but no record was kept of which way any member voted.) A single member can challenge the chair's decision as to which side won a voice vote and demand a division. If this happens, all the members voting aye stand and are counted; then they sit and the nays stand. There is little or no warning for either the voice vote or the counted division, so the only participants are members who happen to be in the chamber or those who can hustle in from the adjoining lobby.

If the outcome of a division is unsatisfactory to at least twenty members of the Committee of the Whole (forty-four if the full House is sitting), they can demand a teller vote. Prior to 1971, this was one of the most ludicrous spectacles in official Washington, and it's not much better now. Under the old routine, the chair would appoint two tellers, or counters, one for ayes and one for nays. The two men would stand at the back of the House on opposite sides of the center aisle, and the members would line up, sheepishly, and file by the teller of their choice. The teller would clap each member on the shoulder as he or she passed, counting all the while.

Reporters in the gallery would try to spot congressmen from their home state to see which way they voted, for no record was ever kept. It was always difficult because the lines faced away from the press gallery, presumably in the interest of just such anonymity, and one House member tends to look a good deal like another from the rear. Some members would hang back until the last minute and then try to slip in at the end of a short line unobserved. Once on a critical vote, Speaker Rayburn came down to the floor and stationed himself at the head of the aisle so that every Democrat voting against the proposal would have to face him, man to man, in the process. History, unsupported by record, tells us that only one was so bold.

It is not just that the teller vote was an egregious waste of time, which it was, taking twenty minutes to reach a simple decision. It is not that it was an embarrassing way for grown men to behave, which it was, shambling through the great Hall of the House in a sort of backslapping, Rotarian parade. It was really that this unbelievable ceremony was used to decide momentous issues of government, to vote billions in public money, while the nation's elected representatives almost literally hid their faces from the voters, furtively cloaking what was left of their convictions from the people who had entrusted them with the power to govern.

The Congressional Reorganization Act of 1970, a few deep scratches through a field that needed a power cultivator, did make a major constructive change by requiring the recording of teller votes. Beginning in 1971, teller votes have taken at least as much time and look very nearly as silly, but they now leave on the record the names of those members who voted for the amendment and those who voted against it. (They still line up, but file down separate aisles, dropping signed red or green cards into a box at the end, and are spared the backslapping.) Almost immediately, this change made itself felt in the House. Veteran observers are convinced that the surprising first defeat of the supersonic transport program, achieved early in 1971 on a recorded teller vote, would not have occurred if the old system had been in effect and any member who kept his head down could not have been reported as pro or con.

It had better be said without further delay that there is no intention in this examination of Congress to probe extensively into the rules of either house. That would require a book in itself, and an involved, special, and dull one it would probably be. House procedure, in particular, is infinitely complicated, and for the first 100 years no one there really knew what the rules were. Or, more accurately, no one knew how they had been interpreted by a series of Speakers who, by so doing, had written many important new precedents into those rules.

Finally, in 1907, Asher Hinds, a heroic parliamentarian if that is not a contradiction in terms, published five volumes of carefully collected and indexed precedents. Previously, the House had spent about a third of its time in session bickering over procedure rather than legislating, but this source of instant authority for the Speaker reduced that particular type of wasteful argument sharply. It seems only fitting that four years later Maine elected Hinds to membership in the House.

In 1936, another parliamentarian who by then had also become a House member, Clarence Cannon of Missouri, updated these rules with three volumes more. (Cannon ultimately rose from his humble clerical origin to become chairman of the House Appropriations Committee, and he proved, understandably, to be as prickly about protocol and procedure as any congressman of his era.) The latest 500-page edition of his *Procedure in the House of Representatives* ranges between serving as an index to his longer compilation and providing a working script for some of the more routine floor maneuvers.

Cannon's rules not only furnish the basic procedural pattern for lawmaking but a treasury of insights into past House arguments, such as "the death of Members who have signed petitions to discharge committees does not invalidate their signatures unless withdrawn by their successors." (In the House, the dead can bind the living.) Or, a member can raise a question of personal privilege on the floor based on "newspaper charges of falsehood" but not based on "criticism by the President." Or, "the reading of papers other than the one on which a vote is to be taken is subject to the will of the House, and any Member may object." The last is a widely ignored inheritance from the British, who regard the reading of speeches in Parliament, as opposed to extemporaneous delivery, as distinctly infra dig.

While perhaps not essential to the survival of the institution, it would certainly be helpful if Congress created a special committee—or two, if the two houses insist—with expert technical staff, to compile, rewrite, condense, modernize, and otherwise civilize the rules of the two houses. It is probably too much to expect that some sort of uniformity between Senate and House rules could be effected, so that a spectator, reporter, or member who understands one could move into the other without experiencing cultural shock. But there is no reason why a freshman member of the House should not be given upon admission a book of reasonable size that explains in language he can be expected to understand how the body operates. There is, for all practical purposes, no way to obtain this information today except by sitting in the chamber and asking questions of those who have been sitting there longer. It is hard to believe that one of the great parliamentary bodies of the world is operating, in terms of procedural continuity, by the prehistoric method of word of mouth, but it is very nearly true. Even a freshman representative who studies House procedure firsthand is in for trouble. For he will find the Speaker basing day-to-day rulings on precedents that cannot really be challenged because they have not been collected in decipherable form in any public document since Cannon's effort of 1936.

Technically, all such rulings appear somewhere in the millions of pages of the *Congressional Record*, but the only place they are sorted out and indexed is in the private notebooks of the House parliamentarian, Lewis Deschler. The 1970 reorganization law provided for publishing a revised up-to-date rulebook every five years—but only after Deschler produces a compilation of the previous thirty-five years or more, a project that is under way but advancing almost imperceptibly.

Deschler has held his job for more than forty years, through all shifts in House political control. As long as the latest compilation of precedents remains unpublished, he remains the single source of sound procedural information in the House, at $42,000 a year. Until the project is completed, ignorance prevails, a state in which senior members are perfectly content to leave their juniors, having spent so many years there themselves.

Although there is some grumbling from time to time, most House members regard their opportunities for floor debate and amendment as adequate if not exactly generous, when taken in the light of the schedule the body must maintain. A major reason for this is that hardly anyone today believes that debate still serves its historic function of clarifying the issues so the members can vote intelligently.

You have only to watch a small closing segment of debate and a roll call in either house to see why. Unless it is one of the major bills of the session, there will be about 10 per cent of the members in the chamber for the closing debate, probably fewer in the Senate and more in the House. Nearly half of those in their seats are not listening to the speeches. In the House, one or two are likely to be asleep; senators, fewer and thus more conspicuous, try to confine napping to the privacy of their offices. Then the roll call is ordered, and bells ring in the Capitol and the huge adjoining office buildings to summon all those absentees.

(Almost perverse in their refusal to conform, the Senate and House have different bell codes; a roll call is one long ring in the Senate, but two in the House.) Within a few moments, members begin pouring into the chamber as the clerk reads the names slowly, giving those down the alphabet more time to get there. Senators tend to materialize more rapidly than representatives. More of them have hideaway offices in the Capitol, near the floor. Also, both Senate office buildings have electric subway cars that scoot members over to the floor when the bells ring. Only one of the three House office buildings, the monstrous Rayburn monument, has a subway. From the other two, a member must walk, and that can involve as much as four floors and three blocks. The close-in Capitol Hill restaurants make a small ceremony of announcing the bell signals over their public address systems, implying a congressional clientele, but it is relatively unusual to see a customer set down his drink and scurry for the floor.

In any event, it is fairly obvious that when three-quarters of the congressmen voting have not been present for the closing debate—although some of them may have heard earlier portions —they are not basing their vote on the arguments, however cogent, in the speeches just concluded. They are responding instead to the Republican or Democratic position, to the liberal or conservative line, to the importuning of lobbyists, to the clear voice of their constituents, or to their own reasoned conclusions, based on staff research and a review of all the facts available, including the *Congressional Record*. But live debate? No, debate cannot really have had much influence. As a result, the fact that the House restricts the over-all time for floor speeches, divides it between parties, and then parcels it out in a niggardly fashion to individual members is not a subject of serious concern most of the time. The function of informing the members is taking place in other forums, as we will see, so a relatively routine public exploration of the issues suffices.

An exception arises when there has not been an adequate opportunity for the members and the public to know what is in a long, complicated bill before it suddenly appears for judgment on the floor. A classic example: the welfare reform program proposed by President Nixon and reshaped by Representative Wilbur Mills in his House Ways and Means Committee for nearly four months in 1971. Mills never held public hearings on the bill. His committee had worked over a similar measure the year before, only to see it die in Senate committee, and he apparently thought the members already knew enough to proceed.

One of the most interesting and complex men in Congress, Mills is a strong chairman who, as we have noted, likes to appear permissive, with his committee believing it is under a loose rein. He is very skillful at masking his own conclusions while maneuvering his members into a consensus position. That position usually is where Mills was heading all along; at the least, it is the closest he could get to his preference and still keep a solid majority behind him. Working in this fashion, Mills prefers to reach "informal agreement" on legislation section by section in committee rather than take a series of potentially polarizing votes as he progresses. While the Ways and Means Committee worked over the welfare bill, week after week, Mills refused to report what they were doing, claiming they had not taken any final action. He may have been technically correct because all formal committee votes, which are supposed to be made public as they occur, were postponed until the last few days before the bill was reported. But the result was that decisions vitally important to the nation's governors, mayors, and welfare commissioners were being made but kept secret. And so it was very difficult for the interested groups most concerned, the social workers and the antisocial workers, to get information on the massive piece of legislation that was taking shape.

A few reporters developed reliable contacts inside the Ways and Means Committee and in the welfare lobby, producing periodic stories on the way the bill was being secretly written. But unless you were a reader of the *New York Times* or the *Los Angeles Times* or the *Baltimore Sun*, the costly, complex, and sweeping welfare bill that finally burst out of committee darkness into the sunshine of publicity came largely as a surprise to you. And, only a relatively few days later, the 780-page measure reached the floor under a rule that prohibited any amendments and permitted only three votes: on the controversial welfare plan itself, on an opponent's motion to recommit, and on final passage. No other changes at all.

The use of the closed rule that denies the House the right to change a committee draft, only permitting its rejection as a whole, is probably justified on some technical and politically sensitive bills, such as the tax and benefit legislation that Ways and Means deals with regularly. But it is highly dubious treatment for any bill to which there has been no public access during its final drafting.

In the case of the welfare bill, all the public officials and private groups with the best background, the strongest opinions, and the biggest stake in the issue were almost totally shut out of any opportunity to influence the measure until it was frozen into a final take-it-or-leave-it form. Any information that outside experts got while the bill was still potentially changeable was acquired in spite of Congress and Wilbur Mills. When a tentative version of the bill was printed by the committee midway in its deliberations, copies were numbered, marked confidential, and distributed one to each committee member, with specific instructions not to show them to anyone. This may have made it easier for Mills to conduct smooth, cooperative committee sessions, but it certainly did not help the public to have any influence on the new welfare law.

Longer floor debate could have helped ventilate the questions implicit in the welfare bill, but the problem goes deeper than that. If the House is not going to be able to change a bill on the floor, to reflect public opinion or private expertise, then there must be an earlier opportunity to give some information and consideration to outside authority before the committee reports. It may seem a drastic remedy by congressional standards, but why not require a committee seeking a closed rule for a bill to conduct its "mark-up"—the line-by-line, section-by-section review before reporting—in open session?

Open committee mark-up has been tried, frankly with mixed results. The House Education and Labor Committee, dominated by liberals, admits the press and public to all its sessions, but it pays a price. Some observers are convinced that the resulting grandstanding by members wastes time and generates confusion without really producing sounder legislation than would have been drafted in executive session.

But if committee chairmen like Wilbur Mills—and there are plenty of others—continue to circumvent the rule that closed committee decisions are matters of public record, then the only recourse may be to open up their meetings or, alternatively, to open up their legislation to amendment on the floor. Perhaps, the most acceptable solution would be denying a closed rule to any bill if there had not been full and regular public reports of the progress of its drafting in committee.

Floor procedure in the House, orderly if somewhat arbitrary today, has not always been so. In the rowdy closing decades of the nineteenth century, when they took their politics seriously, the minority party used every parliamentary device at hand to tie up the body and obstruct action by the majority. It took one of the giants of Congress, although a man little recognized elsewhere in history, to end the practice permanently.

For many years, as the slavery issue tore the Congress apart along with the nation, House dissidents developed the technique of stalling with roll calls: demanding a quorum call to establish that a working majority of members was on hand, then moving to adjourn, which required the same roll call over again, then going back to a quorum call. Although the House was somewhat smaller then, each roll call must have taken fifteen or twenty minutes. On a single day in 1850, during the debate on the admission of California, there were thirty-one roll calls.

Another popular device for the obstructionists was the disappearing quorum. Members would answer a quorum call, but then, on an ensuing roll call, the minority would remain silent, not voting. Unless the majority could produce every last member, which was unlikely then as now, there would not be enough votes on the roll call to constitute a quorum, and the bill or motion would fail.

Speaker Thomas Reed of Maine, a great balding bear of a man, took care of that. Shortly after his election in January, 1890, the House was voting on whether to seat the Republican candidate in a disputed West Virginia election. At that time a quorum was

165. On the roll call, there were 161 ayes and 2 nays, with more than 100 Democrats present but refusing to vote. The Democratic floor leader called out, "No quorum," but Republican Reed calmly instructed the clerk to record the names of those in the chamber who had not voted, and the Speaker read off some three dozen he could see himself. Amid cries of protest, Reed announced that a quorum had indeed been present and the resolution seating the new member had been approved.

A month later Reed won approval for a new set of House rules that formalized his method of dealing with the disappearing quorum and also empowered the Speaker to reject as dilatory motions for adjournment and other purposes that were obviously directed only at delaying the proceedings. His enemies, whom he did not hesitate to taunt, called him "Czar Reed," but he was responsible almost singlehanded for converting the House from a snarling zoo into a working legislative body.

Reed had wit and character as well as courage, but he never cultivated the popularity to achieve higher office. Asked if he would seek the Presidency, he said of his party's national leaders, "They might do worse, and I think they will." (They did. When Reed made his only bid in 1896, the convention chose a former House leader, William McKinley of Ohio.)

The House rules being so extensive and complex, there is still considerable room for those who know them to outmaneuver those who don't. For example, House Democrats outwitted the Republicans on a Kennedy housing bill by submitting on the floor a substitute for one of its sections that prominently included one of the proposed Republican amendments. After they happily approved this move, the Republicans discovered they had lost the right to attempt a flock of further changes because a substitute, once adopted, cannot be further amended.

Sometimes pressure can be applied to advantage where the rules offer alternative courses. The last weapon the opposition has on the House floor before the final vote is the motion to recommit. It can take two forms: a flat motion, which has the effect of killing the bill by sending it back to committee, or a motion to recommit with instructions to report the measure back with specific changes made. This is really just a last-gasp way of trying to achieve a major amendment, one that may already have been defeated on the floor.

This motion is the property of the opposition. It is ordinarily made by the leader of the minority party or, if he supports the bill, by a minority member who opposes it. Generally, it is much easier to persuade the House to recommit with instructions, preserving some of the bill, than to recommit flatly, destroying everything. Thus, backers of a bill sometimes work behind the scenes to get the opponent making the motion to choose flat recommittal, the move less likely to succeed. Just such a maneuver, engineered jointly by the Eisenhower Administration and Democratic House leaders, succeeded in preserving a 1958 trade bill intact.

Sometime in the summer of 1972, the House was scheduled to install its first electronic voting equipment, only about forty years too late. The problem had been conspicuous for a century: a full roll call of the 435-member body conducted by the tally clerks always took just over a half-hour, much of it waiting for members not in the chamber when their names were reached the first time. In 1968, as a sample, the House was in session 726 hours, and 196 of them were spent on roll calls and quorum calls. If the new system provides for virtually simultaneous voting by all members a certain time after a warning bell—there remained ominous reports that names would still be called one at a time with members pushing a button rather than answering—the actual voting time could be reduced to a matter of seconds, and the House could save between one and two months' worth of working days every year.

The old slow system was kept for so many years after state legislatures were routinely using high-speed equipment for intrinsically political reasons. It gave members who refused to be tied to the floor a leisurely twenty to thirty minutes in which to stroll over to the Capitol from their offices and avoid any stigma of absenteeism. (In Congress, statistics on how *often* you voted are sometimes regarded as more important than *how* you voted.) In addition, the confusion of the slow roll call, almost impossible to monitor accurately from the gallery, gave the leaders cover to switch a few votes at the last minute on close tallies—a move that will be a good deal more obvious when the totals are flashed instantly on an electronic scoreboard.

One of the little understood and least defensible features of congressional voting is the practice of permitting "pairs," which involves putting on record the vote of an absent member, sometimes even giving it effect in the outcome of the vote, despite all rules to the contrary. A pair consists of two members who would have voted on opposite sides of a given issue had either of them been present. At the bottom of the roll call will be found two lists of names: "paired for" and "paired against," each with an equal number of the names of absentees.

This practice is not seriously offensive when it does not affect the outcome of the vote and only permits a member to record in the most prominent place how he would have voted if he had taken the trouble to be in the chamber. It remains, however, a piece of petty fraud. By arranging pairs, absentees create the spurious impression that they participated in a decision of the House when precisely the opposite is true. Perhaps only the unsophisticated are deceived, but there seems to be no valid reason why a member who did not care enough to be present should be entitled to have his name and position recorded on the roll call.

Much more objectionable is the "live pair," under which a member who is present agrees to let an absentee cancel out his vote. In the Senate, where the floor procedure is explicit, a member rises at the end of the roll call and says, "On this vote, I have a pair with the senior senator from Backwater. Were he present and voting, he would vote in the negative. I have voted in the affirmative. Therefore, I withdraw my vote." Arithmetically and morally as well, this is an outright gift of a vote to the side of the issue that the giver claims to oppose. The only justification is that it represents an extension of courtesy to a colleague who was unavoidably detained elsewhere. But it also says something about the man extending the courtesy. If he were really voting his convictions, he would not so lightly give his vote away; if he in fact favors the opposition cause, why not drop hypocrisy and vote that way in the first place?

The practice of pairing goes back to the 1820's. At one time, it even covered two members who were in such thorough disagreement that they agreed to pair on all votes "until further notice," eliminating the necessity for showing up in the chamber at all. There is still no official sanction for the practice in the House; in fact, the rules say it is not in order for a member to announce how he would have voted after failing to answer a roll call or to announce how absent colleagues would have voted. But pairing continues nevertheless, and sometimes inspires both sides of a closely contested vote to intrigue and maneuver.

On the memorable 1941 House vote to extend the draft, the Democratic leadership barely managed to round up a 203–202 majority after a highly emotional debate. But majority leader McCormack was prepared for the possibility that the bill might be one vote short after the roll call. In the wings he had two members who had voted against the measure but who were prepared to take live pairs with absentees who favored the draft extension. The withdrawal of these two votes would then have given the leadership a one-vote victory.

The same debate focused public attention briefly on a common congressional procedure that continues to mystify the galleries to this day. Jefferson's *Manual* provides that a final vote on a bill can be reconsidered only within the next two days and that, if a motion to reconsider is made and then tabled, that will constitute "a final disposition of the motion." Thus, in both houses, when a bill is finally passed, a member who voted for it automatically moves to reconsider the vote and another then moves to table that motion. When the tabling motion is approved by voice vote—it is rarely challenged since the winning side has just demonstrated its majority on a roll call—the approval is permanently sealed and the issue cannot be raised again.

On the 1941 draft vote, with its precarious margin subject to being upset by the arrival of one more member in the chamber, Speaker Rayburn immediately announced the result, which shut off any further voting. Then he said, "Without objection, a motion to reconsider is laid on the table," although no one had made either motion. One of the antidraft leaders, Representative Carl Anderson of Minnesota, rose and asked the Speaker whether the House had voted on the tabling motion. Rayburn snapped back, "The Chair does not intend to have his word questioned by the gentleman from Minnesota or anybody else." And that was the end of that.

# 8 · The Senate: Cave of the Winds

In the House, the rules enable a large cumbersome machine to operate. In the Senate, with superficially similar rules, an apparatus that would seem more manageable moves in fits and starts, then stalls, occasionally spurts forward, but more often crawls almost imperceptibly down the legislative course.

The difference is simple but fundamental. The Senate operates on the principle of unlimited debate, and all other rules give way before it. As long as one senator has the floor and wishes to speak, whether on a motion, a bill, an amendment, a treaty, a confirmation, or his own fancy, there is literally nothing that can be done to stop him and proceed on any sort of schedule. If a group of senators decides to continue speaking, acting in concert to delay action indefinitely, there is nothing to stop *them*, short of collective exhaustion.

The Senate has been going on this way ever since 1806, when the motion for the previous question, which ends debate if it passes and is not debatable itself, was stricken from the rules in the interest of freedom of expression. For reasons history does not record, no one thought of using this new freedom as a parliamentary weapon until 1841. Then, a group of senators objected to a bill to hire printers for the body and decided to talk it to death. Ten days' debate later, the bill was put aside, the printers (who had apparently been slipped onto the pay roll in time-honored political fashion) were dismissed, and the Senate went back to business. So, humbly, the first filibuster was born.

The derivation of the word is curious. *Filibusteros* were nineteenth-century pirates who preyed upon shipping in the Caribbean. Later, privately led military raids into Central and South American countries were known as filibustering expeditions. Somehow, for obscure reasons, this violent sort of unauthorized activity passed its name to the far less swashbuckling practice under which a minority can defeat a majority in the Senate by lung power and persistence alone. No swordplay involved.

Except for the Civil War, when debate was restricted on emergency measures, the Senate talked on, completely untrammeled, until 1917. Then, after diplomatic relations with Germany had been broken, a filibuster against Wilson's bill to arm merchant ships, led by his "little group of willful men," prompted the Senate to action. It overwhelmingly approved Rule XXII, which has been a subject of contention ever since. The rule, little changed thereafter, now provides that a petition signed by sixteen senators can force a vote on shutting off debate. If two-thirds of the senators present and voting approve such a motion for cloture (the accepted term in Congress, although *Webster's New International*, second edition, prefers "closure"), then ensuing debate is limited to one hour per senator, and a final vote follows.

The trouble with Rule XXII—or its value, depending on your viewpoint—was that it rarely succeeded in limiting debate. For one thing, senators who felt themselves in the minority for one reason or another—Southerners, conservatives (and lately, sometimes liberals), Republicans, men from small states—were reluctant to vote for cloture, no matter what the issue. They foresaw the possibility that their particular minority might be the one threatened the next time, and they did not want to weaken the powerful parliamentary weapon of the filibuster, just in case. In addition, the original Rule XXII applied only to debate on a bill but did not interfere at all with debate on a motion to take up a bill, which must come first. When the minority discovered this loophole and began filibustering motions, the rule became totally ineffective. Before that happened, cloture had been voted four times within ten years, initially to get a vote on the ratification of the Treaty of Versailles in 1919. But from 1927, when a prohibition measure was involved, until 1962, when liberals attempted unsuccessfully to block creation of the Communications Satellite Corporation (Comsat), the Senate did not invoke the rule and vote to limit debate once.

The rule was changed in 1949, to apply to motions as well as bills, but this liberalization was balanced by changing the number of votes required for cloture from a two-thirds majority of those present and voting to an absolute two-thirds of the Senate membership, or sixty-four votes at that time. In 1959, this was changed back to two-thirds of those present and voting, so that cloture must now be approved by sixty-seven senators if everyone is there, or a smaller number if there are absentees. The "present and voting" language no longer means much; cloture votes are regarded as so important, even today when they occur with some frequency, that every able-bodied member is on the floor and everyone votes.

Since the Comsat bill in 1962, the Senate has voted to shut off debate four times, on civil rights bills in 1964, 1965, and 1968, and on an extension of the draft in 1971. But, for more than twenty years, the effort at the opening of each new Congress to reduce the size of the majority needed for cloture has failed. Many senators, most of them liberals, believe that a simple majority should be able to cut off debate, just as it can in the House, by approving the motion for the previous question. Their more limited immediate goal, however, has been reducing the majority required for cloture from two-thirds to three-fifths, or sixty senators if everyone is present.

The procedural problem has always been that, when the motion to change Senate rules is made, the defenders of the filibuster drag out their trustworthy old machine and start talking. As a result, under Rule XXII, it takes a two-thirds majority to cut off debate on the question of whether it *ought* to take a two-thirds majority to cut off any future debate, and the revised rule has never passed. Times are changing, filibusters sprout up like dandelions after a spring rain, and cloture petitions are filed almost as routine documents. But all this activity may only stiffen the resolve of the Senate not to relax its insistence on preserving un-limited debate. It is a tradition that dies hard.

Most people are aware, at least dimly, of the basic impact of the filibuster: how it enables a minority to prevent a majority from working its will. But relatively few voters are concerned over its devastating secondary effect: preventing the Senate from proceeding, even at a snail's pace, with all its other business, which continues to pile up as the House and the Senate committees work away, until a log jam of weeks and even months of legislating is backed up behind the bill being filibustered.

There is one way to cut off any debate that threatens to become a full-fledged filibuster, but it is only delicately achieved. It involves what is known as a unanimous consent resolution. The Senate can do anything by unanimous consent of its members. It can ignore all its rules, except the one governing roll call and voting procedure. It can call up bills that a committee has never cleared because an artful chairman buried them deep in a crowded agenda. It can move on the calendar, off the calendar, take up amendments that have not been printed, approve conference reports that are still warm from the Senate-House compromising session. All, by unanimous consent.

The effect of a unanimous consent agreement is a good deal like a rule from the House Rules Committee, although less constricting. It spells out how much debating time each side shall have on a given bill, how much time there shall be for each amendment, and, sometimes, the hour for the final vote. Once it is adopted, it enables the Senate to work in a relatively orderly fashion, on some sort of predictable schedule. But such an agreement can only be reached if every senator on the floor accepts its terms. One objection blocks it. Thus, before the majority leader proposes such a move, he must clear it with all possible objectors: the leaders of the minority party, the chairmen and ranking minority members of the committee and subcommittee involved, and any other senators who have played significant roles in the debate. This is not an easy proposition, with so many bases to be touched and egos to be massaged. One of the essential qualities for a Senate majority leader is the ability to sense the time when various factions have exhausted their random noise-making and are ready to proceed toward a resolution. Sensing that time, drafting the agreement, and bringing it to successful floor approval are almost the only skills that keep the Senate moving at all some days.

For those occasions when unanimous consent simply cannot be obtained, Senator Mike Mansfield, the current Democratic leader, has devised an ingenious alternative, "the two-track system." When a group of senators is firmly committed to filibustering a bill before the Senate, that measure is allocated half the working day, during which the speeches go on, untainted by legislative action. During the rest of the day, other bills are brought up, debated, and passed, in more or less normal fashion, perhaps even a little more rapidly than otherwise because of the time pressure of the concurrent filibuster. This unorthodox arrangement, of course, requires unanimous consent, but that is normally not too hard to get. The senators staging the filibuster are usually content as long as they are blocking the specific bill to which they object, and those not directly concerned with the bill are happy to get on with other pressing business. The only ones not so happy are the senators favoring the bill being filibustered. The two-track system takes a good deal of pressure off the filibusterers; it cuts down their working, or talking, day, and it makes them limited instead of total obstructionists. True, they are deliberately frustrating majority rule, but they are only doing it on a single bill and not bringing the great legislative machine to a halt, as in the past. Their protest takes on much more of an aura of principle, which doesn't help an embattled majority much.

When Lyndon Johnson was majority leader, he tended to regard filibusters as a personal challenge to his stewardship. Instead of making an end run around the combatants with the rest of the Senate business, he often preferred to break the filibuster by keeping the house in session for long hours, even around the clock, and forcing the minority ultimately to give up in exhaustion. This is not Senator Mansfield's way. The Johnson method was a different one, but it can hardly be classed as a better one, from the viewpoint of trying to run a modern legislative body in the last quarter of the twentieth century.

It seems clear to many observers that the Senate cannot continue to function in a modern society on the principle that a two-thirds majority is required for any *important* action, when a minority of a half-dozen men can define what is important on any given day. It seems equally clear that, tradition aside, the Senate should have more extensive opportunity for debate than a highly structured rules system would allow. As long as the House is forced to keep floor discussion to a minimum, the Senate should provide a broader, more hospitable forum for all points of view. Between these two guideposts stand a few viable possibilities for change.

As a minimal exploratory step, the Senate should revise the cloture rule so that a three-fifths, or 60 per cent, vote of those present can shut off debate. The historical reluctance of the Senate to vote cloture is not dissolving rapidly enough to provide any encouragement that the two-thirds majority now required is going to be readily available to discourage the growing popularity of the filibuster. Reducing the cloture requirement would make it easier for the Senate to halt obstructive debate and get on with its business, but it could also have the discouraging side effect of arousing more filibusters (which the Johnson Treatment did not). As the cure becomes more effective, the disease becomes less socially objectionable; an easily sidetracked filibuster may be no worse than a bad cold. Just how well a three-fifths cloture rule would work is difficult to predict, but the way to find out is to try it.

If such a change strikes a reasonable balance between the right to extended debate and the need for legislative progress, well and good. But if the filibuster remains a major source of interference, then the Senate should revise its rules again to permit shutting off debate by majority vote. The procedure, however, could be materially different from that in the House, where a motion for the previous question is not debatable and forces final voting without further discussion.

To preserve a healthy measure of Senate tradition, most of the present cloture machinery could be retained: the initiating petition, perhaps with an even higher requirement for signatures, and two days more of debate before the motion comes to a vote. If it is then approved by a simple majority, the present procedure would follow: continued debate of up to one hour for each senator before a final vote on the issue. On the nine instances in which the Senate has voted cloture in the past, the defeated filibusterers have normally not pressed for this additional talking time. They were beaten, exposed as a minority of less than one-third, and had so antagonized most of the other senators that further debate would have been unlikely to win converts. Also, they were usually tired. Under the revised system, members of a stubborn minority might want to use their extra time. At the least, with a rule guaranteeing up to 100 hours of debate on an issue between cloture and any final vote, it would be hard to argue that the Senate was arbitrarily cutting off anyone who wanted to be heard. Restricting unlimited debate, yes, but giving every senator a reasonable opportunity to state his case.

This sort of change is not going to be easy to obtain. The senators who are self-conscious about representing a minority are intensely proud that their vote counts as much as those cast from New York or California. But they remain fearful that their particular interests—mining, farming, segregation—will be ignored by the majority and their cause submerged. The filibuster is their symbolic weapon, often most valuable as a threat. Do not ride roughshod over our interests, these senators say, or we will bring the entire majestic Senate to a grinding halt.

The ultimate question is this: should any minority that is sufficiently belligerent be able to thwart the will of the majority, or even be able to force that majority to trials of endurance unrelated to any issue? The answer is no, not under the democratic system we profess. If the minority, given a fair chance, cannot get the votes, then the minority loses. That should be all there is to it. There is no traditional American right to deny order and obstruct progress because you can't get your own way, and the filibuster, sooner or later, must give way before the absence of any such right.

The Senate's devotion to the tradition of unlimited debate is even more difficult to defend if you are familiar with what passes for debate in the chamber. It is best to be frank about it: Senate debate no longer fulfills the basic function of illuminating the issues and directing the final vote, if it ever did. What it mostly fills is time. The Senate abhors a vacuum. Its leaders, operating under pressure of some prehistoric consciousness, become uneasy if the Senate does not go into session each day at noon and if some sort of business does not *appear* to be taking place on the floor for the next several hours.

It is true that the chamber must be open daily for a certain amount of routine activity: the receipt of messages from the President and the House, concurring in noncontroversial House actions, and the like. But much of this could be handled either by a clerk at the desk, without the necessity of the Senate being in session, or by a small flurry of activity at the beginning of the next day's session.

The Senate does not see it that way. It would rather be in session, conducting its deliberations before the galleries, even if those deliberations consist of a single member reading a forty-page speech to an empty chamber, or a clerk very slowly calling the names of the senators to determine whether a quorum can be mustered to provide technical justification for continuing the nonsession. (Attendance has been a Senate problem from the very beginning. The first Congress convened in New York City on March 4, 1789, but it took the Senate until April 6 to raise a quorum.)

"Debate" on a major bill almost always consists of a series of end-to-end speeches by senators, each constituting the member's personal position, many often overlapping those that have come before and those yet to come. Very few senators come to the floor to listen to such speeches. They claim they read them in the *Record*, but few ever do. Their staffs will occasionally glean an interesting point or two from the great undigested mass of verbiage, but that is about as far as it goes. Since hardly anyone is on the floor, the instances are limited when one senator interrupts another with a challenging question and provokes an exchange that could qualify as debate. Even when this does happen, the interplay between viewpoints is rarely heard by more than a half-dozen other senators, so it can hardly be said to have been influential. It does appear in the *Record*, of course, but if the exchange had any bite at all it was probably edited out by the participants in the interest of mutual self-esteem.

Senators' votes, very simply, are not influenced by floor debate.

They *are* influenced, as we will see, by their knowledge of what is in the bill, mail from constituents, pressure from lobbyists, the views of colleagues more expert in the area, the doctrinal liberal or conservative position on the issue, their wives, their mistresses, their staff, and their indigestion. But not by debate.

Then why waste so much time on it? Well, there are some constructive functions of floor debate that are unrelated to influencing votes. When a bill is ambiguous, it is important that the members clarify in debate what they intend it to do; if the law is later challenged in court, the judge will lean heavily on this so-called legislative history in making his decision. And each senator feels, with some justification, that he has the right to place his personal position on the public record. The Senate frowns on the accepted House practice of inserting wholly undelivered speeches in the *Record*, so they occupy floor time. (Once in the *Record*, they can be reprinted and distributed to constituents at very low cost.) But, mostly, debate serves the purpose of slowing down and spacing out the legislative process. Deliberation is literally the key to the Senate approach. Senators like to have plenty of time to see how an issue is jelling—with the public, in the press, in the dim recesses of their own minds—before they vote. And they are busy men, with much other business to conduct. If debate stretches out the schedule and makes strict attention to the floor less frequently necessary, it accordingly makes life a good deal easier.

Some orthodox theorists believe that Congress could complete its legislative duties in the first six months of each year if the system were really tightened up, and that steps in this direction are desirable. What would be required are more frequent committee meetings, a full five-day week of working floor sessions instead of three or four as now, elimination of fake Senate debate, and full-time concentration on lawmaking at the expense of all the other time-consuming congressional responsibilities.

Assuming all this were possible—and that is debatable—what advantages would result? The great majority of senators and representatives would then feel obliged to return to their home states and districts for the rest of the year. Many of those who now regard Congress as their full-time employment would take on outside work during the second half of the year, work that would almost inescapably tend to intrude later on the first half of the year. The members' capacity to provide services for their constituents would certainly suffer. During the session, all efforts would be devoted to lawmaking; in the off-season, with the senator or representative in his Washington office only occasionally, the pressure would be off, no matter how dedicated his staff was. Away from the Capitol half of the year, the members would lose touch, have even less contact with the President and the huge executive establishment than they do now. In most cases, their local newspapers would provide a far sketchier picture of the course of government during the off-season than they get reading the Washington papers.

The intense, high-gear, six-month session may sound more efficient, but thoughtful observers in Washington no longer agree with Woodrow Wilson that "the nation breathes easier when the Congress adjourns." They conclude instead that serving in the Senate and House has properly become a full-time professional occupation, that the men and women who do it should spend most of their time where the action is, in Washington, that it does no harm to space out the legislative side of their work over four or five more months a year than is absolutely necessary.

This is not to say that an immense amount of unproductive effort cannot be cut out of the congressional lawmaking process, saving time and energy. It can. But simply compressing the time span within which a given bill is shaped, from first draft to final White House copy, rarely achieves anything, and it may easily produce a poorer law. Debate has become obsolete as the force behind congressional decision-making, but all the other forces that have replaced it need time to operate. A reflective Congress does not have to be an inefficient or a lazy one.

The conclusion, then, is that Senate debate, although rarely edifying or effective, is harmless enough, as long as some new provision for reasonable time limits is adopted. If debate no longer wins dramatic converts on the floor in the fashion of a revival meeting, it at least postpones a final decision long enough so that the conscientious men who must make it have time to study the question and weigh the alternatives, in relative privacy at their own convenience. How much more can we ask of an ancient parliamentary custom?

Beyond the filibuster, the Senate suffers from a serious procedural malady: a chronic deficiency of germaneness. The rule of germaneness, as it is honored in the House, prohibits attaching a bill on one subject to a bill that deals with an entirely different one. Such a union is almost always attempted as a political maneuver, trying to promote a weak measure by hooking it onto a stronger one. Late in the 1970 session, Senator Russell Long advised his colleagues that a Finance Committee bill was likely to be "the last train out of the station," to which anyone with a pet project would be well advised to couple it. Ultimately, the measure proved too heavily laden to get into motion at all.

It may seem obvious to most people that each major proposal for change in the government should be judged individually, on its own merits, but it does not seem obvious to Congress. A more haphazard, old-fashioned practice was called logrolling—you vote for my bill today, and I'll vote for yours next week. In its modern refinement, the possibility that such promises will not be kept is eliminated; one bill is attached to the other, and only one vote is required. Meanwhile, members who strongly support one of the two different measures have little choice but to vote for the combination.

The House maintains a reasonable measure of control over this sort of thing by flatly prohibiting floor amendments that are not germane. In committee, more than one subject can be included in one bill, as long as all fall within the committee's carefully defined but often broad jurisdiction. But once that committee bill reaches the floor, all amendments must deal strictly with the subject matter. The House germaneness rule has created a whole library of precedents: a bill to exterminate the boll weevil cannot be amended to include the gypsy moth; a one-year proposal cannot be amended to make it permanent; a bill to retire an officer cannot be amended to grant him a pension. However, a bill to support several Indian tribes can be broadened to include one more and a bill to build new ships for the Navy can be amended to require their construction in government rather than private yards. And so on, and so on.

The Senate escapes the need for compiling precedents by having no germaneness rule at all. (Sometimes a requirement that amendments be germane is written into a unanimous consent agreement, but that only affects one bill and can be blocked to begin with by a single objection.) As a result, it is perfectly in order for the Senate to add any sort of rider at all to any passing legislative horse, usually a House-passed bill that majorities in both chambers are anxious to see enacted. The only exception is an appropriations bill, which is off limits for any amendment that has general application or is not germane. Even the Senate has to have some standards: appropriation bills must be passed to keep the government running and would almost certainly be loaded with a whole host of outlandish amendments if germaneness were not enforced.

The Legislative Reorganization Act of 1970 took a significant step toward curbing irresponsible Senate use of the rider. It provided that when a bill or conference report reaches the House with a nongermane Senate amendment attached, the House will have an opportunity for a separate vote on the merits on that amendment alone, rather than a single, take-it-or-leave-it decision. This change does not mean that the Senate will stop tacking miscellaneous provisions on bills; it simply makes it much easier for the House to cut out those of which it does not approve.

The absence of a Senate requirement for germaneness is defended by liberals on understandable but essentially expedient grounds. For many years, some Senate committees—Judiciary is a good example—have been so dominated by conservatives in both the chairmanship and membership that certain kinds of legislation—civil rights, in this instance—have had extreme difficulty in getting out of committee and onto the floor. When a majority of the full house supports such a committee-blocked bill, its sponsor can simply propose the entire measure, long or short, as an amendment to some luckier bill that has reached the floor and is almost certain to pass and be signed by the President. Liberal senators are very reluctant to contemplate giving up this method of circumventing the committee system. But they are wrong.

In the first place, there are several other ways to solve the problem of an obstructive committee with a stubborn chairman, without resorting to the birth of a legislative two-headed calf.

There are rules under which a committee may be forced by a floor vote to disgorge a bill, although the tradition-bound membership regards such an assault on committee prerogative as improper, if not actually indecent. There are also rules under which a House-passed bill may be stopped at the Senate desk rather than referred to committee, and then moved onto the calendar.

In the second place, once again, replacement of the seniority system by a merit system would go a long way toward eliminating committee blockades. A chairman who knew he was subject to replacement, rather than only reverence, would be far less likely to bottle up a popular bill in committee. Even with a majority of his committee behind him, such a chairman would be acutely aware that his authority might only be temporary; the party leaders, reflecting the Senate rather than the committee position, would have the power to reduce or eliminate the chairman's control by filling committee vacancies or by adding new members if the size of the party's Senate majority increased.

The worst recent example of the kind of hydra-headed legislation that Senate procedure incubates was the 1970 bill that the Finance Committee delivered to the floor only a few weeks before adjournment. It included extensive, expensive, significant revisions in social security, medicare, and medicaid, some important if temporizing welfare changes, and in the same package, selective and highly controversial revisions in the nation's trade and tariff policy. On the floor, conservative opponents of broader welfare reform filibustered the bill from one side, while liberal opponents of restrictions on free trade filibustered from the other flank. The result, hardly surprising given the Senate's inability to cope with relatively simple problems, was a complete impasse. Under the pressure of imminent adjournment—the session ran right through to the January 3 constitutional deadline—the entire package died. Good, bad, and indifferent parts all met the same fate.

If there had been separate bills on social security, on health and hospital insurance, on welfare reform, and on trade, the Senate could have exercised some sort of reasoned independent judgment on each of them. But there weren't. It might be argued that the muddled, nearly uncontrollable Senate procedural system proved indirectly valuable here by defeating all these complex proposals instead of passing them in a single undigestible gulp. But the argument fails. A good deal of that great hulk of legislation was worth passing—at least worth serious consideration, which it never got on the Senate floor—and its total demise postponed action on many of the pressing problems involved for at least a year.

It must be conceded that even the House rule on germaneness would not have prevented the 1970 monstrosity from reaching the Senate floor. All the subjects involved were within the official purview of the Finance Committee, so they could be combined in a single bill that would survive any procedural challenge in either house. The same sort of heterogeneous bills come out of the House Ways and Means Committee upon occasion, without hindrance.

Parliamentary motions to divide a bill into two or more sections are and always have been available, but are simply never used. Instead, opponents of one part of an omnibus bill usually try to amend it or substitute their own version altogether. The leadership rarely encourages a motion to sever, regarding it as an assault on the integrity of the committee system or, at the least, a rebuke to the chairman involved and thus unseemly.

The only really effective way to resolve this problem is to impose a rule of germaneness on the committees in both houses, prohibiting them from joining in a single measure two subjects that are palpably unrelated, for instance, social security and foreign trade. If a committee violated this rule, the resulting bill would be subject to a point of order on the floor that could block its consideration from the beginning. Germaneness rules are easy to write but hard to apply, and such a limitation would involve building up a long series of precedents in each house as to what sort of subjects can and cannot be joined in one bill. But, in the end, this is the only way to restore a measure of order and reasonableness. After the rule had been on the books for some time, it is possible that committees would regularly report separate rather than omnibus bills, to avoid taking any chance on the floor and focusing attention on the weaker of the partners in a legislative forced marriage.

This new restriction on committee practice would perhaps be more palatable if it were imposed on both houses, as it should be, along with the present House requirement for germaneness of floor amendments. Unfortunately, the Senate tends to believe that it properly enjoys a license for license, to talk as long as it pleases and legislate without regard to reason or order if it sees fit. As a result, the introduction of germaneness, a gentle and altogether logical discipline, into the Senate is likely to be attacked as a gross violation of the members' privileges.

But germaneness is the only weapon that will enable an honest, diligent Congress to chop down the Christmas tree—the sturdy bill so heavily decorated with amendments of all sizes, shapes, and colors that it is scarcely visible under the enticing load. Ending this traditional exchange of presents among members will not prove popular, but, in the interests of civilized, responsible, reasonable lawmaking, it is time somebody shot Santa Claus.

# 9 · Conference: The Time of the Crunch

There is more law made by fewer men with less public understanding in the conference committees of Congress than in any other part of the legislative system.

The conference committee is almost inherently mysterious and secretive. It consists of a relatively small delegation of senators and representatives, often five or seven of each, named by the presiding officers of each house, usually without the consent or even the knowledge of most of the rest of the members. It meets only in closed session, and no record is ever kept of its deliberations. Some conferees literally refuse to tell reporters afterward anything that went on during the meeting.

A temporary creature with no home of its own, the conference committee meets in unlikely places, often without any public announcement. It votes in an odd fashion, by house rather than by individual member, and no record is kept of that either. Finally, having completed its deliberations, it hands up a report that until recently has been almost unintelligible and drops out of existence, hoping to be absolved of responsibility and identity. All that then remains of these unusual deliberations are the House and Senate chairmen of the conferees, who must sell the conference report to their respective colleagues on the floor as the best secret compromise that honorable men could devise.

All this takes place because the Constitution reads: "Every bill which shall have passed the House of Representatives *and* the

Senate, shall, before it becomes a law, be presented to the President [italics added]." This stricture is interpreted as requiring that the two houses approve a single bill, with no variances or versions, before there is anything to go to the White House. And the Senate and House, being jealous, contentious bodies, very rarely approve identical versions of any legislation of importance, at least on the first go-round.

The use of a conference to reconcile bills at variance goes all the way back to the British parliaments of the fourteenth century, as they first became clearly bicameral. In the early congresses, conferees were chosen without reference to committee—there were no standing committees—but by 1850 or thereabouts it had become accepted that the senior members of the committee involved served as managers in the conference as well.

As a purely parliamentary matter, it is possible for the House to pass a bill, the Senate to add certain amendments and pass it, and the House—the bill having been returned—to vote its approval of the somewhat altered product. Then a single bill has passed both houses and can properly be sent across to the President. But it is seldom that simple. The Senate has more than likely struck some provisions of which the House was particularly fond; some of the new Senate language may easily prove obnoxious to the House. Rather than bouncing the bill interminably back and forth between the two houses, changing it in one and changing it back in the other, some mechanism for compromise is obviously essential.

The result is the conference committee, with each house dispatching to a neutral meeting place a set of emissaries empowered to debate, barter, and ultimately draft a recommended combination of the differing Senate and House measures. All provisions that are precisely the same in both versions of the bill are adopted automatically, and the conferees have no power to alter or drop them. Where a provision varies in the two versions, the final product—the Senate language, the House language, or something in between—must be approved by a majority of the Senate conferees *and* a majority of the House conferees, with each group counted separately. Their final collective recommendation, sometimes reached with great difficulty, is then presented to both houses pretty much on an all-or-nothing basis: Either you accept this admittedly imperfect compromise or you get no law at all, because the opposition is not going to give in any further.

One serious problem of the conference system is the private and unresponsive way in which conferees are chosen. It all happens in a moment, when a slip of paper is sent to the desk of each house and a list of names unquestioningly read. Officially, the conferees are selected by the presiding officer of the Senate, who may be the Vice President at that moment, but probably is not, and the Speaker of the House. They regularly accept the recommendation of the chairman of the standing committee involved, and he almost always recommends the three or four senior members of his party on the committee—including, of course, himself—and the two or three senior members of the minority. (In many congresses this tends to give the minority more conference strength than its numbers warrant; if the majority conferees happen to be divided on an important issue, the decision may be controlled by the minority.)

Exercising their actual, if unofficial, appointive power, committee chairmen have full discretion in choosing conferees and may bypass senior members if they see fit. When the House went to conference on the campaign finance bill in 1971, Chairman Wayne Hays of the House Administration Committee skipped over the next senior Democrat, Representative Frank Thompson of New Jersey, whose votes on some amendments had displeased him, and picked the third- and seventh-ranking members instead. A chairman can even select as a conferee a member who is not on his committee at all but has played a major role in floor debate on the bill, although such a choice is unusual. Generally, the entire process of creating the conference is unilateral and almost imperceptible, with the senior men on the committee or subcommittee automatically becoming the interhouse bargaining team.

In theory, this team of conferees has now magically become nonpartisan, with any memory of how its members voted on the bill or key amendments wiped out. Their collective duty has become to represent the Senate version of the bill against the House version, or the other way about, whether or not they happen to agree with the particular provisions in dispute. "In appointing the conferees," Speaker Joseph Byrns declared in 1935, "the chair is always willing to accept the suggestions of the chairman of the committee which has charge of the bill, assuming that the members who are appointed will stand for the House measure because they represent the House in the conference. The chair would not assume that gentlemen would accept a position as a conferee and not stand for what the House wants."

Congressional gentility aside, human nature does not always operate that way. "There is a little line in the instructions," one House member observed, "which says that the chairman of the conferees will attempt to carry out the will of the House regardless of his own personal feelings about it. Now, I have never seen that rule observed."

A classic example was the 1970 controversy over continuation of the program to build a supersonic transport plane. The House had appropriated $290 million to keep the debatable project going, but the Senate voted by a narrow margin to end the program altogether by cutting off funds. Obviously, a conference was necessary, and the seven senior senators on the appropriations subcommittee on transportation were named as conferees, in the time-honored fashion. But four of the seven, headed by the subcommittee chairman Senator Warren Magnuson, had argued and voted *for* the SST on the floor and wound up in the minority; now they constituted a majority of their half of the conference. (Magnuson, whose hometown of Seattle is a major center of the aviation industry, is sometimes identified off the floor as the Senator from Boeing.) When the conference report was completed, it contained $210 million for the SST, a fiscal compromise from the House point of view, but a sellout in the eyes of the Senate majority, which thought it had killed the program. Magnuson insisted on the floor that he had fought like a tiger for the Senate position, but, with no record to sustain him, the SST opponents were understandably skeptical. Ultimately, the issue was set aside until the following year when the giant plane was permanently grounded by negative votes in both houses. But, in the interim, the conference system had come perilously close to enacting a program that half of Congress had flatly refused to authorize.

Much the same sort of problem has arisen in recent years when the Senate has repeatedly approved amendments to the annual defense authorization bill that would cut back on offensive weapons systems or subject the Pentagon to a higher level of legislative scrutiny. The House version of the bill has not contained comparable provisions, and the Senate conferees have been, as a matter of course, the ranking members of the Armed Services Committee, men and women who have almost universally fought these same restrictive amendments on the floor. As a result, almost none of them survive in the conference report that is the final form of the bill, because there has been no one in the conference to make a case for them.

It is very difficult indeed to persuade either house to defeat a conference report simply because one or two provisions have been cut out of it. Only an issue of the magnitude of the SST can induce a majority of either body to reject the kind of detailed compromise that the bicameral committee produces. Often, conference reports reach the floor in the closing weeks or days of a session, when there is little time to send them back to the conferees for more reworking. Often, the conferees virtually refuse to reconsider the draft over which they have already struggled so long.

Only about 10 per cent of the laws produced by a given Congress are products of a conference committee, but this does not lessen the importance of this uneasy system of compromise. All appropriations bills, which form the skeletal structure of the entire legislative product, and almost all other measures of any serious import do go to conference, making it essential that this last reshaping and refinement be conducted by adequately representative members working within established ground rules.

Aside from its composition, the conference committee is most often subject to criticism for legislating outside its jurisdiction. It is not uncommon for these small secret meetings to strike from a bill identical language already approved by both houses, although this is strictly forbidden. Upon occasion, they also introduce completely new material that does not represent a compromise between Senate and House provisions at all. Under their rules, conferences may change dollar or other figures as long as they do not go higher than the higher figure or lower than the lower; ordinarily, in appropriation bills the House sets a figure, the Senate increases it, and the conference strikes a balance about midway between. As early as 1790, however, a conference committee set aside a salary figure for American ministers abroad that had been approved by both houses and substituted a higher one.

Perhaps the most politically explosive example of a conference exceeding its authority came in 1917, when a committee harmonizing tax legislation saw fit to write in an income tax exemption that covered members of Congress. Historians would have us believe that the Senate and House approved this conference report oblivious of its new benefit for them. In any event, there was a considerable uproar when the public learned of the move, and one of the first acts of the 1918 Congress was to bar conference committees from inserting new material in bills. Despite this flat prohibition, the practice has continued. In 1965, to break a two-month conference deadlock on the agriculture appropriation bill, Senate conferees agreed to accept some items that had never appeared in any version of the bill before. The first: $100,000 to begin construction of a $1 million sedimentation laboratory in Oxford, Mississippi, which just happened to be in the district of the chairman of the House conferees, Representative Jamie Whitten. As recently as 1970, a conference committee wrote into a federal salary bill a provision giving the President new power over government pay increases, one that had not appeared or even been suggested in either the House or Senate versions of the bill. Critics raised strong procedural objections on the Senate floor, but the report was approved, 40 to 35, anyway.

Under the present rules, when a conference goes beyond its authority in striking agreed language, inserting new material, or raising spending figures, its report is subject to a point of order when it reaches the floor. If only one member in one house makes such an objection and the chair sustains him, the report goes right back to conference. The problem is that this is rarely done, and a good part of the reason, other than congressional reluctance to rebuff its own committees, is that the reports themselves have been almost unintelligible. Until 1971, only the House required the conference report to be available in printed form for final floor action. The Senate passed laws for 180 years, incredible as it may seem, on the basis of word-of-mouth descriptions of what the conference had produced, a touching demonstration of faith in the Senate conferees. And even the House report, for all that time, was a jumble of references to the two conflicting bills, from which it was very difficult to derive the factual details of the compromise itself.

The Legislative Reorganization Act of 1970, in one of its major contributions to congressional sanity, required all conferees to prepare a joint statement for both houses that would be "detailed and explicit . . . as to the effect which the amendments or propositions contained in such report will have upon the measure to which those amendments or propositions relate." The result has been a radical improvement in the information available to members when they vote on conference reports, a heartening demonstration that Congress is capable of straightening out its obviously inadequate processes once in a while.

But problems remain. The 1970 law prohibits the House from taking up a conference report until three days after the report and explanatory statement have appeared in the *Congressional Record*, except during the last six days of a session. But there is no comparable safeguard in the Senate, where the new statute apparently can be satisfied if the report and statement are printed at any point in time, even after the conference compromise has been voted.

The House has at its disposal a parliamentary weapon with which to prod a conference that fails to reach agreement. If the conferees do not report in twenty days, any representative may move on the floor to discharge and replace the House managers or to instruct them to take a given position in an effort to resolve a deadlock. It was on such a motion to instruct that the House finally was maneuvered into a substantive vote on withdrawal of troops from Vietnam late in 1971. The motion failed, but by a razor-edge 103–101 vote.

The perennial debate over which house is more influential in conference is one more chapter in the long history of Senate-House rivalry. The argument for greater House influence is based on the theory that representatives have fewer committee assignments, often only one, become better informed specialists in their area than senators do, and thus are able to argue them down in conference. Representative Thomas Curtis of Missouri maintained, "They're trying to man the same positions with 100 men that we are with 435. They can't master the subjects. The House imposes its view on the Senate most of the time because the House knows more about most subjects than the Senate." (This proud claim did not deter Curtis from running for the Senate in 1968 and probably gave him little solace when his defeat dropped him out of Congress altogether.)

Less often expressed publicly is the theory that representatives suffer from a massive inferiority complex with respect to senators, and in conference—one of the rare occasions when members of the two houses mingle—become assertively stubborn to demonstrate that they are indeed equals and can legislate just as well as if not better than the more publicized, more prestigious "other body."

The balancing contention on behalf of Senate influence is that senators frequently capitalize on the threat of the filibuster to get *their* way in conference. Representative Oscar Underwood of Alabama, before his ascent to the Senate, complained that he had often outdebated Senate conferees "and they would calmly tell me that they would not yield because a Senator So-and-So would talk the bill to death if I did not accept his amendment, and, with great governmental issues at stake, I have been compelled to accept minor amendments to great bills that I will not say were graft, but they were put there for the purpose of jeopardizing good legislation in America." (The astute congressman's name still rouses faint echoes among those Americans old enough to have listened to the first national convention ever broadcast by radio, that of the Democrats in New York City in

1924, when "Alabama casts twenty-four votes for Oscar W. Underwood" opened the nominating roll call for 103 interminable ballots.)

The opportunity for polite blackmail provided by the survival of the Senate filibuster is still very much alive. As recently as 1962, the Senate added $2 million to the House-passed Public Works Appropriation bill to begin work on Bruces Eddy Dam in Idaho. While the conferees met, Senator Frank Church of that state promised, "If they strike out Bruces Eddy, I shall hold the Senate floor as long as God gives me the strength to stand." Apparently more impressed by the senator's power supply than by his previous opposition to the filibuster, the committee yielded.

If the conference committee sometimes preserves special favors for members, it can also protect the Union against petty lawmaking. It is not an uncommon practice in Congress to adopt an amendment in one house, often at the impassioned pleading of a single member, with the unspoken understanding that it will never survive conference. This can be a great political boon to the Distinguished Representative from North Columbia; he can carry home to his constituents the story of how he won the fight to save the veterans' hospital on the House floor, only to be denied victory at the last minute, in a secret meeting from which he was barred, by a cabal of heartless senators.

A conference committee's cancellation of pet provisions is not always taken with good grace. For a number of years, the House attached to education bills a provision that no money should be used to bus pupils from one area to another to achieve racial balance. For an equal number of years, the Senate deftly eviscerated this language, and the conference committee sustained the Senate position. Many House liberals were aware that this was in the cards and thus did not become overly exercised about the antibusing amendment. But some segregationist conservatives have continued to protest loudly that they have been betrayed and the will of the House thwarted—which sounds just as good back home as the story of how one brave congressman almost saved the veterans' hospital.

What the conference committee system needs most is more understanding—by the participants, the press, and the public. Without question, increased attention must be focused on the way conferees are appointed: who gets on the committee, who doesn't, and what can be done about it. At the other end of the process, the conference report has finally been made intelligible to the members and all that remains is getting them to read it. (Nearly a year after the change, one senator said on the floor that the Senate did not require written conference reports.) But between the committee's creation and its report, the issue of revising conference procedure is a more complicated and controversial one.

Much improvement in the formation of the conference could be achieved if the committee chairmen involved were required to give a day or two's notice of their intention to propose conferees, along with their names. Then other interested members, such as the sponsors of major successful floor amendments, could appraise the proposed conference make-up and see whether it was likely to reflect the position of the house. If it didn't look promising, a substitute list of conferees could be drawn up for a floor vote on which members the Senate or House really wanted to represent them. Faced with such a prospect, a committee chairman might often prefer to negotiate an acceptable panel of conferees in advance. In any event, each house would have the opportunity to decide to whom it is delegating this all-but-final legislative authority.

The generally laudable theory that government conducted in public always governs best does not, unfortunately, help much with the special problem of the conference committee. The very nature of its proceedings, a confrontation between two groups pledged to mutual hostility, argues that there can only be a settlement if the full details of who surrendered to whom are not spread before the other senators and representatives and the world at large. If each set of conferees has been hand-picked by its house as doggedly representative of its position, it seems likely that a conference conducted before the press and public would simply result in a series of speeches of unrelenting loyalty to the Senate or House position, followed by a series of deadlocked votes and very little compromise at all.

In the present closed conference meetings, such pro forma combat can be partially taken for granted and reduced to a minimum, if not eliminated. The conferees know they must reach a compromise, and they can talk freely about how to get there, without being quoted by the press in a manner that might suggest betrayal of the colleagues whose chose them. There is ordinarily not much problem where dollars or other figures are involved; such questions are almost always easily resolved by splitting the difference, or something close to it. But where there are substantive issues in question—a new tax, a new government agency, special treatment for an industry—it is hard enough to hammer out an acceptable middle course when the conferees feel free to make any argument they choose.

Former Senator Albert Gore of Tennessee, an informed critic of conference procedure, would keep the meetings closed but require a record of all votes to be made public the day after a conference concluded its work. He says conferees should be aware that they will be judged afterward by their constituents and their colleagues; specifically, he feels that "Senate conferees would be inclined to put up more fight if they knew they must individually be held accountable for their votes."

It seems more likely, however, that publication of all votes would simply ensure a long series of recorded deadlocks, followed ultimately by the same compromise solution in the conference report. Why not save time and effort and presume—as is now often the case—all those stubborn deadlocks? In the long run, recorded votes seem more apt to discourage than promote viable compromise, which, at this stage of the legislative process, is what is chiefly sought.

A one-man, one-vote, majority-rule system might seem advisable to inject a little democracy into conference procedure, but it also has serious drawbacks. For a small point, both houses would have to agree to name the same number of conferees, an unnecessary inconvenience. For a more serious one, there would be even greater danger that a controversial stand, such as the Senate vote against the SST, would be wiped out in conference.

If each conferee had one vote and a simple majority of the entire conference controlled, there would be even less likelihood of the Senate managers actively pressing a Senate position with which some of them did not personally agree, and the same for the House. Remember, conferees are committee chairmen and ranking members, senior men and women likely to be generally conservative in their outlook and unsympathetic to an innovative position that may represent the majority view in their house. On the whole, the present voting system is probably more serviceable.

It is true that the problems of the conference committee could be eliminated at a stroke if Congress became a unicameral legislature, with only one house. By the same token, these problems could probably be reduced markedly if Congress decided to establish joint standing committees that sent identical bills to the floors of both houses. But there is absolutely no realistic possibility of either of these changes, on the grounds of jealousy and preservation of identity alone, so we had better learn to live with the conference committee, better constituted, held more strictly to its function, and its end product fully circulated before a final vote.

# 10 · Decisions, Decisions

One day in 1821, the House was anxious to vote on a pending bill, but Representative Felix Walker held the floor, resisting all entreaties to yield on the grounds that his constituents expected him to "make a speech for Buncombe," a county in his North Carolina district. Walker's feel for the voters back home did not prove keen—he was defeated for re-election the following year—but he left behind him on Capitol Hill the generic term for idle congressional speeches: buncombe or, more simply, bunk.

Bunk it may have been, but as early as the days of Daniel Boone, with whom Walker had helped colonize Kentucky, a congressman felt the need to reassure his constituents that he was on duty, impressing the House with his people's views, conveying their sentiments to the decision makers. Members of the House 150 years later have still to resolve the very real quandary: how closely must a congressman listen to the voice of his district, how far may he pursue his own sense of what is best for the national community?

Both senators and representatives, even the most insular and self-contained, must do a great deal of listening in any event. For each moment spent voting in committee or on the floor, there are hours of listening—not merely to witnesses and colleagues but also to constituents, personally and by mail; to the Administration; to party leaders; and to lobbyists for both private interests and public causes. Out of this great mass of fact, theory, suggestion, demand, plea, and advice, the individual member must somehow filter a decision. Some understanding of how all these multiple sources of pressure affect a member of Congress, ultimately combining to influence his vote, is essential to an examination of how the legislative process works and where it fails.

The people back home deliver their single, direct, and unanswerable communication to the members of Congress every two or six years on election day. In between time, they write. Some visit Washington in delegations. Others invite their congressman home to a meeting and lecture him. But mostly, they write. Every day, thousands of letters, cards, and telegrams are dumped on Capitol Hill, patiently sorted into 535 piles and each delivered to a member. Are they read? Yes. By the senator or representative himself? Not likely, unless the letter is from an identifiably important person, a political leader, a close friend, a contributor, or the head of an organization. The rest are skimmed by staff.

Letters from outside the district or the state frequently do not get counted or answered, unless the congressman happens to have broader political ambitions. Some members don't count or acknowledge mail that is obviously the product of an organized campaign: coupons pasted on postcards, or form letters. Others regard these as legitimate communications. Scant attention is paid to the crank, obscene, and anonymous letters, of which there is a steady flow not discernibly related to the phases of the moon.

In most Hill offices, the mail count is considered important. If the mail on a given issue is running heavily against the congressman's position, he is not likely to come about abruptly, but he is likely to re-examine his thinking, read some of the letters, and make sure he has sound answers to the questions they raise. In some instances, such as voting to confirm a controversial Presidential nominee, a senator may withhold decision until he sees how his constituents feel. Although the mail probably does not control decisions directly on many occasions, it plays a major role in focusing the member's attention on areas that are causing concern among his voters. If a significant portion of it suddenly begins to feature a particular issue, like gun control or busing or the Middle East, the senator or representative is on notice that he had better develop a credible position or take a second look at the one he already has. No one should expect that letter-writing campaigns, particularly if they are short or obviously contrived, will persuade a Congressman to reverse suddenly a long-held conviction or prejudice. On the other hand, there is no question that the gradual shift of Vietnam sentiment from hawk to dove, first in the Senate and then more grudgingly in the House, was heavily influenced by constituent mail. It takes a strong congressman to hold out against a clear, continuing majority of his voters on the single issue that most concerns them, particularly if there is an election on the horizon.

Very few letters get an individual, freshly written answer, but almost all of them get some reply. A letter from someone who agrees with the congressman gets a warm word of appreciation and a concise restatement of his position; a letter from a critic gets a "thank you for your expression of interest in this very important area, and rest assured I will take it into consideration." There are form answers in each congressional office file for all the current burning issues, and great care is often taken to splice them together when a constituent writes on more than one subject.

Even greater care is taken to avoid any impression that form letters are being used. In the basements of all the congressional office buildings, great banks of automatic typewriters clatter on, night and day, printing "original" copies of letters whose full text or component paragraphs have been fed into them on punched tape. For many years it was a closely guarded secret that the Senate had a signature machine, a device that produces an "authentic" autograph of any senator at the bottom of his letter, not stamped or printed but "written" in ink by a mechanically guided pen. Any constituent who doubts that he has a real, live reply from his senator can touch the signature with dampened fingertip and, sure enough, ink!

The issue of how loyally a member of Congress should reflect the collective views of his constituents will never be successfully resolved by a neat, easily applied formula. For some men and women on the Hill, the state or the district always comes first, any inclination toward moral or intellectual independence giving way before the clear dictate of that specific segment of voters and their immediate economic needs and social views. Others are so seized by a sense of cosmic responsibility upon first attaining entry to the halls of Congress that they set aside the honest convictions and day-to-day problems of the people who elected them as unworthy of more than passing consideration compared to the Great Issues with which they now, as Lawmakers, Must Grapple.

Dr. Philip Donham and Robert Fahey, a couple of serious but narrow-gauge management consultants, in their book *Congress Needs Help*, sum up the provincial theory of representation this way:

> A Congressman is obliged to consider neither the views of people who do not vote within his fixed geographical area nor any historical play of far-off forces; it is his voting constituents' immediate needs and views that most influence his thinking.

At the risk of using a cannon against a cockroach, it is impossible to consider this question of a lawmaker's responsibility to his constituents without going back to Edmund Burke. In his classic statement to the electors of Bristol, he conceded that a legislator must give weight and respect to the opinions of the people who choose him. "But," he maintained,

> his unbiased opinion, his mature judgment, his enlightened conscience, he ought not to sacrifice to you, to any man, or to any set of men living. These he does not derive from your pleasure, no, nor from the law and the Constitution. They are a trust from Providence, for the abuse of which he is deeply answerable. Your representative owes you not his industry only, but his judgment; and he betrays, instead of serving you, if he sacrifices it to your opinion.

Next case.

It is hardly surprising, however, that many members of the

House of Representatives, haunted by the brevity of their two-year term, cannot quite manage Burke's lofty view, much as they would like to. In *Forge of Democracy*, Neil MacNeil tells of a California Democrat who was left, after the latest reapportionment, with a district that still did not contain a clear-cut majority for his liberal views.

"I could have been a statesman if they had cut off a few of those conservatives," the House member complained. "Now I'll have to continue going this way and that way, back and forth. I'm a cracker-assed congressman, and I could have been a statesman."

There is a single group of constituents whose views weigh very heavily with a member of Congress: the men and women who gave him enough money to conduct the political campaign that got him there. There is no blinking the fact that contributors have little difficulty in getting their congressman's attention, out of courtesy for past favors and in fervent hope of future ones.

"Now I don't think that a congressman looks back and votes according to campaign contributions received," one member said, "but he can't help being indirectly influenced by what his friends think. He knows that his friends are the ones who back him financially in a campaign, so indirectly they are going to influence his decisions."

To put it more bluntly, suppose you are a House member who received a $5,000 campaign contribution two years ago from a corporation executive in the district, and a bill is up on the floor that would directly affect that man's business. The executive has written you a perfectly proper letter—which rose to the top of the correspondence pile as if by levitation—asking you as a constituent to oppose the bill, pointing out the potential adverse economic impact on the district.

You are of two minds about the bill. Viewed dispassionately, it has some good features and some bad ones. But you are up for re-election in another eight months. If you vote against the bill, there is a good chance you will get another such campaign contribution from the same man; if you vote for it, there is every likelihood you will not. That money would finance a large part of your campaign, perhaps as much as a fifth, and free you from the ordeal of finding fifty other constituents willing to put up $100 each. Which way do you vote?

As long as we retain our system of privately financed campaigns, that question will arise time after time for every senator and representative who does not represent a secure one-party state or district and who is not independently wealthy. Which is a lot of the members of Congress. We will explore later the implications of government financing of political competition, only noting here that campaign contributors can be among the strongest influences on congressional decision-making.

How, under the present system, can it be otherwise? It is not necessary to regard a campaign contribution as inherently evil, a cross between a bribe and a retainer fee. Can anyone reasonably expect a wealthy contributor to continue helping a congressman who does not share his views? As long as candidates must turn to such men and women to survive politically, they can be expected to reflect the contributors' special interests, whatever they may be.

The greatest outside influence on congressional decision-making, next to that of constituents, lies with politicians: the White House with its phalanx of persuaders headed by the President, and the party leaders in each house, bearing promise of preferment for the cooperative. Although chief executives have complained of impotency from time to time in their efforts on Capitol Hill, the office alone invests the holder with awesome power to impress his views on senators and representatives. And where the President cannot successfully invoke logic, prestige, or party loyalty, he may be forced to descend to a little politicking.

A classic episode involves Lincoln's devious maneuvers to win congressional approval of the Thirteenth Amendment to abolish slavery, a move he believed would shorten the Civil War. There were not enough votes on the Hill in 1863 to pass the amendment, so the President proclaimed the territory of Nevada a state, overlooking the fact that it was still short on population. To line up the new members of Congress that resulted, Lincoln sent a Cabinet officer to the Hill, telling him, "Whatever promises you make, I will perform." (The strategy was successful and the amendment passed, but one of three patronage pledges made in the President's name was still outstanding when he was assassinated. President Andrew Johnson refused thereafter to honor it, declaring piously, "I have observed in the course of my experience that such bargains tend to immorality." Is it any wonder that the House voted three years later to impeach him?)

Presidents rarely try to pick up votes in Congress by promising jobs any more. Inflation has driven the price considerably higher than a single appointment, short of the Supreme Court or a major ambassadorship, would be likely to cover. The White House can do better by offering to put its weight behind a piece of special legislation that is attractive to a whole bloc of congressional votes. President Eisenhower, seldom regarded as an adroit Hill manipulator, was running into trouble in the Senate on trade legislation, but when the Administration suggested the possibility of a bill for "minerals stabilization" (a euphemism for subsidies on lead and zinc), several Western senators altered their views on reciprocal trade and, in the words of one observer, "things just went a-scooting."

The Kennedy years presented a special problem for the White House. Congress was under Democratic control and thus, presumably, subject to the new President's wishes. In fact, the Democratic majorities were arithmetical rather than philosophical, suspicious, after the Johnson-Rayburn era, of the more liberal initiatives of the New Frontier. Kennedy recognized the latent hostility, and the ambassador he sent to the Hill, Lawrence O'Brien, became a model of sensitivity and tact. O'Brien invited every member, Republicans included, to a series of cocktail parties in congressional committee rooms. Then they went to the White House in groups for coffee, with each committee chairman rating a half-hour private audience with the President. O'Brien, later to exercise his talents as Democratic National Chairman, was careful to avoid any appearance of pressure; he never sat in the Senate or House gallery, for example, lest his appearance be interpreted as White House surveillance. But for all this careful treatment, Kennedy had been unable, at the time of his death, to bring enough influence to bear to achieve major parts of his program. His key proposals for medicare and federal aid to education left Congress unmoved, and late in 1963 tax and civil rights legislation threatened to pile up in a massive stalemate reminiscent of the Truman days. Through it all, the new President continued to negotiate and pacify, instead of attacking the Congress as obstructionist and taking his case to the people.

Lyndon Johnson never had to consider going over the heads of Congress to the people; the senators and representatives *were* his people. Seated in his White House office, he played the Congress like a mighty Wurlitzer, intimately familiar with every pedal, stop, and key. Once, early in 1964, after the Senate Finance Committee had adopted a tax cut amendment he regarded as premature, Johnson personally phoned all seventeen committee members during their luncheon recess, and, when they reconvened in the afternoon, the amendment was brought up again and defeated. To a significant degree, it was Johnson who helped put steel in the spine of the Senate during the historic civil rights debate of 1964, culminating after fifty-seven days in the first vote in history to shut off debate on that sensitive issue. The President steadfastly refused any compromise on the bill, which had been considerably strengthened beyond the original Kennedy version, and he won. The leader of the Southern opposition, Senator Richard Russell, had been asked months before whether Johnson's accession to the White House might signal a compromise on the civil rights bill. He knew his man. "No," the Georgian replied, "the way that fellow operates, he'll get the whole bill, every last bit of it."

President Nixon, like his two immediate predecessors, had been a member of both the House and Senate, although much more briefly, but he faced a very different set of problems in dealing with Congress. Where Kennedy and Johnson could seek the cooperation of at least nominally Democratic congresses, Nixon had nothing close to a Republican majority in either house for four years. What's more, he lacked the strong public mandate and personality that had helped Eisenhower deal with the Democratic congresses of his last six years. And the Democratic leaders Nixon faced on the Hill, particularly in the Senate, were less inclined to consensus lawmaking than Lyndon Johnson and Sam Rayburn had been in the Eisenhower days.

Granted all this, it is difficult to argue that the Nixon White House did not set some new record for ineptness in its early attempts to influence Congress. One of the President's first real tests, his campaign to win Supreme Court confirmation for Clement Haynsworth, was lost, at least in part, by clumsy lobbying. Among other mistakes, the White House decided that one way to reach Northern Republican senators on behalf of a Southern judge was to go over their heads to influential contributors and political leaders at home.

Senator Richard Schweiker, only a few months removed from four House terms, began getting telephone calls from important Republican figures back in Pennsylvania, suggesting that he would be well advised as a freshman to accept his President's nominee without further ado. Perceiving that he was not being treated like a senator but was, in fact, being pushed around, Schweiker became angry. He decided to work harder and expand Republican opposition to Haynsworth, and, when that nomination was beaten, he went on to play a similar role against the President's next less-than-choice nominee, Harrold Carswell.

Sometimes, the White House was only irritating. In 1971, Representative William Scherle, a conservative Iowa Republican beginning his third term, got a letter on White House stationery informing him that "in view of the large number of highly qualified applicants in comparison to the relatively few positions to be filled, we are unable to offer you encouragement at this time. . . . Your file, although inactive, has been placed with a selected group in our talent bank." Scherle, who had just won a seat on the House Appropriations Committee and was not exactly looking for work, angrily called the mistake "incomprehensible."

There were times when it almost seemed that the Nixon Administration was deliberately baiting one of the Senate's more austere Republican personalities, Margaret Chase Smith of Maine. In 1970, the chief White House lobbyist, Bryce Harlow, attempted to win confirmation votes for the Carswell Supreme Court nomination at the last minute by telling other Republicans that Mrs. Smith was going to support the Florida judge. The senator denounced this claim, voted against Carswell, and then demanded and got a written apology from Harlow, who said he was confessing error "as directed." Only eleven months later, when a critical vote on funding the supersonic transport plane was scheduled on the Senate floor, the White House sent Mrs. Smith a letter, notifying her that the President had reversed a Lyndon Johnson decision to close down the Portsmouth, New Hampshire, naval shipyard, a major employer of her Maine constituents. Mrs. Smith angrily made the letter public and then went out and voted against the SST, which lost by a close margin. A few days later, she issued a statement denying that President Nixon had "crassly and crudely sought to buy my vote" and insisting that the timing had been "only chronological coincidence." Whatever else it might have been, the episode was as clumsy and ill-planned a piece of White House congressional relations as had been put on exhibit in a number of years.

As Congress now operates, its leaders largely lack intrinsic power to influence their members and their votes directly. The days of the party caucus, when a majority or two-thirds vote of the members of one party in closed session bound all of them inflexibly to vote one way on the floor, are long gone. At its peak of influence, King Caucus enabled a strong leader who could control little more than a third of the full house— two-thirds, say, of a party with a 55 per cent majority—to impose his will on the entire body. This prospect grew so repugnant to those who were being imposed upon that the powers of leadership were whittled down to a narrow wand with which the Speaker and the Senate majority leader may now occasionally rap a member lightly on the knuckles.

The power to make or heavily influence committee assignments and transfers remains one of the chief sources of the leaders' authority. It is deeply undercut, however, by the fact that once a senator or representative has been rewarded with the committee of his choice, there is no way for a party leader to impede—or, indeed, promote—his progress toward influence on the mindless, moving belt of the seniority system. The deed has been done, the favor conferred, and the ancient political principle of "What have you done for me lately?" comes into play again.

In the House it remains possible for a Speaker to favor one

member over another on the floor through application of the elaborate system of rules. Although it does not frequently prove controlling these days, the Speaker's unchallenged right to recognize one member and ignore another was an awesome weapon in earlier times. Speaker John Carlisle of Kentucky (1884–89), otherwise little noted, developed the screening technique for exercising this power. When he saw a member standing on the floor bidding to be recognized, Carlisle would inquire, "For what purpose does the gentleman rise?" If the answer did not conform to his plan for the House at that time, the Speaker would refuse to recognize the member further. And, under the rules then and now, no point of order can be raised against the Speaker for such arbitrary action, nor can his ruling be appealed. Today, the Speaker asks the same question of members seeking recognition, but almost entirely as a matter of tradition. Rare indeed is the occasion on which he refuses recognition as a matter of personal authority alone.

Special parliamentary situations may occasionally arise in the House when a Speaker has an opportunity to reward an ally with a favorable ruling, but this is not a reliable source of power. In the Senate, where the leader is on the floor and not in the chair, and procedure plays a lesser role, this kind of gift is even more rarely bestowed. In both houses, rulings are actually made by the parliamentarian. He whispers up to the presiding officer on the rostrum, who then announces the decision as his own. While, politically speaking, the parliamentarians are arms of the majority party in each house, they are so circumscribed by past precedents and the need for instant decision that they normally play a role in augmenting the leader's power only when a careful parliamentary strategy has been laid down in advance.

Party leaders can win their members' loyalty most effectively by special legislative consideration for their pet projects. Within the framework of the party program, it is often possible for a bill to be whisked onto the calendar at the request of one member or delayed for a week or two for another. The leaders can be persuasive with committee chairmen on the inclusion of important amendments or appropriations in a bill and on its prompt reporting. In the Senate, a floor vote may be postponed for several days to accommodate a member's private travel plans—and too often is. Minor bills, of little moment to the Congress but important to the sponsor, only reach the floor with the assent of the leaders.

Beyond the relatively limited area of committee assignment, party leaders have only slim rewards to offer in terms of advancement within the institution. In the Senate, the only two consequential posts in each party are elective: floor leader and assistant leader, or whip. It is possible for a leader to promise his aid to one candidate for whip when a vacancy opens or a challenge arises, but this has not been attempted in the Senate in recent years, with leaders in both parties obliged to harmonize competitive liberal and conservative factions. Thus, Senator Mike Mansfield, the wise and careful Democratic leader, kept hands off when Senator Edward Kennedy surprisingly unseated Senator Russell Long as whip in 1969 and when Kennedy was, even more surprisingly, dethroned by Senator Robert Byrd only two years later.

There is also a cluster of Senate posts in each party that are more ornamental than functional: chairman or secretary of the policy committee, chairman of the party conference, and the like. These are normally token rewards for senior members, recognizing with titles but no real influence senators of the party faction that lost the last leadership contest. Thus, in the Ninety-second Congress, the Republican leadership officially included two staunch conservatives, Gordon Allott of Colorado and Milton Young of North Dakota, and a moderate conservative, Margaret Chase Smith of Maine; but the real power was in the hands of Hugh Scott of Pennsylvania, a liberal, and Robert Griffin of Michigan, a moderate edging leftward as his re-election campaign approached.

In the House, the Speaker and floor leaders are elected, and the majority leader has the right to appoint the majority whip. But this is a one-shot proposition, and the dim future prospect of gaining this favor is not likely to endow the floor leader with much extra authority in the eyes of each of his 200-odd charges. Each party in the House also has a group of regional whips, men assigned the task of checking in advance how a key vote is likely to go and then rounding up the troops when it takes place. Appointment to this job is an honor of sorts, but its distribution does not really contribute much to leadership influence. (The minor prestige accorded these posts may account for the fact that whip-counts in the House have not proved very reliable in recent years, with predicted figures for one side or the other sometimes dissolving when the roll is called.)

The congressional leaders of the party that holds the White House are automatically a full measure more influential with their members—or at least they ought to be. Distributed skillfully, the social cachet, transcendent publicity value, and dense political impact of the Presidency can go a long way toward molding an unruly congressional delegation into a mannerly, manageable team. The leaders can usually best suggest to the White House how to apply social invitations, personal phone calls, minor appointments, and private consultations, in order to make friends on Capitol Hill. But when his own party leaders are barely consulted on such matters by the President and his congressional liaison staff—as was often true in the early Nixon years—this source of influence tends to evaporate.

Occasionally, congressional leaders can bring to bear negative power, invoking disciplinary action against a member for political betrayal or failure to observe what amount to the lowest standards of the body. Thus, in 1965, Representatives Albert Watson of South Carolina and John Bell Williams of Mississippi were stripped of committee seniority for failure to support the candidacy of Lyndon Johnson the previous fall. (Another man with a smaller landslide and matching ego would probably never have pressed the point.) But two years later, when House Democrats decided to remove Adam Clayton Powell as chairman of Education and Labor for multiple transgressions, the action was opposed by Speaker John McCormack. Exercise of disciplinary authority is even rarer in the Senate; when Harry Byrd, Jr., of Virginia deserted the Democratic Party in 1970, ran as an independent, and won, he was welcomed back into the Democratic caucus, his seniority, though trifling, unimpaired.

The official disciplinary strictures of the two houses, as we will see in more detail later, are invoked so rarely that they have almost atrophied from disuse. The Senate has not seen fit to expel a member since 1862; the House, since 1861. All six cases in those years involved support for the Confederacy. The Senate, only responding to severe pressure, has censured seven of its members, the most recent, Thomas Dodd of Connecticut in 1967. The House has censured eighteen members, but no one since 1921.

The disciplinary powers available to congressional leaders are simply not brought into play often enough to make them a real factor in the decision-making process of the Senate or House. This is not to say that they should be invoked more frequently, although there are those who will argue that point. It remains a fact that members are not significantly influenced in their own decisions by the prospect that their public or private behavior may subject them to some form of punishment or dishonor within the institution.

The result of all this is that the members of Congress today operate very largely outside the influence of their party leaders. Their vote is not bound by any caucus or conference. Once on a desired committee, they advance inexorably. Special favors exist, but not in significant numbers. There are only a handful of appointive subleadership posts. It is unusual for anyone to get punished. If you are a member, this situation promises a high degree of independence, should you care for that sort of thing. If you are a leader, it is something else altogether.

As things stand today, a congressional leader dedicated to the advancement of the commonwealth—a blend of his own vision and that of his party and its President, if any—is going to have considerable trouble advancing that cause efficiently or rapidly. Those leaders who have succeeded in the past forty years or more have done so because they had a very rare capacity to piece together a large number of small sources of influence into a single mass of power. We have seen how few tools a Senate majority leader or a Speaker has at hand to seal the loyalty of the members of his working majority, even if only for a single bill.

Lyndon Johnson could do that. Not because the system gave him the power by direct grant, but because he knew how to find every small pressure point, personal or political, that existed in the Senate and was never reluctant—hell, he was *proud*—to lean or stomp on any one of them when the situation demanded. Johnson regarded it as the function of a congressional leader to keep track of every aspect of the public and sometimes even private life of every senator and use all that information to threaten, cajole, wheedle, or persuade each of them into voting his way. Without even thinking, Johnson could put in a single, offhand line his consummate legislative self-confidence, his scorn for others who fancied they understood Senate power, and his disregard for operational nicety. In 1959, a liberal Democrat warned the majority leader that he was putting together a bloc of votes behind a certain proposal. Johnson was not impressed. "Why," he observed, "Harry Byrd can get more votes by standing in the back of the chamber and nodding than you can with a detective."

Another fabled Texan, Sam Rayburn, could do it too, which, considering the fact that his field of operation was nearly five times as large, was nothing short of astonishing. (For a dozen years, from 1936 to 1948, Representative Johnson watched Rayburn work, as Democratic floor leader and Speaker; he learned many lessons, upon which he stamped the imprint of his own particular drive and style.) Rayburn was a great Speaker because he could assemble, vote by vote, a patchwork majority of Democrats loyal to the party, Democrats loyal to him, ideologues, men for whom he had done favors, men to whom he could make special appeals, men to whom he could hint some sort of recognition down the road ahead, and those who accepted his time-honored thesis that the way to get along was to go along.

Conjuring up this sort of majority, day after day, year after year, required the light touch for which Rayburn became famous. When a member has been permitted, even encouraged, to "vote your district first" on a series of bills with local impact, he becomes a good deal more responsive to an occasional request for party loyalty on a national issue. On a typical occasion, a House Democrat told the Speaker he would go with the party if his vote made the difference, but he asked permission to wait until most of the roll call had been completed; if it was clear then he was not needed, he would vote against the party and with his district. "That is fine," Rayburn responded, "that is all I want."

There always remained some members whom Johnson and

Rayburn could not reach with their most compelling arguments, and the breed has not died out since their time. Sometimes, it is a matter of making a fetish of independence. Senator Margaret Chase Smith has refused for years to reveal how she will vote on anything until the roll is called, and probably gotten more publicity out of silence than news; she speaks so softly, however, that it is often as difficult to learn her position after she has voted as before. On a different sort of indecision, a House member described a colleague "who goes to church to pray for guidance on difficult issues. The leadership can't do much with that vote."

Sometimes, the most successful devices of persuasion are the most informal. For nearly fifty years now, House leaders have operated what has been known under various sponsors as "The Clinic," "Downstairs," and, its once and present title, "The Board of Education." This gathering of key congressional figures over a few drinks in a back-corridor Capitol office in the late afternoon has been used both to work out major legislative decisions in a relaxed atmosphere and to sell those decisions to individual members who were flattered to have been asked to drop by. The Board of Education is basically a Democratic group, although in its early days it was bipartisan. In the 1950's, there was a Republican parallel, but no longer.

John Garner, the Texan who moved from Speaker to Vice President only to find the latter job "not worth a bucket of warm spit," was one of the founders of the Board of Education. He explained its tutorial function this way: "Well, you get a couple of drinks in a young congressman, and then you know what he knows and what he can do. We pay the tuition by supplying the liquor." Although the Board, like the conference committee, keeps no records, its chief social stimulant over the years has been reported to be that Southern staple, bourbon and branch water. From inside accounts, it seems likely that anyone who asked for a very dry martini would shortly have found himself on the Committee on Merchant Marine and Fisheries.

It was under Rayburn's skillful guidance that the Board of Education reached its peak of utility, even providing one of the rarest services in congressional history, a point of coordination between the House and Senate. For when Lyndon Johnson moved north to the Other Body, he continued to drop in of an afternoon, keeping far better track of what was under way in the House than Senate leaders had seen fit to do before or since. As a House member, Johnson had been a Board regular; he was there with Harry Truman on that fateful day in April, 1945, when a call for the Vice President told him that Franklin Roosevelt was dead and he was the leader of the nation and commander in chief of its warring forces. "Jesus Christ and Andy Jackson!" was Truman's reported reaction. What Johnson said, at a similar grim moment eighteen years later, no one has yet recorded.

As Democratic floor leader, John McCormack had been a regular Board member, but after Rayburn's death elevated him to the Speakership in 1961, he slowly let the custom decline. (A most conservative man in many respects, McCormack lived through most of his forty years in the House in a modest downtown hotel suite from which he and his wife rarely ventured for social exchange.) When Carl Albert became Speaker in 1971, he reinstituted the Board of Education, with the encouragement of his convivial floor leader, Hale Boggs of Louisiana, but they had difficulty infusing it with the old spirit and influence of better days and stronger men.

Both houses have a number of other informal groups of members, gathered by party, seniority, political philosophy, or a combination thereof, and some of these enjoy real influence. The best organized and most effective is the Democratic Study Group, a band of some 140 House liberals that was established in 1959 in an effort to counteract the coalition of Southern Democrats and conservative Republicans that dominated the House then and sometimes still does. For an ad hoc organization, the DSG has become almost institutional. It has full-time professional staff, conducts research, keeps its members informed on pending legislation with well-written memos, even has some internal politics of its own, with competitive elections for chairman. Roughly comparable, but smaller and correspondingly less influential, is the Wednesday Club, a voluntary association of Liberal House Republicans. The same name is used by liberal Republican senators, but their organization tends to be more a luncheon club than an action group.

The fact that it takes the political skill and diligence of a Johnson or Rayburn to bring the role of Senate leader or House

Speaker to life, to invest with real legislative authority offices that lack statutory power, is a source of serious concern to members like Representative Richard Bolling, who would like to see the machinery run more smoothly and productively. In his book *House Out of Order*, the congressional critic decries the fact that the Speaker can achieve some sort of working leadership only by his willingness to attend to a wide and sometimes ignoble range of individual concerns of his members. He wrote:

> To maintain personal influence, the Speaker is forced to engage in a savage political scramble involving sectional interests, local claims and personal advancements, all of which are more fondly regarded by the inner circle of the House [of which he has long been a member] than party loyalties or vital national issues. All too often, wise and just legislation becomes a subordinate issue and frequently a total casualty.

There is little question that the Senate and House leaders should be granted a somewhat stronger hand than they have enjoyed in the recent years during which Congress has tottered downhill into greater inefficiency and unresponsiveness. Substitution of a merit system for the seniority system, as already discussed, plus an open and official role for the leaders in making committee assignments, would tend to increase their authority over the membership, although not so drastically as to limit a desirable measure of general independence. Once congressional advancement becomes a competitive rather than an automatic matter, the leaders' power to bolster up a sagging chairman or encourage an insurgent challenge will become a considerable factor in the power structure of each body.

Over a period of years, a bold and aggressive leader will be able to put together a team of cooperative committee chairmen: existing chairmen anxious for his support in retaining their authority and new chairman whom he has helped move up in contests based on merit. Backed by such a team, a leader will be much better able to move his party program, with less necessity for piecing together a public majority through time-consuming attention to private problems.

One of the few things that can be said with certainty about the use of paid agents to influence congressional decision-making is that we know very little about it. For one thing, neither the lobbyists nor the senators and representatives they are trying to influence like to talk about the process very much. It suits the public posture of both groups to deny that any such influence exists, or, at least, that it is really effective.

For another, Congress did not even approach the question of collecting information about lobbyists and regulating them in the mildest way until 1946. If this seems incredible, it simply provides evidence of the concurrent reluctance of the members to acknowledge over the years that special-interest pressure was being applied, widely and expensively, and of the lobbyists to acknowledge to anyone but their employers—for whom, of course, they magnify their influence—that they were indeed laying a heavy thumb on the delicate scales of the legislative process.

The 1946 statute—nothing has been done since—deals entirely with disclosure, requiring individuals and groups whose "principal purpose" is to influence the passage or defeat of legislation to list their major contributors, all but their smallest expenditures, and the salaries and expense money paid their agents. There are penalties for failure to report, but no limits on any kind of activity. Theoretically, then, we should now have comprehensive lobbying statistics covering more than twenty-five years; in fact, the law has been avoided, evaded, and unenforced, so that those lobbying reports tell us very little about the proportions of the situation, much less the problem.

The best evidence of this is that the total of reported lobbying expenditures in 1954, when the law was still warm, was something over $10 million, probably a fraction of the real figure but reasonably credible nevertheless. By 1964, in the face of inflation and a multiplying population of Washington agents, the figure had dropped—*dropped*—to $4 million, and in the early 1970's it only ran about $5 million. Obviously, lobbyists were sitting in their Connecticut Avenue offices and thumbing their noses at the statute. It did not charge anyone with enforcement, so no one was enforcing. A check of the filed reports any time in the past year showed both minor operators and major law firms that provide Washington "representation" listing new clients but refusing to report any figures for compensation or expenses.

Only rarely does a blatant example of corrupt lobbying hit the headlines. Bribe-takers do not ordinarily make announcements, and even the senator or representative who is inclined to report an illicit offer he has just rejected does not like to identify himself publicly as the sort of member lobbyists apparently think they can reach. He is much more likely to refuse the lobbyist, ruling out any future dealings but remaining quiet, salving his conscience with the thought that there may have been some sort of misunderstanding. Underlying extreme congressional reluctance to blow the whistle on flagrant lobbying is the distinct possibility that the inevitable investigation would bring to light less scrupulous colleagues. In the curious moral handbook of the Hill, protesting out-of-line lobbying is regarded as fouling a portion of the nest in which all must cluster.

Contrary to this code, Senator Francis Case of South Dakota reported in 1956 that an oil lobbyist had promised him a $2,500 campaign contribution to oppose the pending natural gas bill, a gesture the senator interpreted as a bribe. He abstained on the roll call and the bill passed, but President Eisenhower vetoed it as the product of "arrogant lobbying." In subsequent criminal action, the oil company was fined $10,000 and two of its agents $2,500 each, on the whole probably a bargain for all three.

There are some levels of lobbying that will never be subject to congressional control, although they are regarded in some quarters as bordering on sharp practice. The American Medical Association has conceded privately, for example, that it enlists the help of the family doctors of senators and representatives to talk these men and women into line on major votes. Less personal but often equally powerful, the AFL–CIO need only speak softly to gain the full attention of members from industrial districts and states. Andrew Biemiller only escaped obscurity as a two-term Democratic House member from Wisconsin because of his considerable size; now, as the labor movement's chief lobbyist, he looms even larger as a Capitol Hill power figure. Speaker McCormack acknowledged that he cleared all Education and Labor Committee appointments with Biemiller, a procedure that has produced the only solid liberal majority on any House committee.

In that great, unmapped limbo between the outright bribe and the heartfelt plea, lobbyists have developed a whole range of rewards for the congressman worth courting. The location of a defense plant in a House district, for example, can provide permanent economic help for its residents and pay commensurate political dividends for the congressman. Naturally, the complex series of public and private decisions that locates a new plant in Oklahoma instead of Iowa or Georgia is certain to make a particular lawmaker mighty grateful. He may be unwilling or unable or both to express his gratitude in concrete terms. Or he may not.

One afternoon early in 1963, Bobby Baker, then the Democratic Senate patronage dispenser, placed a telephone call from the Washington hotel suite of the lobbyist for North American Aviation to one of the most politically powerful Oklahoma oil barons, seeking his intercession with the National Aeronautics and Space Administration on new plant locations. "Carl Albert feels he has to have something in his district to survive politically," Baker declared.

The conversation, recorded as part of FBI surveillance and later reported by Drew Pearson in his column, seems almost absurd. Albert, then majority leader and now Speaker, had carried his district by 43,900–4,400 in 1958, by 56,100–18,800 in 1960, and by 56,000 to nothing (he was unopposed) in 1962. There is no evidence that Albert had raised the question with Baker or ever acted in response. But, subsequently, North American Aviation and then General Dynamics opened new plants in the congressman's district, in the lonely rural southeastern reaches of Oklahoma. Lobbying? Who is to say? And, even if it were, who could spell out a code that would prohibit a major industry from choosing a plant site in the district of a politically influential congressman?

Attempts to write realistic and effective lobbying laws are likely to leave the draftsman between a rock and a hard place. The criminal statutes already cover any sort of attempt to buy votes with money or something of value, and the First Amendment's free speech guarantee goes a long way toward protecting anything less. One constituent can certainly threaten to deny a senator his vote in the next election, on the basis of a single issue, without any question of impropriety. So can the president of a fifty-member rifle club, on behalf of all the group. So, surely, can the well-paid lobbyist for the 2.5 million member American Legion, although his claim of infallible delivery may be somewhat more suspect.

Again, who is so deft as to draft a statute that would prevent a grateful corporation or association, a few months or years later, from placing an annual retainer with the law firm of, say, Senator Everett McKinley Dirksen, the former Republican floor leader? Who is to say that the client does not wish general legal advice emanating from Peoria, Illinois? Dirksen, magnificent in outrage, denied to the last that this kind of arrangement had ever been made, but he also refused to dispel the thickening cloud of rumors by any report of the clients who *did* find their way to Peoria from the greedy world outside.

The most that can apparently be done, at least with our present limited and shrinking knowledge of the extent of lobbying, is to tighten and then enforce the existing disclosure law. A 1971 proposal would have broadened the definition of lobbying to include indirect and part-time activity, transferred report supervision from the secretary of the Senate and the clerk of the House to the less reticent comptroller general, and doubled the fine for failure to report. This could be a first step, never yet really taken, to make sure that all members of Congress are aware of who is spending how much on what side of which issues, in periodic, well-organized, complete reports from a responsible agency not afraid to exercise enforcement powers.

Perhaps before too long, when Congress has made the essential move to a computerized information service, it will be possible to require reports from lobbyists shortly before the vote on a major bill and then to circulate summaries. Just as campaign spending reports could enlighten the voters on election eve, members of Congress could weigh lobbying activity, objectively and quantitatively, before reaching a final decision on a floor vote. There is not a good deal of satisfaction, after all, in discovering six months later that the drug industry, let us say, poured tens of thousands of dollars into an "education campaign" on a House bill on which you unwittingly voted the industry's position.

What can be done to raise congressional resistance to the lobbyist with a clearly improper offer is another matter. How many members refuse the special rate offered them on new cars by at least one major manufacturer, called a "VIP discount" to promote the theory that it is an advertising gimmick rather than an implicit down payment on future favors? No one can really do much about the congressman who is willing to betray his trust and take the lobbyist's sovereign; codes of ethics irritate but do not stop him. What is most discouraging are the members who play it both ways: they maintain their own innocence by piously rejecting other than customary graft, but they keep the faith with their less scrupulous colleagues by refusing to report any questionable propositions that they realize might have proved irresistible to others.

The broad questions of congressional ethics will be examined later. Suffice it to say here that the only long-range solution to the lobbying problem lies in elevating the standards of the institution generally, imbuing its members with some pride based on a sense of excellence, making the Senate and House, in fact rather than fancy, such centers of quality that the men and women who compete for membership would be hopeless targets indeed for the paid agents of any special interest.

# 11 · Just Give Me the Facts

The computer age did not exactly break over the Senate of the United States like a thunderclap, in a sudden, illuminating moment of revelation. What happened was that the lead plates used to address senators' outgoing mail got so numerous and heavy that the mail room floor began to give way, so the secretary was forced to buy a light-footed computer to do the job on tape.

The advent of computer technology in the House was only a little more enlightened. When the House Administration Committee seized jurisdiction of the single computer the clerk had resourcefully rented, the chairman discovered that the machine was costing $42,500 a month for about five hours' work, so the committee decided it should be assigned more duties. (The fact that the House computer was accomplishing in three hours a job that had formerly taken three weeks—making out the payroll—did not particularly impress the members, who still tended to regard the machine as lazy and overpaid. Nor did House success with automating the pay roll impress the Senate, which continued to hold the questionable honor of being the only federal agency to pay its employees—there are 4,500 of them—in cash.)

These tentative, exploratory steps gave the 1969 Congress a computer capability of three—one machine in each body for housekeeping chores and one working overtime in the Library of Congress on information. At that time, the executive branch had

4,600 computers humming away downtown, about two-thirds of them in the technology-conscious Defense Department.

This yawning gap, essentially just as large today, does not seem too surprising if you take a close look at what currently passes for a communications system in Congress. For example, members are notified that their committee will meet the next day by hand-written, hand-delivered slips of paper. A senator *may* be able to discover the floor agenda for the day by searching the *Congressional Record* for the day before; normally the leaders make some announcement late each afternoon, which goes into the *Record* but appears no place else.

The *Record*'s index is published only every ten days or so. By the time it arrives, much of the current information to which it could lead a member is no longer current. And, as indexes go, it is better at guiding a member to his own speeches than as a key to the large amount of valuable information—statistics, summaries, and tables—that are scattered among the thousands of pages more or less indiscriminately.

Copies of bills are stored on the Hill as they must have been for nearly two centuries, in metal boxes stacked on shelves, with sleeve-gartered clerks scurrying up oaken ladders to retrieve the high numbers. A House member who phones the document room for a bill may get it within an hour, if he is lucky; there is no way he can get a summary and explanation of its provisions unless the sponsor has prepared one privately or a committee has already approved the bill and written a report on it.

When the bells ring in the Capitol and office buildings to summon members not on the floor—almost always the great majority —for a vote, the *only* source of information on the imminent decision for these absentees is word of mouth. Although they do not like to admit it, members often vote on the basis of a last-minute whisper or even a hand signal from someone they trust to have superior information—a committee member, a party aide, even the doorkeeper, who may greet a latecomer with "Committee voting aye," to identify the majority position.

Reporters covering recorded teller votes in the House can watch uninformed members cluster in the well of the chamber, uncertain whether to turn up the "aye" aisle or the "no" aisle with their voting card, while leaders of rival factions lobby among them. The fact that this scene is more rarely played in the Senate does not demonstrate a greater mastery of information there, but the facts that (1) Senate roll calls, while occasionally languid, tend to be brisk by comparison with House votes, leaving little time for indecision, and (2) unlimited debate inevitably spaces out floor votes, with intervals long enough so that most members manage to find out, at least roughly, what the issue is before it comes up.

The telephone is the most sophisticated instrument of congressional communication. You can always call the cloakroom to find out what is being debated on the floor. You can call the leader's office to get a rough idea of the floor agenda. You can call a committee to determine the status of a bill. You can call a department in search of background on a bill within its jurisdiction. Sometimes you get an answer, sometimes you don't. When you do, you usually have to write it down and have someone type it up.

It is really not too far from the truth to say that the communications level of Congress is accurately symbolized by the equipment on each Senator's desk in the chamber: a wooden penholder with a removable metal point, an inkwell, and a shaker of sand to use for blotting.

Lack of information due to inadequate communication has created such obvious problems for Congress that you would think the members would have rebelled against their own uncertainty, inconvenience, and ignorance years ago. But they would have been forced to admit imperfection.

Increasingly over the past few decades, Congress has become a processing agency for the programs of the executive branch rather than an originating agency for programs of its own—a trend that distresses thoughtful members. A root cause of this situation is the difficulty that individuals and committees have in obtaining information—current, accurate, concise, relevant information. The clumsy and time-consuming committee hearing has become an information-seeking session rather than what it should be: an opportunity for Congress to challenge government agency heads and outside authorities with an arsenal of facts already in hand.

It stands to reason that, if Congress is not well enough informed to draft its own legislation, it is also poorly equipped for the less demanding role of reviewing and evaluating the programs that are sent to the Hill from the White House. If they are to do any kind of a job, the members need not only those selected facts that the Office of Management and Budget and the departments are willing to disgorge, often to serve their own purposes, but a solid background of information from outside as well as inside the government, to set against the claims and protests of bureaucracy.

As has been said many times, the problem is not that Congress gets too little information but that too little of the great mass it gets is relevant and readily, rapidly available. Were it not for janitor service, the House and Senate could suffocate in a single day, deep under the vast masses of paper that are dumped on Capitol Hill from government agencies, public and private interest groups, and ordinary citizens. Buried in this information glut are useful facts and provocative arguments, but the members and committees of Congress, with limited manpower and no mechanical assistance at all, have rarely been able to separate the worthwhile bits from the great mass of repetition and special pleading and then store those bits where they can be readily found.

The Library of Congress has striven manfully over the years to keep the Senate and House informed, but, until very recently, it has been nearly as old-fashioned as the legislature it served. After all, the same Congress that has been reluctant to seek electronic assistance for itself has governed the Library and furnished its funds, so perhaps it is surprising that it managed to begin computerizing some information as early as 1967. A major part of the credit for progress, then and now, goes to Robert Chartrand, the Library's persistent and effective computer specialist.

It is difficult to escape the conclusion that the congressional power structure must share some of the responsibility for the basic information shortage in both houses. Information produces knowledge, which is power, and the leaders and committee chairmen have always seen to it, as a natural thing, that they were better informed than the rank and file.

One of the chief supports of the seniority system, in fact, has been the theory that it took years to learn enough to become a committee chairman. A younger member was to absorb wisdom at his elder's knee, as gradually as possible, until he was finally educated for leadership at an age when most men were forgetting at least as much as they were learning. If a freshman committee member suddenly has at his disposal all the same information as the chairman, this last, flimsy argument for the seniority system becomes as groundless as the rest.

Generally speaking, there are no technical problems involved in providing Congress with a complete, up-to-date, fully automated information system that would be invaluable for both lawmaking and housekeeping. The equipment is virtually all in existence now or will be by the time Congress decides to make use of it. Technologically, current advances are simply reducing the amount of physical space, power, and money required, while speed and capacity increase. Basically, the congressional equipment would consist of a bank of computers, which need not be on crowded Capitol Hill at all, and a series of terminals or consoles in the leaders', committee, and members' offices. Routine incoming information would appear automatically via a high-speed typewriter or an even faster printer. Requests for stored information would be submitted on the typewriter in a simple, condensed code, with the reply coming back from the data bank in printed form without any discernible time lag. There is no need for experiment, except as to what types of service seem more useful to the particular needs of the national assembly. More than twenty state legislatures have already acquired some computer capability, with Florida, Indiana, Iowa, Missouri, North Carolina, and Pennsylvania among the most active. If members of Congress can stand a little laggard embarrassment, they can go out and watch the equipment at work in state capitols all over the country.

The potential impact of full electronic assistance on how Congress conducts its business and makes its business and makes its decisions is almost incalculable (except, perhaps, by computer), but these are a few of the benefits we can be sure of:

DECISION-MAKING. When a bill or amendment is approaching a

floor vote, every member of the house would receive on his office console the number, sponsor, and a summary of the provisions and their effect. The same basic information would be available on similar printers in the lobbies of the chamber and also projected on a screen there. No longer would roll calls be punctuated by this sort of whispered exchange:

> *Senator Backlash (striding into the lobby):* What are we voting on?
> *Senator Goodwell:* It's the Hangdog Amendment.
> *Senator Backlash:* The Hangdog Amendment? What the hell does that do?
> *Senator Goodwell:* I'm not sure, but labor is against it.

The print-out information on anything up for a vote could be considerably more comprehensive, including a summary of the positions of the President, leaders of both parties, and the main organizations involved. Also immediately available would be background on how the issue had been resolved in committee, in the other house, and in past sessions when it arose.

VOTING. As this is written, the House is scheduled to begin voting electronically in mid-1972, substituting button pushing for the interminable oral roll calls, with the results for each member, each party, and the entire body flashed instantaneously on screens in the chamber. Even allowing time for members to get to the floor, the present thirty-five minutes for every House roll call should be cut in half, perhaps reduced even more if an early warning system for votes can be developed. In addition, a full print-out of the vote, including breakdowns by party, will be available in a matter of seconds in the press gallery, at the leaders' desks, and to any members who call for it. Once stored in the data bank, a roll call can be recalled at any time by a member or committee.

Automatic voting raises at least one very troublesome question: why should an absent member, who has not heard the debate but who has read the basic information from his office console, be required to come to the floor and vote? That absentee is no different from a current member who only comes to the floor for votes and does not hear debate on a bill at all, except that he would be much better informed. Why not remote voting stations in the congressional office buildings so that the total time and effort for each roll call could be even further reduced?

There are obvious surface objections. Remote voting stations would be expensive, even if there were only one or two on each office building floor. A security system would have to be devised to ensure that the vote was cast by a member and not one of his aides; a key or card would not be adequate but a scanning device for a fingerprint or a voice pattern might. (In a number of congressional offices, it would probably not affect the result much if the chief staff man or woman cast the vote, since the member and his aides tend to interact and wind up sharing the same opinions. Nor would it necessarily be a bad thing, for many of these aides tend to be younger, better educated, better informed and more issue oriented. But they are not elected, and the members are.)

The real problem here is that off-floor voting would be an official acknowledgment of the impotence of debate as a factor in congressional decision-making—an admission that Congress is almost certainly unwilling to make in public, however accurate it may be, until some informational and procedural substitute for floor debate has won wide public acceptance. That time seems some considerable distance ahead.

LOBBYING. The present reporting requirements for lobbyists are both ineffective and unenforced, but a tough, new registration system could operate hand in hand with computerized information retrieval. A member approached by a lobbyist could have an aide check in seconds through his console as to whether the agent was properly registered, who his clients were, and what he was spending on his various campaigns. A scrupulous member would presumably refuse to talk with an unregistered lobbyist and would report his lack of credentials to the official with jurisdiction over the system. A few experiences like this, and most lobbyists would register and file reports or look for another line of work.

If the lobbying reports were made detailed and frequent enough, a congressman could check the record through his console whenever a controversial bill reached the floor, discovering who had lobbied on each side and how much they had spent, hopefully up to date within a few days. This legitimate variety of decision-making information, akin to the identity of large campaign contributors at election time, is almost totally lacking today.

RETRIEVAL. By consulting the console, a member could obtain at any time the title, number, sponsor, and summary for any of the 30,000 bills before Congress and a statement of its status. Mechanically, this and more detailed information could also be requested by dialing a special telephone-type panel, or it could be received on a small television screen, from which high-speed photocopies could be made.

Committees would store summaries of all the bills under their jurisdiction in the bank, and the computer would sort out and prepare any kind of calendar the chairman wished, by subject, time of introduction, priority, or what have you. Two or three House committees are already using this service and saving hundreds of hours of clerical handwork and printing time.

Also stored in the congressional information bank could be figures on federal aid grants and federal contract awards for each state and district. Such information is obviously useful to demonstrate claimed achievements during a political campaign; it could also alert constituents to the fact that they aren't sharing in the federal largesse and send them off in legitimate search of it.

Public and private data banks have stored a good deal of useful legal material, both statutes including the entire U.S. Code and a significant amount of case law, including decisions of the Supreme Court. A compatible congressional system could tap these sources and provide members with a statement of the current law on any question in printed form, in their offices within minutes, or with a list of where to look it up in seconds.

With an investment of time and money, indexes could be built up of the *Congressional Record*, of all hearing transcripts and committee reports, of documents printed by the departments and agencies, and, where executive privilege did not interfere, of data stored in executive department banks that could be reached directly. In every instance, a member could obtain almost instantly either a copy of the document itself or a direct, time-saving reference to the information he sought.

A "profile of interest" would be prepared for each member, covering the jurisdiction of his committees, economic and social issues in his district, and other subjects of particular concern to him as a lawmaker. Over in the Library of Congress, the Congressional Research Service would reduce this to a set of key words that would be stored in the computer under the member's name. So would summaries of books, articles, and records as they arrived, and each week the senator or representative would receive a computer-generated list of material likely to be of interest to him.

There is no technological reason why each member could not also have his own personal file, one that could only be tapped by his console, containing his speeches and statements and information on such important constituents as campaign contributors and volunteer political organizers. Once the members discover how rapidly and accurately they can summon up public information, they are sure to want the same kind of service for more private facts.

NOTIFICATION. An information system would make currently considerable congressional housekeeping tasks routine. The committee meeting schedule for each day would zip out of each member's console the previous afternoon, with individual notices to members of specific committees of witnesses to be heard or legislation to be taken up. On the machine early every morning would appear a summary of floor and committee action in both houses the day before, with votes, references to the *Congressional Record*, and the approximate agenda for each house for the day. The agenda would be updated at noon when the Senate and House normally convene and changes are often announced. Similarly, preadjournment reports of the next day's schedule would appear within minutes in each member's office. After each committee hearing and executive session, a summary of the witnesses' statements or the action on legislation would be fed to all members, for the benefit of those who could not attend.

Obviously, all this is going to require fast, accurate reporting by information aides attached to both houses and all committees, but existing staff, liberated from many routine duties by the new system and given modest training, should be able to handle much of it. Most congressmen will probably need one professional staff member who has been trained in computer analysis, someone who understands the techniques of flagging useful facts, storing them, and calling them back up. Professor John Saloma III of the Massachusetts Institute of Technology, one of the academic authorities in the field, believes a new breed of congressional aide will develop, one who can combine political science and public administration experience with the economics, physics, and engineering background of the systems analyst.

No important change comes without problems. There remains on Capitol Hill, despite awesome displays of computer ingenuity or perhaps because of them, an instinctive fear that someone is trying to replace members with machines, which must somehow violate the Constitution. This uneasiness, bred largely of ignorance, has certainly contributed to past congressional reluctance to move into the computer age. But computers, says Dr. Kenneth Janda of Northwestern University, another academic authority, "propose not to eliminate the congressman as a decision-maker but to increase his capabilities for making decisions by telling him what he wants to know." Although the computer can catalogue, sort, and reproduce facts, speaking broadly, it cannot weigh values. Finally, men and women must make the judgments, and Congress will clearly be able to do so more rationally and probably more rapidly with the assistance of these machines under its control.

The cost will be substantial, enough so that supporters of a full computerized information and support program tend to dodge the issue as not helpful to their cause. They prefer to cite less alarming figures for the small introductory system that is certain to precede any more ambitious version. They decline to estimate the expense of a full system unless told precisely what "full" means. Nevertheless, it is possible today to say that a relatively modest information system, serving congressional leaders and committees but not individual members, would cost about $4–$5 million a year, with the figure rising with the demand for more sophisticated levels of information. A system with a console in every member's office and the necessary massive computer configuration to provide a wide range of services would probably run between $20 and $25 million a year, almost certainly more by the time Congress arrives at a decision that this is what it really needs.

If that seems like a lot of money, consider the fact that the federal government spent as much in 1971–72 on research on how to build more efficient ocean-going vessels. And again on the statistical reporting service of the Department of Agriculture. And again on a 250-mile strip of the Darien Gap Highway in Panama and Colombia. Surely, a better-informed Congress is at least a comparably wise investment.

There will be limits not dictated by cost on what information the new system can give Congress. Obviously, members will not be able to tap casually into the Pentagon's data bank and draw out classified information. But ready access to legitimate facts on the cost and performance of the Defense Department can be of incalculable value to an increasingly questioning Congress, which will have to be on the alert for any attempt to cloak routine information with a security blanket.

Similarly, the doctrine of executive privilege, first invoked by George Washington in 1796 to keep treaty information confidential, will surely be revived to try to limit the amount of information that Congress can draw from the data banks of the executive branch. Particularly if opposing political parties are involved. But basic facts should be fully available, while tentative policy recommendations, interpretation, and analysis properly remain among the private records of the President and his Cabinet.

During recent debates on limiting campaign spending, members of both houses bemoaned the fact that incumbent congressmen have demonstrated a steadily increasing capacity to defeat all political challengers. The introduction of a computerized information and support system will do nothing to reverse that trend; most thoughtful observers believe it would make unseating a senator or representative, once he gets to Washington, even more difficult than it is now. The incumbent will be stronger in campaign debate than ever because he will know more. He will be stuffed with figures to prove what the government, presumably at his behest, spent in the district. He will have an elaborate computer-based mailing system through which he can reach, largely or entirely at the taxpayers' expense, different professional, social, and geographical groups among his constituents, with appeals tailored to their interests. (The Senate already has such a setup, and the House version is in the design stage.)

A good deal of this added advantage for the congressional office-holder is unavoidable. No one is going to hold down the information level and potential competence of a lawmaker in order to give his next opponent a better chance to defeat him. What can be done is to limit a congressman's purely political communication with his constituents during campaigns, both primary and general, when some or all of the cost comes out of the Treasury.

This task will not be easy. Separating an informative newsletter from a political appeal for re-election is so hard that it is not even attempted now, and each member, weighing whether to buy stamps or frank campaign mail free, is left to the dismal company of his own conscience. There is a fundamental free-speech issue involved in limiting the number of letters a congressional candidate can mail to his real or would-be constituents, just as there is in limiting his time on television. But this electronic selective mailing capacity is, or will shortly be, a fact of life, and future abuse is sure to provoke investigation and invite restrictions.

Is Congress finally moving toward adoption of an electronic information and support system? At last, years behind industry, state government, and the executive branch, the answer seems to be yes. Despite slow and feeble beginnings, most experts believe it is only a matter of time and money until a comprehensive computer capability is at work on Capitol Hill, with the time diminishing and the money increasing as members discover what this equipment is capable of.

The first bill proposing a congressional data processing system was introduced early in 1967 by Representative Robert McClory of Illinois. A year later the Library of Congress began storing bill titles and descriptions in a computer memory bank. A year after that, in early 1969, the House Banking and Currency Committee acquired a terminal to provide members with virtually instant summaries and status reports on all the bills under its jurisdiction. By early 1972, three more of the twenty-one House committees had similar facilities running, too.

If this is not exactly a pell-mell rush into the computer era, it is at least progress. Under the aggressive leadership of Representative Wayne Hays of Ohio and his House Administration Committee, the House voted late in 1971 to spend $1.5 million for further advances toward electronic voting, computerized mailing, and assistance on legislative status reports and bill drafting. By contrast, the Senate was barely in motion. In 1971, with only a computerized mail system in operation, it produced a study indicating fifteen ways in which electronic equipment could be helpful. The leadership decided to begin implementing one of them, an automated payroll, and to give further study to another, a tracking system to determine the status of bills. The total investment: a paltry $225,000.

Such cooperation as has existed between the Senate and House on this critically important and very expensive subject has been unofficial and almost furtive. Officially, the two bodies have characteristically pursued their own obstinately separate courses. It was almost pure luck that the two houses and the Library of Congress wound up with compatible equipment from the same manufacturer so that they can all work together

In the summer of 1969, when a House subcommittee was beginning serious study of the computer potential, Senate leaders of both parties were invited to contribute personnel to a working group study, a first step toward coordination. The invitation was not even acknowledged, much less accepted. Senator Mike Mansfield, the Democratic leader, who can be as starchy as much less intelligent colleagues upon occasion, reportedly felt that the offer should not be recognized unless it came from House leaders rather than a lowly subcommittee chairman.

Thus Mansfield could hardly have been shocked when that chairman, Representative Joe Waggoner of Louisiana, later led a floor fight to kill a proposal for a Joint Committee on Legislative Data Processing, arguing successfully that the House was so far ahead of the Senate that a joint endeavor would delay its progress by at least three years. This debate reflected as well the long-held House fear that senators dominate joint committees for the Senate's purposes. So bitter were subsequent recriminations that, at last report, the chairmen of the two committees with computer jurisdiction, Representative Hays of House Administration and Senator Everett Jordan of Senate Rules, were literally not speaking to each other.

Although the joint data-processing committee was dropped, the Legislative Reorganization Act of 1970 did create a Joint Committee on Congressional Operations, with a mandate easily broad and flexible enough to involve it in coordinating electronic data-processing activity between the houses. In addition, its chairman, Representative Jack Brooks of Texas, has long been among the most active supporters of the whole concept of uplifting Congress with modern technology.

Political as well as substantive factors seem likely to accelerate Congress's belated entry into the computer age. Professor Saloma of MIT believes more pressure will result from the explicit rivalry between authorizing and appropriating committees, each in search of better information; from Congressional fear of losing still more authority to the President; from interparty competition for the most compelling set of facts; and from what he calls "the generational divide between activist and high-seniority Congressmen." (In the past, however, the seniors have rarely given in to the pushy freshmen.)

Historically, and not without reason, Congress has been reluctant to construct its own legislative bureaucracy with which to challenge the vast legions of the President. But the advent of a solid computer capability on Capitol Hill, increasing the quality and capacity of the legislative staff but not its size, may at last begin to redress the imbalance of governing authority between the dominant White House and the recumbent Congress.

# 12 · Your Man in Washington

It must have been on March 4, 1789, the first day of the first Congress, or very shortly thereafter, that the first member discovered he was the Washington representative of his constituents for a startlingly broad range of activity with almost no discernible relation to making the nation's laws.

A merchant in Exeter, New Hampshire, let's say, still had not been paid for woolen goods he provided the militia during the Revolution, so he wrote to Representative Nicholas Gilman, asking if the congressman did not believe the new federal government had an obligation to meet the costs of the conflict that had resulted in its creation. Representative Gilman, sensing a legitimate question and anxious to gain the favor of a constituent, penned a letter to the Department of the Army, inquiring whether any funds were available to meet such claims. After all, the congressman reasoned, if he did not intercede with federal authorities for a good New Hampshire man, who was going to?

These may not have been precisely the circumstances of the first constituent request to Congress, but they are close enough to give you an idea of the hundreds and then thousands and now millions of pleas for help that inundate Capitol Hill every year. The citizenry, then as now, is understandably apprehensive about coping with the faceless bureaucracy of the executive branch. Addressing a letter about an overdue tax refund to the

Director of Internal Revenue, Washington, D.C., seems roughly equivalent to corking it in a bottle and tossing it in the Mississippi River. But if you happen to live in San Fernando, California, such a complaint to Representative James Corman is likely to be a very effective move. Corman is a member of the House Ways and Means Committee, which initiates and heavily influences all tax legislation, and the Internal Revenue Service, like all of the Treasury Department, is most solicitous of its members. In addition, Corman represents a district that has been politically close in the past, and he is unlikely to let a chance to please a constituent slip by.

Not all members of Congress occupy the precise political pressure point most effective for a given request—a member of the House Judiciary Committee is not likely to get as prompt service from the State Department as a member of the Senate Foreign Relations Committee—but just being a member in the first place carries a remarkable amount of weight. In most departments, a letter from a senator inquiring about a constituent's problem must be answered by a written report, even if only a temporizing one, within twenty-four hours. If you really want action from a federal department, make your inquiry through a representative who is on the Appropriations subcommittee that clears that department's budget. The speed and courtesy will astonish you.

The problems that voters expect congressmen to help solve are varied and numberless. A veteran who moved stops getting his pension check. A serviceman overseas has been denied emergency leave to come home to help cope with the effects of serious illness in the family. A social security pensioner has been ruled ineligible for new higher benefits. A student traveling abroad has run afoul of local authorities and could use State Department help. The Federal Aviation Administration has shifted an airport traffic pattern to envelop a once-peaceful suburb in noise. The Postal Service has located the mail box for a nursing home on the wrong side of a busy intersection. An inmate in a federal reformatory, while protesting his innocence in the appellate courts, wants the authorities to return his burglar's tools (a real case). All this, in the congressional lexicon, is case work, the processing of constituents' requests for help in dealing with the unfathomable Washington apparatus. They key word is help.

Case work is unquestionably a legitimate exercise, although it appears nowhere in the official roster of congressional duties. It rights wrongs that would probably go unchallenged without the intervention of a senator or representative. It permits members to use their considerable power in a constructive, satisfying way. It keeps the federal bureaucracy at least a little on its toes. Once in a while, when the problem turns out to be more than merely inept administration of existing law, it can even lead to new legislation to eliminate the problem in the future. It makes friends for congressmen back home. But, in the average Capitol Hill office, it siphons off an almost unbelievable amount of time and effort.

A House member's office typically has two full-time case workers, who occupy a sort of professional limbo below the administrative or legislative assistant, and above the secretarial staff. In a moderately large Senate office, there are likely to be at least three people working on constituent service and a fourth helping out part time. On the political level, case work is much more important to a representative than a senator because it can touch a significant proportion of his constituents and, for them, lift him from anonymity. For an average senator, with at least five to ten times the number of voters in a House district, doing personal favors simply cannot have the same impact.

Case work, although demanding, is only part of the service work load a congressman has come to assume. Most large-state senators, for example, have another full-time assistant charged with what might be called public case work: ensuring that the home state, its cities, and its citizens get their fair share of federal projects and grants—even a little more, if possible. The job can also involve smoothing the path to a federal research grant for a scientist or helping a local industry obtain a defense contract. Some of this activity merely involves providing information, making sure that every person, business, and community knows what it's entitled to and where to line up to get it. But critically important, too, is the member's responsibility to use his muscle to make sure that the new post office or beach erosion project gets into the public works bill. These things do not happen accidentally; they happen because someone on the staff is paying attention.

Every Senate office must also have a patronage aide, someone to deal with the federal judgeships and customs posts, postmasterships having been mercifully removed from politics by the recent reorganization of the old Post Office Department. This aide's duties involve collecting information from some people who want to be appointed and others who should be, trying to guide the White House if the senator is of the same party, negotiating with it if he is not. (By tradition, a senator can block confirmation of any appointee from his home state if he sees fit; this blackball, infrequently cast, does not enable a Democrat to suggest to President Nixon whom he should name as a federal judge, but it enables him to indicate very strongly whom the President should *not* name.)

At the most routine but still important level of constituent service, every congressional office must have someone to answer the requests for autographed pictures of The Man, Washington tourist information, copies of *How to Buy a Beef Roast*, and the hundreds of other federal publications that members of Congress can distribute free to their advantage. The same staffer, often a decorative receptionist, hands out gallery passes to the Senate or House chamber (or both, if the members have a reciprocal agreement) and sets up White House tours—the special, early morning, no-waiting-in-line variety—for privileged constituents.

All this service—for individual voters, for office-seekers, for businessmen, for mayors and governors—takes a heavy toll on the amount of time and effort that a congressional office can devote to what congressmen are supposed to be doing. One estimate in a moderate-sized Senate office is that case work and constituent service make up about 40 per cent of the work load. In House offices, where there is less political security and, ordinarily, a narrower range of legislative interest, the errand-running percentage runs higher, often well above 50.

This discouraging situation has led some congressmen to propose that they be relieved altogether of the responsibility for case work, that a new agency be created in the legislative branch to deal, professionally and efficiently, with all those letters from constituents looking for help. The idea has considerable appeal for congressional aides anxious to devote more time to legislation and politics. In a House office, those two case workers could be replaced by a lawyer and the professional capacity of the staff multiplied; in a Senate office, even more productive time could be freed. And, theoretically, a new agency would do the work faster and better, staffed by experienced case workers familiar with all types of problems and organized into smooth-running, specialized units. Political credit could be preserved if the answering letters went out over the congressman's name.

It's a nice, orderly idea, but many people who think case work is worth more than a lick and a promise believe it won't really work. Each office would have to retain one case worker, probably full time, to shuttle all requests over to the new agency—flagging politically important ones—and then keep checking for prompt action. Under the present system, a case worker calls the Congressional Liaison Office of the federal agency involved, which then goes to work. Under the proposed reform, a third person in the new agency would make that same call. But the third person, inescapably, would feel less responsibility to the congressman to get a satisfactory resolution than would his own staff worker, and the federal department would feel less pressure because it was dealing with a politically anonymous group of civil servants. A new layer of bureaucracy would have been inserted between the Congress and the Executive departments, and the resulting responsiveness of the latter to the former would almost certainly be reduced. As things stand now, a case worker fully armed with the influence of her senator—they are mostly women—and devoted to improving his record for service can only reverse about one decision in ten reached elsewhere in the government. The most knowledgeable people are convinced this slender percentage would fall even farther if a new agency took over the job.

The answer lies, instead, in recognizing case work as a legitimate major responsibility of every congressman and not a sort of marginal favor-granting operation that a few legislative secretaries can do in their spare time. If a representative's staff salary allowance, now about $145,000, were increased by $25,000 for the specific purpose of providing constituent service, that same office could then afford a legislative as well as an administrative assistant at a professional salary level, instead of only one of the two. For a big-state senator, this new case work allowance should probably be $40,000 or $50,000, actually a smaller percentage increase in his staff salary total of about $480,000.

The resulting rise in the congressional budget would only be about $15 million a year—a small investment to enable the members to help their constituents on an efficient and professional but personal basis, without neglecting their lawmaking duties. There are few enough places in Washington where individual complaints can be raised, heard, and, upon occasion, even answered, and the best such agency, imperfect and fragmented though it may be, should be recognized and strengthened rather than shuffled off into the faceless bureaucracy.

The adequacy of the allowances for staffing and operating congressional offices is debatable; the character of the argument depends on whom you talk to. For a hyperactive senator with a huge constituency like Jacob Javits of New York, the money nearly always seems insufficient. A staff salary total of $478,000, the figure for states with a population of 17 million or more, may appear reasonable enough until you discover that senators with less than 3 million constituents get 296,000. Obviously, Senator Mike Gravel of Alaska, where only 80,400 people voted in the last election, is better able to operate his office with his allowance than is Senator Alan Cranston of California, where 6.4 million did, with his.

(Until very recently, Congress maintained a fictitious salary schedule for its staff, with absurdly low figures still officially on the statute books to which a long series of percentage increases had to be applied to discover the real salary for any job. Under this clumsy, deceptive practice of some 100 years' duration, a House administrative assistant who earned $27,500 appeared to be getting only $7,500. Over the years, Congress has lived in deadly fear that the voters might learn how much it spends on itself and regard the investment as less than a bargain. To this day, the members' staff and expense records, while technically open, are made as inaccessible as possible. In the House, anyone seeking this information must copy it in longhand from the ledgers; the Senate prints an accounting of sorts every six months, but it is a lengthy, unorganized, unindexed list that must be examined item by item for several hundred pages, for example, to check one member's travel expenses.)

How far a member's stationery allowance will stretch also depends on how many people he represents and whether his state or district is politically competitive. House rules provide that a member may draw up to $3,000 worth of supplies from the stationery room every year, or take the money in a cash lump sum. If a thrifty or uncommunicative member does not use all this money for stationery, he is supposed to report the balance as taxable income, but there is no recorded instance of the Internal Revenue Service peering into a representative's stamp drawer. The $3,600 Senate allowance may serve some small-state members well, but not an outgoing, outspeaking man like Senator Javits, who used up his entire 1971 fund before the end of March and had to finance his stationery expenses for the rest of the year out of his own pocket.

Occasionally, a wealthy congressman will use personal funds to hire an additional staff member or two or, more likely, to supplement the federal salary schedule so that he can bid for a higher level of talent. A politically prominent senator with a national future, as a number now think themselves to be, can command a considerable amount of valuable volunteer service, with speech writers and academics outside Washington undertaking research, writing articles, and drafting legislative proposals, all because they support the senator's cause and future and want to make a personal investment in it.

But the traditional means of building up a congressional staff as the member's interests and responsibilities multiply involves those twin pillars of the Capitol establishment, the seniority and committee systems. For a senator or representative who does nothing more than retain his seat moves automatically up the ladder on his committee, never passing anyone who is alive—heaven forfend! —but gently and reassuringly levitated as the members with longer service above him die, retire, or are rejected by the voters. After a period of waiting, much shorter in the Senate than the House, a member may rise to fifth or sixth rank on his committee and qualify for the chairmanship of a subcommittee, providing he is a member of the majority party. And it's a rare subcommittee that does not have some staff. (Even the two-member Senate Judiciary Subcommittee on Federal Charters, Holidays, and Celebrations, a private creation of the late Senator Everett McKinley Dirksen, had a staff of one, named by him.)

Sometimes committee chairmen insist on appointing the staff of the full committee and all subcommittees as well. They are not popular with their colleagues. More frequently, a subcommittee chairman is given the right to name most or all of his staff, subject to the chairman's veto. On a typical Senate subcommittee, this could mean two or three professionals—lawyers or administrative types—and four or five secretarial jobs, including at least one semiprofessional. All these people are formally charged with the business of the subcommittee—say, antitrust laws or national parks or small business—and they organize hearings, interview experts, collect research material, and draft legislation for introduction by the chairman and consideration by the subcommittee.

But, inescapably, this staff also works for the senator or representative who appoints them, and it is frequently difficult to draw a distinct line between their committee duties and their service to him as an individual, helping out with obligations that can be personal, representative, or political, or all three. At the very least, because the committee staff spends a good deal of time on a major area of legislative interest, a member's office staff is accordingly freed of that concern and can work elsewhere. The result of achieving committee seniority is an increase in the number of people a member can call on to help him, more openings, more better-paid jobs to which to promote promising young aides, more information about what's going on, ultimately more influence.

There is some evidence that senators can acquire subcommittees before their ability to cope has fully matured. Shortly after John Tunney of California moved to the Senate from three undramatic House terms, he was asked to preside over a forthcoming Public Works subcommittee hearing because no one else was available. His staff briefed him thoroughly, suggested appropriate lines of questioning, and sent him off to the hearing room on the appointed morning. When subcommittee aides reported him missing a half-hour later, his panic-striken staff fanned out through the Senate office buildings and found him presiding over another subcommittee hearing, happily demonstrating his expertise to a different set of witnesses concerned with a different bill.

When a senator or representative finally attains the summit of a chairmanship, this potential increase in his staff becomes awesome. The Senate Appropriations Committee has nearly thirty professionals and half that many secretaries to staff its fourteen subcommittees. The House Government Operations Committee, continuously involved in investigations of the executive branch, has a staff of fifty or sixty.

Even if you are a member of the minority party—the Republicans, for congressional purposes, ever since 1954—the reward for rising to ranking minority member of a committee is not inconsiderable. On a typical Senate committee, for example, the minority may have a half-dozen professional jobs, each with a secretary. A ranking member who is sensitive to his colleagues' problems will probably allocate two of these openings to the second- and third-ranking Republicans, giving them a little more help than their seniority technically rates and earning a share of their loyalty for future combat, inside the committee or the party and on the floor.

A good congressional staff is not just important for the business of the moment. A senator or representative cannot expect to hold a bright young lawyer more than a year or two, but, by giving him a start and some sound government experience, he can earn his loyalty for the future. Most senators who reward their aides with responsibility and respect as well as salary are building a volunteer campaign staff, available when election time approaches. Frequently, former staff men who have moved on to private practice or business will rally around for the campaign, writing speeches and raising money, anxious to help their one-time benefactor and eager for the exhilaration of political combat.

Rising to the point where the committee system augments your staff can be a long process, particularly in the House. Generally speaking, it takes a representative four or five terms of service, at a minimum, to gain enough seniority to be rewarded with a subcommittee chairmanship. In the Ninety-second Congress, the men who had been elected ten years before were beginning to appear among the chairmen of subcommittees of some consequence; the few who won the title with less seniority occupied positions of less than pivotal power, like chairman of the Subcommittee on Retirement, Insurance and Health Benefits of the Committee on Post Office and Civil Service.

In the Senate, where the average committee is less than half as big and subcommittees abound, a first-term man can often achieve such distinction fairly rapidly. Take Senator Thomas Eagleton of Missouri. Elected in 1968, without previous House experience, he was immediately named chairman of the Fiscal Affairs Subcommittee of the District of Columbia Committee and of the Railroad Retirement Subcommittee of Labor and Public Welfare. Pretty small potatoes by congressional standards, but a lot more authority than any House freshman would see for years. Two years later, he became chairman of the District committee, not everyone's idea of a choice berth, but a chairmanship for all that.

Senator Birch Bayh of Indiana was another fast riser. A year after he took his seat in 1963, he became chairman of the Constitutional Amendments Subcommittee of Judiciary. Later that year, President Kennedy's assassination alarmed Congress into taking up a constitutional amendment to establish a system of Presidential succession, and Bayh as subcommittee chairman became its sponsor. Some of his seniors regarded the brash young Hoosier as a bit presumptuous. When they learned, on the scheduled day of final Senate passage, that Bayh had a plane waiting to fly him to New Hampshire where the state legislature was ready to ratify the amendment, senators began questioning him at length. One after another took the floor, flustering Bayh and ultimately delaying the vote for a day, just, as one of them admitted later, "to make him sweat a little."

Backed by the largest and most talented staff money and influence can produce, armed with his allowances for stationery, telephone, and telegraph, the congressman does not, of course, confine his contact with his constituents to case work. Those occasions when they seek him out with a problem are probably the most important; a voter's voice has been raised, and attention must be paid. But no senator or representative with any sense of stewardship—or any desire for re-election—can avoid maintaining a wide range of communication with the people who sent him to Washington. Not just with those who know his name and address and make use of both, but the far greater group that didn't vote for him at all, or did but can't even remember his name. This massive silent constituency cannot, as a matter of duty or politics, be taken for granted; it must be sought out by every means of communication available, including the congressman himself on the old one-to-one-basis.

Pride, wrath, sloth, and lechery may all be tolerated in a member of Congress—and frequently are. The one unforgivable, deadly sin is neglect of state or district. So it follows that a member must make regular trips back home, to see and be seen. Few Americans today will protest if their congressman feels he can serve them better by moving his family to Washington, in recognition of a full-time, year-round job. But this license demands in return that the lawmaker keep a close eye on the district, retain firsthand familiarity with its problems, sense the views of its people—be attuned enough, in sum, to represent.

The congressional travel allowance still tends to reflect long-past, leisurely days of less lawmaking and more time back home. Members of both houses currenty get two kinds of travel allowance. The first covers one round trip a year from home to Washington at twenty cents a mile, the rate unchanged since 1866; it's a relic of the days when a member came to the nation's capital by horse and then rail at the beginning of the session and returned the same way when it was over a few months later. Today this is a generous rate, about twice the cost of a first-class plane ticket to most cities in the country, presumably reflecting the possibility that the congressman might bring his wife with him. Or his secretary. The second allowance provides every senator with the actual cost of twelve round-trips home each year and House members with one for every month that Congress is in session, usually ten in election years and twelve in the others. (Sedentary members, or those with districts close to Washington, can take a $750 lump sum instead. This is fine for Representative Joel Broyhill of Virginia, whose district just across the Potomac River enables him to commute daily by car and pocket about half the allowance, if he wishes, but it is not advantageous for too many others.)

One trip a month may be enough for representatives who have become fixtures in one-party districts, sufficient to ensure their re-election, if not to keep them really responsive. But it is clearly not enough for senators in politically balanced states, which now means nearly everything outside the shrinking Democratic South, or for representatives with close districts or the need to establish themselves in more solid ones.

Take Representative Harold Runnels, who ousted a Republican from New Mexico's Second District seat in 1970 by only 3,400 votes of over 125,000 cast. A dozen flying trips a year to Roswell will exhaust his travel allowance but not his need to communicate with his constituents. And, having gotten home, how is he supposed to finance travel inside a district that is nearly as large as New York and Pennsylvania combined? Aside from Senator Javits, whose three or more weekly trips to New York exhaust his year's allowance by the end of January, many less compulsive travelers in the Senate, men without private means, find themselves hard pressed to get home as often as they feel is necessary for adequate, well-informed representation.

There are a few ways to get around this problem. Often, senators take speaking engagements in their home states that provide travel expenses in lieu of a fee, and then they expand the visit to include other activity. This is a good deal harder for House members who, except for the nationally prominent handful, are less in demand and usually expected to perform at home without reimbursement. Occasionally, a party organization will provide an air travel card for a senator with urgent political need for frequent home visits —New York Republicans did it for the hard-pressed Kenneth Keating in 1963–64—but this is unusual. Senior members often manage to schedule committee hearings in their home states during an election year, thus ensuring both local publicity and government-paid travel, but this only works for committee or subcommittee chairmen.

In recent years, more and more corporations have acquired

their own jet planes, which can whisk a well-connected senator or representative back to his constituents without charge, but there is always risk that word of such an arrangement will leak out. Airport claims by a deplaning lawmaker that he expects to be charged for the use of the Calgram Distilling Company's jet enjoy about as much credence as they deserve.

Some members quietly accept off-year contributions from their major campaign supporters and put them in a fund to help pay their travel and extra office expenses on a regular basis. (It was this sort of fund that got then-Senator Richard Nixon into political hot water during his first vice presidential campaign in 1952, but he talked his way out of it with that memorable television message on the virtues of poverty.) A number of congressmen have quietly used this system from time to time, insisting for the purposes of conscience that it is really no different from accepting early campaign contributions. But, like the free corporation jet, this only works until the public finds out. Somehow, the voters rarely look with favor on a group of wealthy men, often with powerful interests in legislation, bailing out a lawmaker by covering expenses, however routine and justifiable, that he can't meet himself.

As a result, most members of Congress are forced to dip into their own pockets to pay legitimate travel expenses back to the home state. A New York City congressman with a thoroughly safe district estimates that he spends $2,500 a year above his allowance shuttling back and forth, and that figure would rise considerably for a man facing a serious re-election threat. Such an investment of his own money can get a New Yorker back to his district almost every week. But a congressman from Chicago can only make it about twenty times a year on $2,500, and one from Seattle perhaps eight times. The farther away you live, the more planning you have to do to make each visit home politically productive—and the less time you have for your other duties.

Most active members of Congress are convinced that the current travel allowances are inadequate, reflecting an out-dated era of part-time representation and not the pressing pattern of the 1970's. For today, instead of living at home and commuting to the capital, more and more members live in Washington year round and commute to the home state or district. Such travel is almost in pursuit of the public business rather than in retreat from it. A minimum travel allowance ought to provide half again as many trips as are now allowed, eighteen a year, or one every three weeks on the average. If any member did not feel compelled to make full use of such an expanded travel allowance, the Treasury would be that much richer and his constituents, presumably, that much poorer.

Once a congressman is home, his pattern of communication is fairly standard: a few speeches, a campus visit, drop-ins at the larger social events, local radio interviews, touching base with the party leaders, happily announcing a federal grant or construction project that will generate favorable publicity. Many congressmen hold regular office hours in their district office and at other principal towns so that constituents can come by and raise problems or offer opinions. The district office is usually a rent-free room in the post office or another federal building, but private space can be rented up to $2,400 a year. One well-remembered congressman, Randall Harmon of Indiana, decided to locate his district office on the front porch of his own house and charge the federal government rent, payable to himself. He was not entrusted with a second term.

One never-ending and costly area of constituent contact is the demand for advertisements, a sort of forced donation by a public official that is unlikely to buy friendship but may avert hostility. Everyone comes to the congressman—the high-school yearbooks, the college dance program, the VFW testimonial dinner, the PTA fund raiser, the Patrolmen's Benevolent Society—all asking him to take an ad in the program, surely one large enough to reflect his prestige and position. In a New York City House district, the cost can run up to $3,000 a year, with the sole profit the fact that an ad is often regarded as a satisfactory substitute for the congressman's presence at the annual dinner or ball.

When a senator or representative can't get out of Washington, which is likely to be a good deal of the time if he's paying attention, home contact can, he hopes, be maintained through a number of devices. The most common is the newsletter, dispatched at regular intervals to the best mailing list of his constituents that the lawmaker can compile, purchase, or steal. Newsletters vary widely. Some are a single mimeographed sheet, while fancier versions may run four or more printed pages, with colored headlines and pictures of the senator meeting visitors from the home state on the Capitol steps. (The Capitol steps are not only photogenic, but meetings there are popular with the lawmakers because they are shorter—no chairs—and easier to break off than those in an office.)

The newsletter text usually stresses the congressman's role in major Capitol Hill events of previous weeks or months, no matter how marginal, and includes some chatty copy on his district-related activity. Its principal virtue, in addition to publicizing the member, is cost: more than 80 per cent of the expense of most such mailings is borne by the federal government because they go out, postage free, under the "frank" of the congressman, his imprinted signature substituted for a stamp on the envelope.

The frank, a privilege most voters are only dimly aware of, is one of the most powerful weapons in the arsenal of the congressional incumbent today. (The British abolished it in 1840.) Take Representative Jonathan Bingham of the Bronx, a Democrat in an overwhelming Democratic district, who has always had to beat the party machine in a primary to get his seat and is now competing with fellow Democrat James Scheuer for the same seat because of redistricting. Bingham has regularly sent four or five newsletters a year to some 150,000 constituents. Paper and printing costs run about a penny apiece, so that each costs about $1,500. But if he had to pay the postage—as his opponent in a primary or general election would—each mailing would cost about $12,000 more, for an annual total well in excess of his salary.

Not all House members use the newsletter, and some mail it less frequently and to a smaller list than Representative Bingham. But if the average congressman put half as much effort into this form of communicating with the voters, the total value of the frank to the House—for newsletters *alone*—would run nearly $10 million a year. About 200 million pieces of franked mail are dispatched from the Capitol each year these days, a figure that doubled during the 1960's, although the number of members remained the same. The franking privilege is unlimited: it covers all the congressman's official correspondence, copies of his speeches, re-prints from the *Congressional Record* and federal government publications, as well as newsletters. Each member of the House gets 480,000 brown envelopes a year with his frank printed on them, or $34,400 worth. Similarly franked white envelopes cost him a fraction of a cent each, chargeable against his $3,500 a year stationery allowance.

Taken to full advantage, the frank can do awesome things for a congressman anxious to inform his constituents and impress his presence and activity on them. The staggering range of printed material that can be obtained free from various government agencies—all looking for high circulation figures to justify their efforts—and then mailed out free includes: calendars carrying a picture of the Capitol and stamped with the member's name; a handsome *Life*-sized, 100-page picture magazine on the Capitol and Congress; yearbooks on science and agriculture; pamphlets like *How to Fix Potatoes in Popular Ways* and *How to Control Diseases*; and, most popular of all, the government's books for brides, on infant care, and on the preschool child. A well-run House office will audit birth announcements in the district news-papers, send out the baby book to the list, and then follow with the child care book a year later. There are even free seed packets available, and an otherwise new flag that has the distinction of having flown over the Capitol. The last cost up to $6 apiece, de-pending on size, and most members accordingly charge for them, except when there is considerable countervailing political pressure. How could a congressman send a bill for the flag to his own VFW post back in Centralia?

The flow of all this mail from Capitol Hill out into the hinter-lands and the total investment of staff time in getting it there has persuaded some congressmen that their lawmaking functions have become secondary. "I'm not a congressman, I'm a printer," observed Representative Edward Koch of New York, a Democrat from the district John Lindsay represented as a Republican, and a man interested in the New York mayoralty himself. From Mas-sachusetts, where members often distribute a handy check list of the free publications available, Representative James Burke said, "I'm not a congressman, I'm a mail-order house."

Many members of Congress have gone far beyond the newsletter in sophisticating their communication with the voters back home. At least once a year, a number send out questionnaires that serve the collective purpose of reassuring voters that their congressman is interested in their views, implying that he will accept them as a guide and providing him in turn with a picture of how he should act—or at least appear to act—in order to win re-election. There is some hazard here. Constituents have been known to write back that they elected the senator on the assumption that he had some answers of his own to these questions. But in these days of pre-eminent polling, when George Gallup and Louis Harris psych the entire nation with only 1,200 interviews, most people are flattered to be consulted.

Sharpening the political value of the inquiry, Representative Jerome Waldie of California sends out fresh questionnaires periodically to relatively small groups of about 800, each with a personal letter. He gets back an astonishing average of three out of four, many of them with a handwritten message in the space for additional comment. Another California congressman conducts polls within individual precincts in his San Francisco district and then sends out computerized letters, different for each precinct, based on the result.

Senators and representatives are alloted a certain amount of free long-distance telephone and telegraph service under an involved formula, and they have unlimited access to the nation's telephone lines between 5 P.M. and 9 A.M. daily and all weekend. (This has paid an unanticipated dividend by making otherwise reluctant Hill staff willing to man the skeleton office force on Saturdays; during lulls, they telephone their friends all over the country.)

Skillfully used, the telephone can have great impact. Every weekday afternoon after five o'clock, Representative Lucien Nedzi places four calls to constituents in the Detroit suburbs, notifying them personally of a successful piece of case work, a son admitted to a veterans' hospital, a social security problem resolved. It takes time, but it touches people, and it may explain why this Democrat has been re-elected consistently in a district that includes paranoiacally Republican Grosse Pointe as well as Polish-Democratic Hamtramck.

Many congressional newsletters are cut from pretty much the same piece of political cloth, rehashing old news and heavily stressing the prominence of the author on the Washington scene. One, from the office of Representative Otis Pike of New York, stands out as a refreshing exception for several reasons. It is written by the congressman himself, which few are. Only about 150 copies are circulated; it is designed as a column that weekly newspapers in his Long Island district may use free, and is only distributed otherwise to Washington reporters covering New York affairs and some envious House colleagues. For Pike takes an unconventional view of Congress: about a third of his weekly efforts are lighthearted, poking fun at Washington, and the others incline toward a very realistic look at how Congress operates, with self-glorification by the author at a minimum.

A month before the 1968 election, for example, Pike wrote:

> By the time you read this, the Ninetieth Congress in the history of our Republic will have passed into history or merciful oblivion or whatever you want to call it. It would be nice to be able to report that it went out on a high note, doing lofty things for all the people of America. Candor compels the admission that it went out on a low note, doing tiny little acts for minor political advantage.

An unusual piece of reporting for a member. Candor also compels the admission, however, that the Ninetieth was a Democratic Congress and Pike is a Democrat regularly re-elected in a Republican district.

Use of the postage-free, staff-written newsletter as a political weapon goes unchallenged until the congressman is involved in a primary or general election campaign, mostly because until then there is no one to challenge it. When the question arises as to whether the frank should support only strictly nonpolitical mailings, responses of members vary. In 1970, Representative Leonard Farbstein of New York, the last (as it developed) of the Tammany Hall congressmen, was locked in a better primary fight with Bella Abzug, a fiery, no-holds-barred reformer and feminist. A month before the primary, Farbstein wanted to mail out a newsletter, but he was fearful of criticism and dropped the idea. He lost. Democratic Representative Waldie, in a California district that had been Republican a half-dozen years before, mailed a newsletter early in the same campaign. When his Republican opponent cried foul, he sent another. When the GOP renewed its criticism, Waldie put his frank on a third message to his voters. He won.

Because incumbents have survived the last two or three congressional elections with considerable regularity, they are getting a little self-conscious. Not a lot, but a little. A bill that Senator Hugh Scott, the Republican floor leader, introduced in 1971 would have taken the first step toward equalizing the political advantage of the frank. It would have given both candidates in Senate and House races, the incumbent *and* the challenger, two free mailings during the general election and one during any primary contest. This move would not have affected the incumbent's franking power directly, but, authorizing a limited number of openly political mailings during a campaign, it would have created some official pressure on the incumbent to keep the rest nonpolitical. The suggestion never became part of the otherwise significant 1972 campaign finance law, however. When that bill was on the House floor, Representative Bingham successfully sponsored an amendment that would have included within newly established political spending limits the cost of postage used for direct mail campaign appeals. The amendment was dropped in conference, but during the few weeks it was a tentative part of the law, the House plan to computerize its mailing system was abruptly halted, the leaders aghast at the notion that the use of this powerful new mechanism might be restricted.

For the past dozen years, members of Congress have also enjoyed a sort of electronic frank, a cut-rate method of communicating with their constituents on radio and television that has proved invaluable to many of them. The Senate and the House each has its own recording studio, where a professional staff films television interviews and records radio tapes for any member who requests the service, at cost. The resulting program is then aired by stations back in the district without charge, as part of the public service programming that the Federal Communications Commission requires. True, it frequently winds up with less-than-prime-time exposure, filling gaps in the Sunday morning schedule, but considering the relatively small investment of money involved, most members regard this service as a bargain. If they were to have the same tapes made commercially—as their opponents must during a campaign—the cost would be three or four times as high.

Senators can normally communicate with their constituents more successfully on television than representatives. In most states, a program shown in a half-dozen or fewer major cities will reach a large share of the population, without too much wasted spillage into adjoining jurisdictions. Contrariwise, the House district that can use television efficiently is a relative rarity.

In the urban districts of New York, Chicago, and Los Angeles, it is an almost complete waste of time and money, since more than 90 per cent of those getting the picture are likely to live and vote in somebody's else's district. Similarly, in many rural districts, television is equally impractical. For a classic example, the old thirty-fifth District of New York stretched about two-thirds of the way across the upstate area but did not include a single major city. Thus, if Representative Samuel Stratton— who moved into politics, incidentally, from a role as television news commentator—wanted to use the medium to reach his voters, he would have had to wheedle or buy time from stations in Schenectady, Utica, Syracuse, Rochester, and Binghamton, all of them outside the district and each spraying his message over people three-quarters of whom couldn't care less. There are, however, some House districts well adapted to television, those with a centrally located, moderate-sized city, big enough to have a TV station but too small to rate a separate urban congressional district of its own. Examples are the Wisconsin Second District, centered on Madison; in South Carolina, the First around Charleston and the Second around Columbia; and the Kentucky Sixth around Lexington. Then there are districts like the Colorado First, where the medium is usable but somewhat inefficient, blanketing the urban Denver constituency but also spilling well over into the suburbs and countryside of the Second District.

A few senators have similar television problems. New Jersey has no full-fledged television stations of its own, but looks entirely to New York in the northern part of the state and to Philadelphia in the south. Before 1970, no Senate candidate had seriously tried to use the medium for campaign commercials because well over half the viewers would not be Jersey voters at all but residents of other states. Then Nelson Gross, in a well-financed attempt to unseat Senator Harrison Williams, put some television in his budget. He may have impressed thousands of New Yorkers and Pennsylvanians, but in New Jersey he lost.

Is the $42,500 salary high enough, given the quantity of work a congressman must undertake to represent his constituents adequately, to protect both their individual interests in Washington and their collective interest in the legislative process, and to maintain responsive communication with his district? The answer, unsatisfactory like most these days, is yes and no.

In the First Congress, members received $6 a day, which for the long 1789 session of 210 days meant $1,260. Not much of a reward, even at the colonial consumer price index, for those indomitable men who got the machine into motion. And yet, ever since, the battle for a living wage for the lawmakers has run into stubborn opposition at almost every turn, alternatively from the voters, resenting Congress's power to increase its own reward out of the public treasury, and from the congressmen themselves, anticipating such resentment.

In 1816, Congress voted to move up to a flat $1,500 a year, retroactive to the beginning of the session, and the citizen reaction was volcanic: mass protest meetings, hangings in effigy, and grand jury presentments. In the election that November, all the members from Delaware, Ohio, and Vermont were defeated, and many of those from Georgia, Maryland, and South Carolina, so the next year Congress humbly retreated to $6 a day. It was not the last time anxiety prevailed over poverty. Having gone to $3,000 a year in 1856 and $5,000 ten years later, on the last day of the 1873 session the members voted an increase to $7,500, retroactive to the beginning of the session. So loud was the outcry that the raise was repealed early the next year, and the lawmakers did not venture back up to $7,500 until thirty-three years later, in 1907.

An increase to $10,000 in prosperous 1925 was cut back twice during the Depression and then gradually restored. In the post-war years, the congressional salary really moved up: to $12,500 in 1946, $22,500 in 1955, $30,000 in 1965, and $42,500 in 1969. The only current bonuses go to the leaders, the Vice President, who for salary purposes occupies his congressional role of President of the Senate, and the Speaker of the House. They each make $62,500, and the majority and minority leaders of both houses get $49,500.

Beginning in 1968, Congress purposely stripped itself of some of the responsibility for its own wage level. A federal commission was established to review the salaries of judges, members of Congress, and top executive department officials every four years. Its recommendations go to the President, and his resulting recommendations go into effect automatically in thirty days if Congress does not take contrary action. Presumably less guilt attaches to a Congress that does nothing to block a salary increase than to one that actively promotes it.

A few members of Congress, generally the die-hard economizers, believe the present $42,500 is too high, but they have not been detected returning any of it. Others are sincerely convinced that there should be an increase to reflect the responsibilities of the office, the demanding year-round nature of the work, and the debilitating impact of inflation. Certainly, the productive members of Congress, it is argued with some cogency, do not receive a reward for their public service comparable to what they could command in private life.

On the whole, however, the majority of members would probably as soon retain the present salary level—if certain other financial adjustments could be made. This attitude reflects in part the pervasive congressional fear of self-reward, but it is also based on some sound economic arguments. Under present law, $3,000 worth of salary is tax exempt, theoretically representing the Washington living expenses of a lawmaker who retains his principal residence in his home state. For a congressman who moves his family to Washington, as more and more do, this allowance could cover maintenance of an apartment back in the district. But for the large number who find they must keep two family residences, one in the capital and one in the home state, the figure is completely unrealistic. It could be doubled—President Johnson proposed a $5,500 figure—at minimum cost to the

Treasury and considerable assistance to the members. If the travel and stationery allowances were liberalized as we have suggested, the salary of many of the more active members would stretch a good deal farther than it does now. With these adjustments, the present congressional wage level would satisfy most members, perhaps with one further addition, an escalator clause tied to the cost of living, such as now operates in the social security benefit system.

To enable senators and representatives to handle adequately their collateral role as Washington agents of their constituents, the principal need is a substantial new allowance for case work in each office, on top of the present provisions for staff, recognizing such work as an important congressional function and freeing other aides for legislative activity. It is entirely possible that the over-all staff salary figure for larger states and districts should be raised somewhat, to reflect the amount of service that dense population centers require, but such urban bonuses are always difficult to sell to the rural, small-state element that still seems to dominate Capitol Hill when such issues arise.

The political changes suggested in this chapter in connection with member-constituent communications are not going to be achieved lightly any more than are the financial. Giving the challenger for a House or Senate seat a limited number of free mailings during an election campaign does not seem an unreasonable proposal—unless you happen to be an incumbent congressman. But with the trend toward re-election of incumbents solidifying every two years, some move in that direction is certainly in order.

It is questionable, in the light of our present information, whether newsletters or any other form of direct mail activity should be limited by a campaign spending ceiling. Any barrier, however temporary, to communication between congressman and constituent should be discouraged, if at all possible. Once a full disclosure law is in effect, with each candidate making public all his election spending, it will be easier to tell whether this medium is being abused, like television, by a wealthy candidate trying to "buy" a seat in Congress.

Meanwhile, one modest proposal: the disclosure law should

require an incumbent senator or representative to make public during the campaign period his use of the franking privilege—how often, in what volume, and for what purpose he has dispatched free mail. This provision would exactly parallel the requirement that his opponent report all direct mail expense—printing, stationery, and postage. At the very least, it would be instructive to the voters to learn how many seed packets and baby books come flooding out of the Capitol at campaign time. At the best, such a reporting requirement would deter congressmen from abusing for openly political purposes the legitimate privilege they enjoy for communicating with their constituents.

# 13 · The Endless Survival Game

To a congressman, nothing, not even a campaign promise, seems as temporary as an election victory. No sooner has a candidate sprinted the perilous course of a campaign, fallen across the finish line into the arms of his advisers, and heard himself pronounced the winner than he must drag himself up and start jogging down the track again. For the senator, with his six-year term, there is a period of respite, varying with the political character of his state and himself. But the representative, having successfully outdistanced his pursuer, can almost hear the footsteps of another pack forming for the chase. In some states with early primaries, the victorious House candidate may be little more than a year away from the opening of another contest.

Granted that electoral competition is inseparable from representative democracy, granted that the campaign provides an essential and proper time of testing for the men who would make our laws, it remains true that one of the most pervasive concerns of the members of Congress, one that has only limited relevance to their broad public responsibility, is getting re-elected. For many, the office is never quite clear of the stale air of political intrigue left from the last campaign. The necessity of nurturing the esteem of the voters between elections drains the lawmaker's personal finances, burdens his staff with unproductive duties, and fills hours of his own time that could otherwise be devoted to more legitimate public concerns.

These political pressures are a good deal less severe for senators and representatives whose states or districts are "safe," so dominated by voters of their own party that there is little real competition on election day. For the senators, however, there are far fewer safe states than there used to be. Senator Roman Hruska, who earned a niche in immortality with his argument that mediocre citizens are entitled to a mediocre justice on the Supreme Court, barely scraped past his last Democratic opponent in institutionally Republican Nebraska. After the 1970 election, the Republicans held all four Senate seats in Tennessee and Kentucky and were preparing to mount serious challenges still deeper in the once-solid Democratic South. There are, in sum, only a handful of states left in which a strong candidate of the minority party cannot seriously threaten the majority-party Senate nominee.

The House, designed by the framers of the Constitution to be more volatile in response to public sentiment, has actually become more stable, less mobile than the Senate. Probably fewer than a quarter of its 435 seats are genuinely competitive, although every election produces some unexpected close races; in recent years, incumbents irrespective of party have managed to win reelection 85 to 95 per cent of the time, a showing that is statistically impressive but has led some members to concede reluctantly that the cards may be stacked in their favor.

A different sort of political pressure on the occupants of safe districts has begun to build in the House, however, raising alarming portents for the complacent. A new generation of aroused political activists, not all young or radical, has discovered simultaneously that (1) there are large numbers of vulnerable nonentities in the House, some of them edging ominously toward positions of real power, (2) these men can be unseated with party primary machinery that has grown rusty from disuse in many districts, and (3) this sort of campaign can often be more exciting and rewarding for its organizers than larger, more diffuse efforts to nominate a Presidential candidate or defeat a governor—particularly when it succeeds.

An outstanding 1970 example was the Third District of Massachusetts, where Philip Philbin, a seventy-seven-year-old Democrat, had served with limited distinction but great persistence since 1942. Norman Miller of the *Wall Street Journal*, after a careful examination of Philbin's House service, concluded that he could fairly be called "a party hack," a man of meager talents exercising none in his public office, merely occupying space in the chamber—where, incidentally, he regularly slept during sessions. But there was no likelihood that any Republican could make inroads into the Irish-Italian-Polish constituency that Philbin had courted with endless favors; in his only recent serious contest, he had won 66 per cent of the vote. All this might not have been a threat to the Republic were it not for the fact that Philbin, elevated inexorably by the tide of seniority, was the second-ranking Democrat on the House Armed Services Committee. If anything should happen to Chairman Mendel Rivers (it did; eight weeks after the election he died) this monument of Massachusetts mediocrity would automatically inherit one of the most powerful and pressure-laden jobs in the House, one for which he was almost ostentatiously unfit.

As vice chairman of Armed Services, Philbin had voted consistently with its majority for the Vietnam War and steadily increasing military spending. Using this entering political wedge in some of the dovish Boston suburbs in his district, a coalition of reform Democrats, antiwar groups, and young people persuaded Robert Drinan to run in the primary. He qualified strongly as an outspoken peace candidate and a prominent professional (dean of the Boston College Law School), but he was also a Jesuit priest, and no member of the Roman Catholic clergy had ever represented a state in the House. (In 1842, a priest had been a delegate from the territory of Michigan, but he is regarded for historical purposes as less than a full member.)

Undaunted, the energetic Drinan forces canvassed the district, harnessed computers and college students to their campaign, and won a startling upset in the primary. Elected in November, Father Drinan went to the bottom of the seniority ladder in the House Judiciary Committee, and Edward Hebert of Louisiana became chairman of Armed Services, a dubious over-all victory for the peace cause, perhaps, but a graphic demonstration of how an un-productive congressman can be removed from the system.

House members, fighting almost continuously for re-election, tend to be more insecure politically than senators, but the six-year term in the "other body" is far from a guarantee against constant campaigning. An example was Kenneth Keating, an upstate New York Republican congressman who was carried into the Senate in 1958 on the coattails of Nelson Rockefeller, then making his first run for governor.

Keating had been a moderate conservative in six terms in the House and was virtually unknown in New York City. The only Republicans getting elected to state-wide office then were liberals like Rockefeller and Senator Jacob Javits, who could cut into the massive city vote. Acting from the deepest instincts of self-preservation, Keating immediately began running—and changing. Publicity and emerging liberalism went hand in hand. Counseled by the widely successful Javits, he began stressing his civil rights record, seeking out Negro leaders, flying to New York regularly to speak to Jewish groups, becoming the friend of labor. His staff maintained there were weeks when he attended more bar mitzvahs than Senate roll calls. Through the whole process, six years of virtually continuous campaigning, Keating had to keep reassuring his more conservative constituents that he had not sold out, that spiritually he had never left Rochester, and this effort required regular trips to the cities and hamlets of upstate New York. It was an expensive, exhausting business, particularly for a congenial man who loved both Congress and the Washington social circuit. But, as the closing years of his term approached, it appeared to be paying dividends; Senator Keating had become a widely recognized figure, an emergent liberal who had escaped the label of turncoat. He was clearly going to be difficult for the Democrats to beat.

Then the prodigious Keating political effort was destroyed overnight. Attorney General Robert Kennedy—an outcast in the Johnson Cabinet, effectively barred from Massachusetts politics by his brother Teddy's election to the Senate—decided to move to New York and run against Keating. From then on, the Republican never really had a chance. The Kennedy name and fortune, the molding of a new political personality of force and charm, the impending national Democratic landslide—they were all too much for Keating. But the impact of his long drive showed clearly on election day. Lyndon Johnson carried New York State in 1964 by a staggering 2.7 million majority, but Kennedy only defeated Keating by 800,000. The Republican ran nearly 900,000 votes ahead of his Presidential candidate, Barry Goldwater, an astonishing achievement that says something about both men. It is hard to believe that any senator ever worked harder or longer to win re-election—or diverted so much energy from his public responsibilities in the process—but the six-year term could not save Keating.

A half-dozen years later, New York voters were treated to a condensed, accelerated replay of the same political scenario when Charles Goodell, another little-known Republican upstater, was appointed to the Senate after Kennedy's assassination. He had little more than two years to convert from conservatism and get himself known, and he moved farther and faster than Keating, affecting mod clothes, letting his hair grow, touring Africa in fatigues, and suddenly surfacing in the front lines of the peace movement.

It didn't work. The Republican right became so disaffected with the new, 1970-model Goodell that the Conservative Party ran a candidate against him. On his left flank, too many of the senator's new positions had been held longer and more plausibly by his Democratic opponent, Representative Richard Ottinger. To no good end: Goodell ran a poor third, and James Buckley became the first certifiable Conservative ever to sit in that august body. Once more, the pervasive pressures of politics for two years deprived New York State of full-time representation, and the Senate of the best efforts of an able, intelligent young man.

Persuading between 75,000 and 7 million people that you should continue to represent their interests in Washington is a demanding, complicated, and sensitive process, and no two members of Congress go about it in precisely the same way. In most cases, however, the re-election campaign is an intensified extension of the sort of contact a senator or representative has with his constituents during the off-season, when another term is a general rather than specific goal. All the same elements are involved—travel through the district, handshaking, speeches, mailings, radio and television appearances, summaries of past achievement, promises of future excellence—but the number is multiplied and the time condensed. It is a driving, testing experience, bringing constant pressure on the member to trade modesty for blatant public exposure, to obtain campaign funds by any method available, to overstate or invent a case against his opponent, to insist, sometimes unconvincingly, that he is a vital cog in the great Washington machine.

This is politics. As the system operates today, the race cannot be separated from the prize: the right to try to provide a part of the electorate with responsible, informed public service. But the price is heavy. Regularly throughout his term and intensively during its closing months, a congressman must devote his and others' time, effort, and money to matters that only indirectly involve his competence as a lawmaker, although they directly affect any future he may have in that role.

Something can be done about easing this campaign burden for House members: a four-year term. Doubling his guaranteed stay in Washington would give a newly elected representative a reasonable time in which to establish himself, in his own view and that of the voters, before he must shift his basic concern from government back to politics. If half rather than all the House members were chosen every two years, it would give the larger body a measure of the same continuity and stability that characterizes the Senate, where a third of the members run every two years.

Perhaps most important, it would enable representatives to exercise with more freedom and resolve what Edmund Burke found their most precious asset: personal judgment. "A congressman who must run again in less than two years is not much better than a piece of litmus paper," one House member said. "If his constituents look acid, he turns red. If the next morning he thinks they're alkali, all of a sudden he's blue. That's not representation. Why not have a computer wired up to a scientific sample of homes and offices back in the district? Then those people could all press a button and vote on amendments to the farm bill. But I guess we'd have to elect the man who picks the scientific sample."

It is true that biennial House elections have served the important function of testing national sentiment at frequent intervals, particularly on specific issues dividing the President and the opposition party. For this reason, it would be a serious mistake to elect the entire 435-member body either with the President or midway in his term. Either of these systems would tend to unbalance the House.

If a landslide President carried with him a strong majority in a four-year House, there would be only a limited opportunity to test his program with the people at the next midterm, when thirty-three or thirty-four senators sought re-election. Alternatively, if an entire four-year House were chosen at midterm, the historical pattern under which the party out of the White House makes major gains at that time could be unduly magnified, with that potentially anti-Administration House serving on unchanged through the first two years of the next Administration, of whatever party.

But if half the House members ran in the year of the national election and the other half two years later, there would be more than 200 congressional races each time, certainly enough to reflect important shifts in public opinion and reshape the Congress in response to them.

There are some mechanical problems. In most larger states, simply filling the odd-numbered seats in Presidential years and the even-numbered in off years would tend to ensure that each election included a representative sample of the state, geographically and in terms of urban and rural districts. The half-dozen smallest states, which have only one congressman, could be divided equally between the two elections. Some other adjustments would be necessary because there are presently about twenty or more odd-numbered districts than even, but a formula could certainly be worked out, with a little coin flipping, that divided the House into two representative, balanced halves and left a minimum number of incumbents grumbling over their lot.

Pleasure over the four-year term would go a long way toward holding down resentment over details.

Further complications would arise every ten years when all House districts are reapportioned to reflect population shifts in the latest census. Any redistricting would come at a time when half the representatives in the state were midway through their four-year term and could not be unseated without violating the Constitution. So the new map would have to preserve for each of them a district that included their place of residence while the lines could be revised with somewhat more freedom for those members whose terms were ending—complicating an already complex problem, but not insuperably.

More serious is the political problem of getting the Senate to approve such a change. Superficially, a four-year House term might seem to increase Senate security, making representatives more content in the larger body and lessening the prospect of their challenging their presumed betters. But most senators believe just the opposite, for, under the present system, a representative cannot run against a senator—in the primary if they are of the same party, or in the general election if they are not —without vacating his House seat, since that seat must also be filled in the same election and one man cannot run simultaneously for both. Thus, a representative who tries to move up to the Senate now must make a choice, running the risk of ending his congressional career altogether if he loses. If House members had a four-year term, this would only remain half true. Whenever a senator came up for re-election, half the members of his state's House delegation would be midway through their term, and any one of them could bring a primary challenge against the incumbent senator or seek the nomination to oppose him *without* having to give up his House seat. If such a challenger were to win, he would resign his old House seat; if not, he would go back and serve out the second half of his term, having lost effort and money but not his place in Congress. This is the prospect that makes senators distinctly uneasy. Although few of them could oppose the four-year House term openly on such palpably selfish grounds, many could be expected to argue long and loud that the Constitution was being desecrated and that the full House should remain a sensitive biennial gauge to public sentiment.

Giving representatives more security through the four-year term would inescapably give senators somewhat less, but there is nothing in the Constitution or lesser documents that says a senator is entitled to a free ride, once elected. A senator's awareness that there are two or three representatives in the chamber 600 feet to the south who might like to move up into his chair is not likely to make him perform his duties any less efficiently. If the House needs a measure of protection from prodding, the Senate could probably profit from a little more exposure to it. The four-year term could accomplish both.

Informal campaigning never stops, but it is entirely possible to help members of Congress, their challengers, and other office seekers by shortening the strenuous, all-out period of the official campaign. A five-week contest that opened about October 1 would have advantages for almost everyone concerned. The nominees would raise and spend less money. Incumbent office-holders—the President, members of Congress, state officials—would have to take less time off from their regular duties. The public would be less likely to get bored with the whole enterprise. Voters would be asked to pay strict attention to intense, keenly competitive contests over a reasonable span of time. Speeches would be fewer in number and likely to contain more substance. News coverage would improve accordingly, with less need to provide political filler on the inevitable dull days of a campaign nearly twice as long. Physical demands on candidates and staff would not be so severe.

If the national campaign did not open until October 1, the whole preceding political schedule could be tightened as well. The nominating conventions could be held in mid-September, and, as the states proved willing, the preliminary bouts of the primaries could be regrouped into June, July, and August, instead of strung out over the first half of the year. For the first couple of accelerated election years, it might be necessary for the political parties to draft agreements among Presidential candidates not to compete in primaries earlier than June in order to condense the entire process.

Congress could help enforce the new schedule for Presidential, Senate, and House candidates by making special reduced television rates available only during the five-week period and by tightening campaign spending limits. Once the format was successfully established for federal office, most states could be expected to conform their election practices.

Relatively few people would argue, given today's instant communications systems, that national candidates could not present the issues effectively in five weeks. But many politicians would no doubt object strenuously that this would not be enough time for a challenger, particularly a new face seeking lesser office, to make himself well enough known to counterbalance the incumbent's reservoir of familiarity, if not respect. Such objections might be overcome if campaigning, as now appears likely, becomes increasingly more structured, with regular televised appearances by candidates and spending limits that tend to equalize both parties' access to the voters. It would probably be wise to phase in the short campaign gradually, beginning with the national ticket, then the Senate races, then taking in the House, and leaving open the question of whether local candidates who are unable to command or afford television should have a longer campaign. At the least, an abbreviated campaign could make a major contribution to easing the political work load of Congress.

A major effort, long overdue, is finally under way to cut the cost of campaigning, for the Presidency and Congress as well. In effect in 1972 for the first time in political history were a set of ceilings on how much such candidates could spend, notably for radio and television, and a new reporting system under which they must make public all their contributions and expenditures of any size. The limits were designed to hold down political spending by restricting the most expensive items in most statewide and national campaigns: broadcast advertising. The over-all ceiling was set at ten cents per eligible voter but no lower than $50,000 for small states and House districts. Also covered are newspaper advertising, billboards, and automated telephone solicitation, which generally do not bulk very large in campaign budgets.

The reporting law was intended to put on the public record

the identity of major contributors to any Presidential or Congressional campaign, so the voters will know where and how deep such indebtedness runs, and cast their ballots accordingly. If the law is strictly enforced, it will reinforce the spending limits and show Congress what other types of campaign expenditures, such as computerized direct mail, might also be restricted.

Another new departure in the 1972 campaign spending law limits, for the first time ever, the amount of money that a rich man and his immediate family can invest in his own candidacy —to $50,000 for President, $35,000 for the Senate, and $25,000 for the House. The target here was millionaires like former Representative Richard Ottinger of New York, a Democrat who carried a Republican district in 1964 by spending nearly $200,000 of his own fortune but who failed to advance to the Senate six years later, despite a much larger investment.

Also in effect for the first time in 1972 was a tax credit or deduction for political contributions to a candidate or party. Although it may appear otherwise, this is really a public subsidy for campaigns. The government tells the taxpayers it will provide them with a measure of relief if they make gifts to the Republican or Democratic Party; the net effect is that the Treasury is poorer, the party richer, and the candidates have to raise less from other private sources.

Among other proposals that a more favorable climate for public subsidy has produced is one under which television stations and networks would provide free time for candidates' appearances, singly or in debates, in return for tax relief. This, of course, is nothing more than the government buying the time, if at reduced rates.

Ultimately, the only real solution to the election problem is full public financing of the cost of running for office, a fairly radical idea that may be much closer to realization than is generally believed. In 1971, a Democratic plan to finance the next Presidential campaign with $20 million of federal tax revenue for each major-party candidate passed the Senate and was only derailed when Representative Wilbur Mills, the House Ways and Means chairman, agreed to a unilateral compromise that postponed the plan until 1976 and may have killed it altogether.

Consider what would result if candidates received a public subsidy and were strictly limited to that money or credit alone. Spending ceilings for national and congressional candidates would become unnecessary, disclosure of contributions and expenditures would be largely eliminated, and, most important of all, the distortion that big money—from big business and big labor—introduces into the political process would disappear. A candidate willing to mortgage his public independence to campaign contributors would no longer have any advantage over a man too honest to accept such sponsorship. Both would be on precisely the same footing.

For a minor example of contributors' pressure, take the Long Island Republican who gave Representative Norman Lent $500 for his first campaign and never let him forget it. Planning a business trip to Formosa, he asked for a letter identifying him to the American ambassador as a member of the congressman's staff; he got one asking that he be extended "every courtesy." Once in Taipei, he demanded that the embassy give him a car to carry out what he said was a secret assignment for the congressman, and Lent had to tell the State Department that his angel was an impostor.

Senator Paul Douglas of Illinois, for many years a lonely Senate voice on the issue, put it bluntly but accurately all of twenty years ago:

> The vast majority of the big donors want something in return for their money. Their gifts are in a sense investments. After election, if their candidates are victorious, they will come around to collect. They will want contracts, insurance policies, jobs for friends and relations, loans, subsidies, privileges legislation, and so on. Woe betide the officeholders and the party which ignores their claims, for if they do, then the next time the money is likely to be shut off.

Public financing would free every candidate—*every* one—from any pressure that he reflect thereafter the views of his campaign contributors rather than his own. His postelection conduct would have to satisfy the voters in his state or district, but absolutely no one else except the police. Even party leaders would have trouble threatening his independence they could disown a senator and run a primary opponent against him, but he would still be assured of a well-financed campaign and, again, be answerable only to the voters, which is the way the system has been supposed to work all along.

The Association of the Bar of the City of New York, in its report *Congress and the Public Trust* (see also Chapter 14), argued that the desirability of broad public participation in the electoral process alone, ethical considerations aside, justifies public campaign funding. "The only practical way to involve the public as a whole is by subsidy from public funds," the bar association concluded. "Such spending is for the general welfare, and all citizens should share in it."

The cost of the proposal cannot fairly be regarded as an obstacle. The sidetracked Democratic plan, covering only the national ticket, would have cost about $60 million every four years. A different version proposed by Senator George McGovern, underwriting congressional campaigns as well, would run an estimated $100 million every two years. But even that figure is less than one-twentieth of 1 per cent—or one two-thousandth of the current federal budget—surely a small price to pay for bringing the best-qualified, rather than the most readily purchasable, men and women to Washington.

Very real questions are involved. How much support should a third-party candidate have to demonstrate to qualify for public subsidy and how much should he get? How can some reasonable limit be placed on the number of competitors in a subsidized primary? But these can almost surely be resolved if the underlying principal is accepted.

Probably the most serious practical barrier to public financing of campaigns involves the extreme reluctance of members of Congress to vote, or appear to vote, money directly to themselves. Most incumbents of both parties are almost literally terrified to raise their own salaries, anticipating public hostility focused on them by their next opponent. To pass a share of the taxpayers' money over to two politicians to finance their competition for the right to decide how the rest of it is going to be spent strikes many congressmen just now as politically suicidal, especially when they would be prominent among the beneficiaries. The idea also has the sworn opposition of many top Republicans in

Congress and elsewhere. But the ranks of those who see the publicly financed campaign as the wave of the future are steadily growing, and that future may be nearer than many politicians expect.

For many members of Congress, the costly, time-consuming politics of re-election is only part of the story. All but the most complacent, admittedly not an inconsiderable number, are also inevitably concerned with their own advancement through the structure of the House or Senate to influence, power, and perhaps leadership within the institution. Many must also occupy themselves simultaneously with the future of their party in the home state and its leadership there. Still further, a number of senators and handful of the most prominent House members must work with their national party, channeling its direction, encouraging its better state candidates, and helping choose its national officers and nominees—all politics, all important, all demanding.

Internal congressional politics is less intense but more continuous than the external re-election problem, and, for a newly elected member, it begins even before he takes office. For the most important decision involving his incipient public career, appointment to one or more standing committees, is often made before his first session even convenes. Because the committee structure is the central nervous system of Congress, members frequently rise or fall with the committee assignments their party leaders parcel out in the beginning. No one can be an expert on all the material that Congress deals with, although a few have tried, but committee membership enables a lawmaker to become intimately familiar with one area, and it is vitally important whether that area is of specific interest to his constituents or, perhaps, of broad enough general interest so that eventually he may attract national attention. Sometimes the latter happens more or less accidentally. When Edmund Muskie came to the Senate in 1959, his Yankee independence rubbed Majority Leader Lyndon Johnson the wrong way. As a result, he wound up on the Public Works Committee, not among his three first choices. But over the succeeding years, as air and water pollution developed into major national issues that Muskie came to master, on a committee more likely to attract pork-barrel packers than ecologists, he rose to national prominence from an unpromising beginning.

Generally, a new senator is less likely than a House member to have his career nipped in the bud by a poor committee assignment. A senator gets a minimum of two, and one of them is now normally on a committee of substance, middle if not front rank. But House freshmen usually get only one committee, the one in which they are then expected to carve out a career in the years ahead, and, if it is something like Merchant Marine and Fisheries, or Post Office and Civil Service, that career can be pretty well stymied from the start.

Sometimes this critically important committee assignment can be heavily influenced by events that preceded the election. In 1964, for example, Jonathan Bingham had the temerity to challenge in a primary Representative Charles Buckley, the Democratic leader of the Bronx and, as Public Works chairman, a pillar of the House establishment. A winner in both the primary and the general election, Bingham flew to Boston soon after to pay almost apologetic court to Speaker John McCormack, a long-time Buckley crony. There he put in an early, courteous bid for membership on Judiciary or, failing that, the Banking and Currency Committee. (A former United Nations delegate, he really wanted Foreign Affairs but thought that request would have been presumptuous.) What Bingham got for daring to challenge the system was the Interior Committee, which operates no discernible national parks in the Bronx, and House Administration, near the bottom of the committee ladder. A serious, intelligent, and attractive congressman, Bingham later managed a transfer to Foreign Affairs, but after four terms in the House he only ranked sixteenth of twenty-one Democrats on his chosen committee, and the road toward seniority and influence there was still a long and uncertain one.

Under different circumstances, a freshman's committee experience can be quite the opposite. When David Pryor, a thirty-two-year-old Arkansas attorney, was elected to the House in 1966, he went directly onto the Appropriations Committee, one of the most jealously guarded bastions of power in the establishment. He went there because Representative Mills, the Ways and Means chairman, put him there. The Democratic members of Ways and Means constitute the Committee on Committees for their party, making all such assignments; this was the first time since Mills had become chairman that a fellow Arkansan-Democrat had come to the House—and, what's more, a young man of obvious leadership potential—and Mills took care of him. (It was the first—and, so far, last—time that Mills saw fit to exercise his chairman's prerogative of dictating an individual committee assignment; the Ways and Means chairman is almost certainly the most powerful man in Congress, but he has not reached that pinnacle by promising or withholding choice committee posts.) But even with this running start, Pryor is now only twenty-fifth in the interminable line of thirty-three Democrats on Appropriations. With a few breaks, it is possible that he could reach the chairmanship of the immensely powerful committee while still in his fifties and in full possession of his considerable faculties, a recognition that comes to most House members much, much later in life. (It took the present Appropriations chairman, George Mahon of Texas, thirty years in the House to reach that summit. At seventy-one, he is by all accounts keen and fully competent. Not all House committees are so blessed.)

Once a senator or representative has managed a seat on the committee where he intends to make his legislative future, this particular sort of politicking stops. As we have seen, he is from then on lifted inexorably by the escalator of the seniority system. If he can overcome election opponents and resist pestilence, scandal, and death while those above him, one by one, are not so fortunate, he will eventually be deposited at the top: the chairmanship or the ranking minority post, depending on which party controls the chamber.

A second major area of internal congressional politics, the scramble for leadership, does not operate so smoothly. Here there is only one prevailing rule: the man with the most votes among his party colleagues at the opening of each Congress will be Speaker, majority leader, or minority leader for the next two years. In theory, a senator elected in November could be named majority leader in January if he had lined up enough votes in the interim; in practice, it takes many years and many promises more. In the House, it is even possible to elect as Speaker someone who is not a member at all, but no representative has ever been so rash as to suggest that his colleagues need look beyond their own ranks for leadership.

If virtually all the members of Congress aspire to leadership in a vague sort of way, inclining heliotropically toward the sunlight of prominence, only a relatively small, determined group is willing to add this particularly demanding kind of politics to the others that must be played simultaneously. But to those who choose it, the competition for the handful of power posts in the Senate and House can be the most challenging of all and, occasionally, the most politically rewarding.

Becoming a congressional leader takes hard work, shrewd political judgment, skill, and, frequently, a measure of good luck, but it need not always take time. Lyndon Johnson arrived in the Senate in 1949 on the strength of a still-debated eighty-seven-vote Texas primary victory. In the 1950 election, both the two Democratic Senate leaders were defeated, and in 1951 Johnson was elected whip. In the 1952 election, the new majority leader was defeated, and in 1953 Johnson, nothing near a committee chairman and sixtieth in the Senate seniority, was chosen leader. Senator Richard Russell of Georgia was the real party power in those days, permitting figurehead senators to carry the title. In Johnson, he got something considerably more.

Unlike his brothers who had regarded internal Senate politics as dull and petty, Edward Kennedy of Massachusetts decided to make his first move toward leadership there. In 1969, after a whirlwind campaign for votes, he abruptly muscled Russell Long of Louisiana out of the second-ranking job of Democratic whip by a startling 31–26 vote. Washington reporters, frequently attaching more political significance to this sort of in-house victory than anyone else, proclaimed it the start of the Kennedy Presidential drive. They proved wrong, but for reasons almost no one could anticipate. Kennedy, it developed, could not work up much enthusiasm for the routine, floorwalker duties of the whip, and his involvement in the Chappaquiddick accident six months later dampened both his surviving enthusiasm for the job and his colleagues' for him.

Waiting in the wings was Senator Robert Byrd, a dogged West Virginian and one-time Ku Klux Klan organizer who had risen to the less-than-dizzying eminence of secretary of the Senate Democratic Conference, one of those marginal leadership titles that are created to give the party high command more appearance of breadth and balance. Byrd was the acknowledged master of Senate internal politics at its most routine; he regularly wrote to other senators, congratulating them on birthdays or reporting how pleased he had been to undertake some small piece of floor business on their behalf in their absence. If a senator replied with a letter of thanks, Byrd wrote back to thank him for his thanks.

After taking careful soundings, Byrd challenged Kennedy for the whip's job when the 1971 session opened and surprised a good many people by beating him 31–24. Southern resentment at the ouster of Long two years earlier, Byrd's persistence, and growing Senate doubts about Kennedy's political future had all taken their toll. (On the secret ballot, Kennedy may also have lost some votes among the Senate's half-dozen Democratic Presidential candidates, to whom the prospect of a competitor's public embarrassment may have proved irresistible.)

More often than not, however, campaigns to depose congressional leaders or block their advancement to the next highest post fail. The Senate and House are among the most conservative organizations in the country internally, whatever their rhetoric may sometimes indicate. When any doubt arises, Congress does it the way it did it the time before, and the time before that. If good old Charlie was good and old enough to be elected whip six years ago, why not make him floor leader now? Any other decision might be interpreted as an admission of past error.

Ironically, this sort of conservative attitude can help advance a liberal. In 1969, Senator Hugh Scott of Pennsylvania, who is to the left of Republican dead center but not very far, decided to run for a vacant whip's post. On a strict ideological division, the conservatives should have beaten him, but they chose as their candidate Senator Hruska of Nebraska, whose chief claim to leadership was the fact that he had developed a pale but recognizable floor imitation of Everett McKinley Dirksen. Scott won narrowly, 23–20, and became part of the apparatus. When Dirksen died later that year and the minority leadership became vacant, the conservatives shrewdly picked as their candidate Senator Howard Baker of Tennessee, a young, articulate middle-grounder. But Scott was able to bolster his minority of Republican liberals with colleagues who swear by institutional continuity and win a 24–19 victory. He turned back a second bid by Baker when the 1971 session opened, despite fairly clear evidence that the White House would not have been displeased with the election of a more ardent Nixon loyalist.

In pursuit of a leader's role, a congressman can do favors, flash his knowledge, accumulate political due bills from his colleagues, debate impressively, and assemble a coalition of regional and philosophical supporters, only to find that an unexpected turn of events closes the door just when it seemed ready to swing open. When Speaker McCormack announced his intention to retire in 1970, just such an opening seemed to beckon Representative Dan Rostenkowski, a gregarious one-time automobile salesman who, after a dozen years in the House, was chiefly distinguished as the Washington agent of Mayor Richard Daley of Chicago. Carl Albert of Oklahoma was clearly going to move up from majority leader to Speaker without challenge. Hale Boggs of Louisiana was the favorite to move up from whip to majority leader, with authority then to appoint the new whip. Rostenkowski held the next leadership office in line, chairman of the Democratic caucus. Boggs, in an effort to solidify Northern urban support for his candidacy, privately promised the whip's job to Rostenkowski. But when Boggs was elected majority leader over divided liberal opposition, Speaker Albert vetoed the Chicagoan.

Some associates believe Albert held Mayor Daley heavily responsible for the disastrous 1968 Democratic National Convention, over which the new Speaker had attempted to preside as chairman with only limited effectiveness. Proud Carl Albert knew the Chicago fiasco might have cost him any future opportunity to wield the gavel at a Presidential convention. In addition, on one of Albert's nominating petitions for the Speakership that was circulated among the Illinois delegation, Rostenkowski's name had been conspicuously absent. Forced to break his promise, Boggs named as whip Thomas (Tip) O'Neill, an amiable Bostonian who had endorsed his candidacy at a key moment and, at fifty-nine, seemed unlikely to rise higher in the House hierarchy. Assuming Rostenkowski had been assured of his promotion, House Democrats had already elected a new caucus chairman, so the Chicagoan found himself frozen out of the leadership altogether, a political outcast at forty-three.

The time a member spends building the name and contacts that may some day reward him with a leadership post are not necessarily wasted if he falls short. A senator or representative who is able to make his way into the inner circle of his house, consorting with its official and unofficial leaders, is likely to share in some valuable commodities: inside information on legislative strategy, a voice in key decisions, and the power to get things done for his constituents.

When Representative Richard Bolling of Missouri was a member of the House inner circle in the 1950's, a $32 million federal building was constructed in his Kansas City district and a multi-million-dollar flood-control dam begun upstream. "Both these projects were worthy and needed," Bolling later wrote. "They went to my district because I was an insider, because I was a lieutenant and confidant of Speaker Rayburn. Because of this special relationship, I was also able to vote my convictions on national and international issues. I would have it no other way. But other members have fared less fortunately."

Every congressman is not only a Republican or Democrat within his house, but a member, and more than likely a leader, of his party in his home state. Most senators and representatives want to hang onto such influence despite shifting their operating base to Washington, and this takes time and work. Frequently, particularly in smaller states, a new senator is a former governor, and if he is going to keep the control of party affairs at home that he enjoyed from the Statehouse, he is going to spend a lot of time on the telephone and write a lot of letters, few of them with much reference to his Senate duties.

Senator Robert Kerr reportedly continued to run the state of

Oklahoma from his Capitol Hill office and still found time to be one of the most influential men in the Senate. The fact that he was an oil millionaire several times over probably did not prove a hindrance to either activity. But less fortunate senators who want to retain a voice in their state party have to devote considerable time to contracts, conferences, and conventions back home. If they don't show up, someone else is going to start making all those political decisions, first in consultation with the leader detained in Washington and then later without him.

Some members want to expand rather than merely retain their party influence at home. These generally fall into two categories: House members who would like to run for senator or governor, and senators who would like to run for President. A man in the first group has a tougher job inside his state because there is nearly always keen competition for Senate and gubernatorial nominations, and a massive political effort is frequently necessary to line up enough support to win. A glance at the 1970 Senate election results could make you wonder if such effort is worthwhile. Of the fourteen House members who were nominated for the Senate, only six were elected.

A senator interested in the Presidential nomination has to solidify political support in his home state as a minimum requirement for moving outside it in search of further allies. Any politician who is not assured that he will go to the convention as the choice of his own state is not going to attract much attention from party leaders elsewhere around the country. This was the barrier that faced Senator Charles Percy in 1967–68. He was a wealthy, attractive, articulate, and very interested candidate, but he could provide no assurance that the conservative Illinois Republican organization would back him, if only temporarily, against Richard Nixon, even on the basis of local pride. This being true, trying to launch a national campaign was out of the question.

The proposition that national politics can consume a good deal of a senator's time and effort was never better illustrated than in the Ninety-second Congress, when a half-dozen Democratic senators made up virtually the entire field of competition for the 1972 nomination, trailed by as many more with an eye on the vice presidency. At various times, the declared, undeclared, and hopeful lists for the two openings on the Democratic ticket included: George McGovern, Henry (Scoop) Jackson, Hubert Humphrey, Edward Muskie, Harold Hughes, Birch Bayh, Vance Hartke, Edward Kennedy, Fred Harris, William Proxmire, Walter Mondale, and Ernest Hollings. It could fairly be said that during the effective working life of this Congress one out of five Democratic senators was occupied with national politics, for varying time periods at varying levels of interest, many of them to a degree that could only interfere with the duties with which their constituents had entrusted them in the first place.

Politics is inseparable from service in an elected legislative body, and no one can pretend otherwise. No one seriously advances any proposals to eliminate the initial scramble for committee preferment or the long-term maneuvering aimed at elusive party leadership titles in the two houses of Congress. And the only way to curb a senator or representative who devotes too much of his time and talent to national politics is to retire him to private life at the earliest opportunity or elect him President. But a longer term for House members, a shorter congressional campaign, strict controls on political spending, and a sound public subsidy system for campaign costs could ease the political burden on Congress considerably, freeing its members to devote more of their time and staff assistance to informed, imaginative, and responsible drafting of the nation's laws.

# 14 · Caesar's Dead?
# Let's Run His Wife

For most of the 11,000 men and women who have served in Congress over the past 180 years, power and privilege have come naturally, hand in hand. These people have been, after all, the leading lawmakers of the land, and few of them ever resisted having the path ahead smoothed here and there.

Accordingly, senators and representatives are wrapped today in a whole panoply of privileges that have been raised around the institution, some visible, some not so. They are the beneficiaries of one of the most generous pension plans in America, which permits retirement on 80 per cent of salary after thirty-two years, or $34,000 at the present level. This arrangement does nothing to promote earlier retirement at a lower rate by those members who enter Congress in their forties and fifties, which is most of them. It tends, instead, to ensure that the men elevated to leadership by the seniority system are even older than they might otherwise be, serving time until their pensions come to full bloom.

All members are also eligible for subsidized life and health insurance—$11 a month for $20,000 worth of life protection—and hospital care at reduced rates in the Washington area military installations. Available directly on Capitol Hill are a wide range of goods and services, either free or at rock-bottom prices. There are private stores that sell stationery, supplies, and gifts on a cost basis. There are gymnasiums and swimming pools, and restaurants where the members pay hundreds of thousands of dollars a year less for their meals than they cost.

There is a beauty parlor on the House side for female members, and separate but unequal barbershops for the men. In downtown Washington, haircuts cost from $3 to $5 including tip; in the Senate barbershop, they are $1 50 for staff, with senators, customarily shorn free, tipping the barber $1 for his trouble. In 1971, the House haircut charge leaped from 75 cents to $2, to the groans of increasingly shaggy members For four months of each year, before income tax time, the Internal Revenue Service assigns a four-man team to Capitol Hill, just to make sure the members take all their legitimate deductions.

Even transportation in Washington is tailored to congressional needs. The District government, dependent on Congress for all its funds and most of its laws, obligingly holds the unmetered taxi fares down to one of the lowest levels in the nation. Then it gerrymanders the zones on which fares are based so that you can ride from the Mayflower Hotel, a traditional watering place for members, to the Capitol, a distance of twenty-nine blocks, for only seventy-five cents, even though in heavy traffic the trip can take up to a half hour.

Similarly, residents of the District and its Virginia and Maryland suburbs suffer the discomfort and danger of National Airport, one of the busiest in the country, in the midst of a densely populated area, because the members like to be able to get from the Capitol to the airport in something like twelve minutes. A few years ago, all Washington flights to Chicago and beyond were shifted to Dulles International Airport, a good forty minutes out in Virginia, but congressional protest was so strong that the move was abandoned in a few months.

And when senators and representatives venture abroad, whether on public business, private errand, or vacation, the State Department customarily provides escort and stenographic service, car and chauffeur, baggage transportation, preregistration in hotels, ice and food in the room, plus liquor if requested. Any sort of overseas purchase except liquor may be sent home duty-free in the capacious diplomatic pouch.

Given this encompassing cloud of special privilege that congressmen enjoy at public expense, you might think they would have been particularly sensitive over the years as to the potential use of their considerable public power for private profit. Well, some have and some haven't.

A statistical case can be made that congressional standards of conduct have always been high and remain so. Of the thousands of politicians who have served in the two bodies, only seven senators and eighteen representatives have ever been censured, and a mere fifteen senators and three representatives expelled. But, as we shall see, this says more about congressional abhorrence of self-discipline than about any high level of ethical conduct.

Again, there have been only three major scandals in the past nine years, and one of them incriminated only a Senate employee, leaving the apprehensive members relatively unscathed. Not a very high number, perhaps, considering the hundreds of men and women who passed through the Senate and House during the 1960's, but large enough to make the public wonder how many other cases, equally unsavory, might be hidden from view behind a dense curtain of protective congressional secrecy.

The unspoken requirement that Congress maintain high standards of conduct was clear from the beginning to the Founding Fathers, one of whom wrote in *The Federalist*, "As there is a degree of depravity in mankind which requires a certain degree of circumspection and distrust: So there are other qualities in human nature, which justify a certain portion of esteem and confidence. Republican government presupposes the existence of these qualities in a higher degree than any other form."

That this was only a supposition as far as Congress was concerned became clear almost immediately. During the first session, according to Senator William Maclay of Pennsylvania, his colleagues were privately buying up virtually worthless certificates issued by the Continental Congress while they were publicly considering legislation to redeem them at face value. While Congress was debating whether to charter the Bank of the United States in the 1830's, that institution thoughtfully loaned more than $1.5 million to its members.

During the Civil War, when claims against the uneasy government abounded, some lawyer members of Congress actually advertised in the Washington papers that they could be engaged to prosecute such cases. At about the same time, Senator James Simmons of Rhode Island was offered $50,000 to get a war contract for a rifle manufacturer and accepted two $10,000 notes in part payment. Told by its investigating committee that such activity was regrettable but not illegal, the Senate not only declined to expel or censure Simmons but took no action at all. Presumably unwilling to remain a member of a body with standards like that, the senator resigned.

The most blatant example of congressional corruption ever to surface came after the Civil War, when the federal government was underwriting a good share of the cost of building the first transcontinental railroad, the Union Pacific. Representative Oakes Ames of Massachusetts and some collaborators resourcefully set up the Credit Mobilier corporation, which took on railroad construction contracts, farmed out the actual work to others, and charged the Union Pacific wildly inflated fees, reportedly pocketing something between $7 million and $40 million in three years for no real work at all. To keep such a profitable enterprise operating, federal subsidies in larger and more frequent amounts had to slide through Congress, and Ames decided that a distribution of Credit Mobilier stock among the leaders of both parties in both houses would be helpful. He chose to honor, among others, Speaker Schuyler Colfax, later Vice President; Representative James Blaine, later Speaker; and Representatives James Garfield and James Brooks, the respective Republican and Democratic floor leaders.

Colfax succeeded in blocking one investigation, but political pressures of the 1872 campaign broke the scandal into the open. The Senate conducted an inquiry and the House no less than two. The results seem today all but unbelievable: Ames and Brooks were censured by the House, which ignored a committee recommendation that they be expelled. (Brooks was apparently more guilty than the other bribe-takers because he put his stock in his son-in-law's name rather than his own.) The other five beneficiaries of Ames's largesse went scot-free. In fact, if anything, the Credit Mobilier episode seems to have added luster to their political credentials. Colfax, it is true, was not renominated for Vice

President in 1872, but that had happened before the scandal broke, the result of other political problems. Colfax's successor as the vice presidential nominee, Senator Henry Wilson of Massachusetts, had also taken a bundle of Ames's tainted stock, but he went on to be elected. Blaine continued as Speaker and was later nominated for President. Garfield was nominated and elected. No one ever seemed to think any worse of them at all.

The chief problem in combating congressional corruption has often centered on the men officially charged with suppressing venality everywhere: the lawyers. When a congressman who is a farmer or a businessman accepts money from someone interested in federal legislation, it is a bribe; when a congressman who is a lawyer does the same thing, it is a fee. Or at least he can argue that it is, while all the other lawyers in Congress listen and nod sympathetically.

Daniel Webster's stirring invocation to Congress to "perform something worthy to be remembered" is carved above the rostrum of the House, but his admirers prefer to forget how the famous New England lawyer served the Bank of the United States simultaneously with his constituents, but rather more profitably. In 1833, Senator Webster wrote the president of the bank, noting that his legal retainer "has not been renewed or refreshed as usual," and reporting ominously that another unnamed party had offered him a fee "to be concerned personally against the bank." About the best that can be said for Webster was that he made no secret of the fact that he was serving two masters, the bank and the Congress that chartered and regulated it. During his years in Congress, he argued some forty cases on behalf of the bank before the Supreme Court, a practice that is still open to senators and representatives a century and a half later but rarely taken advantage of in these more sensitive days.

Hiring a congressional lawyer to argue before the government may increase the prospects of winning your case, whatever its merits. After the Mexican War, Senator Thomas Corwin of Ohio represented before the Mexican Claims Commission a client who said his silver mine had been destroyed by military activity, and the senator won him a $500,000 judgment. A few years later, the client was exposed as a fraud and his mine as nonexistent, but by that time Corwin was Secretary of the Treasury in the Fillmore Cabinet, so the Senate did not have to concern itself about his ethics.

In 1906, a series of muckraking newspaper articles revealed, among other things, that Senator Joseph Bailey of Texas had taken more than $225,000 in legal fees from an oil-producing client over a period of only a few months. His defense on the floor became the classic position for oil senators. "Mr. President," Bailey said, "I despise those public men who think they must remain poor in order to be considered honest. I am not one of them. If my constituents want a man who is willing to go to the poorhouse in his old age to stay in the Senate during his middle age, they will have to find another senator. I intend to make every dollar that I can honestly make without neglecting or interfering with my public duty." No one in Texas disagreed. Five months later, they re-elected Bailey to a second term.

In the Eighty-third Congress (1953–54), Senator John Bricker of Ohio, a steadfast opponent of the Saint Lawrence Seaway, held the key position of chairman of the Senate Commerce Committee. Meanwhile, his law firm back in Columbus had as a substantial client—$148,000 in fees over six years—the Pennsylvania Railroad, which fought the Seaway to the end as a potential competitor. Bricker maintained that his $35,000-a-year income from the law firm did not include any part of the railroad money. His reassuring explanation: "Everyone knows I am honest."

In 1961, the New York law firm of Representative Emanuel Celler, the House Judiciary chairman, kicked back $2,500 to Bobby Baker, the ingenious Senate majority secretary, as a "forwarding fee" for directing a $10,000 real estate case to the congressman and his partners. As long before as 1933, the American Bar Association's Committee on Ethics had called it "improper" to split a fee with another lawyer who did nothing more than refer a client.

Concerned by cases like these and a good many others less well known, the Association of the Bar of the City of New York, a group as illustrious as its name is long, embarked on a broad study of conflict of interest and ethical standards among members of Congress. Aided by a Ford Foundation grant, a special committee headed by Louis M. Loeb worked for two years and published its findings in book form in 1970 as *Congress and the Public Trust*. This book is not merely a thorough, well-balanced, well-written, politically knowledgeable study of the congressional ethics problem, it is one of the very few good current books about Congress that exist. Directed by James Kirby, Jr., a former Senate Judiciary subcommittee counsel, now dean of the Ohio State Law School, the bar association survey extended usefully into such fields as the adequacy of congressional salaries and allowances and campaign finance to produce an outstanding work, to which all subsequent writers in the area, particularly this one, are deeply indebted.

The bar association study showed that about half the lawyers in the House who were still nominally practicing took $5,000 or more a year out of their firm, but that many of them did very little legal work in return. These members tended to justify remaining in the old firm, in fact, by arguing that the low work load did not interfere with their congressional responsibilities. But the survey also discovered that other House members, particularly lawyers who had given up their practices, resented this sort of vestigial legal connection as trading on public office and, more bluntly, potential influence peddling.

The bar association recommended closing one loophole by prohibiting members of Congress from arguing cases before the federal courts—for which, just incidentally, they provide the financing—as they have long been barred from practicing before federal agencies. In 1964, Senator Sam Ervin of North Carolina argued before the Supreme Court an appeal from a decision of the National Labor Relations Board, when he could not have taken the case before the board itself. The distinction should clearly be eliminated.

As should the limited but invidious system of "double-door" law firms. Representative Celler, the Judiciary chairman, dean of the House, rounding fifty years' service, is a member of a New York law firm, Weisman, Celler, Allan, Spett, and Sheinberg, which refuses to take any cases involving the federal government. But occupying the same offices and using the same telephone number is another law firm, Weisman, Allan, Spett, and Sheinberg, which will happily represent you before any agency in Washington or in any federal court because it has no partner whose congressional influence might tip the judicial scales. Or does it?

This system has seemed to flourish in the peculiar ethical atmosphere of New York City. During their respective tenures in the House, Representatives Abraham Multer, Jacob Gilbert, and Paul Fino all maintained double-door firms, one for the business that a member of Congress can properly handle and one for the business he can't.

A partnership between two or more lawyers, by its very nature, imposes a sort of commonality upon the partners: they share the clients along with the profits, and information given one partner in the course of a case is given to all. It has never been questioned that a partner is prohibited from taking a plaintiff's case when another partner is already representing the defendant. And the American Bar Association has ruled that "the relations of partners in a law firm are so close that the firm, and all the members thereof, are barred from accepting any employment that any one member of the firm is prohibited from taking." This precedent led the bar association in its congressional study to the reasonable conclusion that the law partners of a member of Congress should be prohibited from accepting any legal business that would amount to a conflict of interest if the member tried to do it himself, no matter whether those partners are nominally operating in a slightly different firm under a slightly different name. The deceit is so patent as to invite suspicion of misconduct.

The bar association divided congressional lawyers into two categories and then neatly disposed of both of them. The first is a senator or representative with a "façade practice." His name is on the door and letterhead, but he seldom if ever engages in any legal activity for the firm. He is a fraud. He is encouraging the public to believe that patronage of his law firm will assure clients of his personal expertise—and, by implication, of the influence of his public office—when it won't because he really isn't doing business behind that door at all.

The second category, congressional lawyers who do continue an active practice, involves a different problem but the same solution. Such men and women cannot avoid acquiring clients whose special interests will cast a shadow over the independent judgment required of all members. Indeed, an established member of Congress acts as a magnet to draw to his firm corporations whose desire, spoken or unspoken, is that he will represent *them* in Congress rather than the great mass of nonclients who make up his real constituency.

The bar association concluded that

> both the theoretical and the actual nature of the lawyer-client relationship are such that it is totally unrealistic to expect lawyers to subordinate their clients' interests when they make decisions as trustees of the public's interest. Temporarily removing the lawyer's hat to put on a public-service hat cannot eclipse the lawyer's duty of loyalty to clients.

The only solution: all lawyers elected to Congress should drop their practice and become full-time senators and representatives. The bar association would apply this rule to any senator elected to a full six-year term and to any House member elected to his third two-year term, allowing them to retain their membership in a firm back home until then as a security blanket against the chilling possibility of political defeat. This seems somewhat harsh. A senator is rarely secure until he has been re-elected once. If the House term were four years instead of two, election to a third term could provide evidence of a reasonably stable future in Washington, but, as things stand today, a fourth term would seem a fairer test of whether a representative should be expected to abandon his law practice to concentrate solely on Congress.

The Constitution threw up a great protective shield around the members of Congress from the beginning. "For any speech or debate in either house," it provides, "they shall not be questioned in any other place." This does not merely free a member from any fear of libel for floor speeches, encouraging him to speak his full mind. The Supreme Court has held that it also prohibits prosecution for bribery of a member who accepts payment for making a speech on the floor; by extension, it would almost certainly shelter a senator or representative who introduced a bill in return for a bribe or sold his vote.

To merit this extensive grant of freedom, the members of Congress were supposed to assume responsibility for a rigorous program of self-discipline, each individual policing his own actions and each body on the alert for any member who was not policing hard enough. Unfortunately, this never came to pass. In fact, it took 179 years of rumors, scandals, prosecutions, and public protest before the Senate and House, spurred by separate events, managed to draw up codes of conduct for their members.

The gentlest form of self-discipline, declining to vote when you have a personal interest in the legislation, has a strong historical foundation but has been largely ignored for more than a century. Vice President Thomas Jefferson provided in his *Manual* that "when the private interests of a Member are concerned in a bill or question, he is to withdraw." Jefferson saw it to be "for the honor of the house" to observe "the fundamental principle . . . which denies to any man to be a judge in his own cause."

This provision was written into the House rules, but in 1874 Speaker James Blaine, who had taken railroad stock in the Credit Mobilier scandal only a few years earlier, ruled that three other Republicans who held bank stock could vote on a bill to estabish free banking. He said it was only necessary for a member to disqualify himself when a bill benefited him exclusively, rather than as a member of a group. Even then, by subsequent House ruling, the decision is optional with the member, and the Speaker cannot challenge his right to vote. As you might expect, there has been mighty little disqualification in the House since.

The Senate rules do not contain any prohibition against voting for your own private interest, but they do provide that a senator who declines to vote may be excused by the Senate after hearing his reasons. Occasionally, a particularly scrupulous senator will disqualify himself on the basis of financial holdings in a particular industry, but it has been a relatively rare occurrence. Senator Robert Kerr, the free-wheeling Oklahoma millionaire, was asked one day why he did not disqualify himself from voting on oil and farm bills. "Now, wouldn't it be a hell of a thing," he replied, "if the senator from Oklahoma couldn't vote for the things that Oklahomans are most interested in? If everyone abstained on the grounds of personal interest, I doubt if you could get a quorum in the United States Senate on any subject."

There are two more serious forms of congressional self-discipline, censure and expulsion, but the first is invoked only in really flagrant cases and the second has been relegated to the role of an historic oddity. Censure charges have only been raised against nine senators and voted against seven of them. Only two of these cases involved ethical considerations: Senator Hiram Bingham in 1929, who put an employee of the Connecticut Manufacturers Association on his payroll to help write tariff legislation, and Senator Thomas Dodd in 1967, who converted campaign contributions to his personal use, of whom more later.

Other censured senators were condemned for revealing secret documents and fighting on the floor. The most famous modern censure case, involving Senator Joseph McCarthy of Wisconsin in 1954, was not based on ethical considerations. Although McCarthy was open to attack over a wide range of behavior, he was ultimately "condemned"—the presumably softer term was substituted —for obstructing the processes of the Senate, impairing its dignity, and bringing it "into dishonor and disrepute." A far more serious offense in the eyes of his colleagues, it would seem, than outright lying or brutal character assassination.

Censure charges have been voted in the House eighteen of the thirty times they have arisen. Only six of the representatives censured were found guilty of violating ethical standards, and no such case has come up at all since the 1873 aftermath of the Credit Mobilier scandal. No House member has been censured on any grounds since 1921, when a highly unusual case involved Representative Thomas Blanton of Texas, who had somehow managed to insert a dirty speech in the *Congressional Record*. Blanton's sly scheme was soon discovered and the offensive material dropped from all but the unbound copies of the *Record*, which are nor mally thrown out in a few weeks to make way for the permanent volumes. As a result, our only clue today to the Texan's lurid prose is in the Speaker's censuring charge that the congressman had inserted

> foul and obscene matter, which you know you could not have spoken on the floor; and that disgusting matter, which could not

have been circulated through the mails in any other publication without violating the law, was transmitted as part of the proceedings of this house to thousands of homes and libraries throughout the country, to be read by men and women and worst of all by children, whose prurient curiosity it would excite and corrupt.

No permanent sense of outrage enveloped either Blanton's colleagues or his constituents, however. He was unanimously censured—who was prepared to vote for obscenity in 1921?—but only after the House refused to expel him. No one back in Texas seemed concerned a bit. Blanton continued to serve in the House, with one short break for an unsuccessful Senate race, until 1937.

For all practical purposes, expulsion has never been used by either house except to unseat rebels during the Civil War. The only three House members ever expelled, of twenty against whom charges were brought, were accused of support of the Confederacy in 1861. Since that time, the technical charge of expulsion has served as a procedural prelude to the slap-on-the-wrist punishment of censure on seven successive occasions.

Expulsion charges have been raised in the Senate twenty-eight times but approved on only fifteen of them, and fourteen of these involved Southern members during the Civil War. The only other case goes back to 1797 when Senator William Blount, down on his luck, took the British sovereign to persuade Indians to join some of his Tennessee constituents in a raid on Spanish Florida—not treason, perhaps, but a bit too much internationalism for his colleagues to take. No attempt to expel a senator has been made in the past thirty years.

Conflict of interest arises from the opportunity to convert public influence into private profit. Often conflict cases do not involve major voting or policy decisions but the day-to-day routine of congressional life. Take nepotism. For longer than anyone can remember, members of Congress have carried relatives on the public payroll. Some of them have been skilled, productive workers, responsive to their employer and willing to put in hours that no one else would. Others were a fraud on the taxpayers and particularly the congressman's constituents, drawing good salaries for little or no work. Still others fell somewhere in between, providing service well below the value of their reward but overlooked because they were wives, sons, nephews, or cousins.

It was obviously impossible for some kind of congressional agency to decide in each of these cases who was earning his pay and who was not. It would have embarrassed the members, which isn't done, and could logically have led to applying the same sort of productivity standards to all congressional employees, a large and probably self-defeating job. So the only real answer was a flat ban on the hiring of kinfolk. Then the question of abuse could never arise.

Some members talked about such a prohibition from time to time, but there weren't very many of them and they didn't talk very loud. So it came as something of a shock in 1967 when Representative Neal Smith, a forty-seven-year-old farmer-lawyer from Iowa, succeeded in doing something about the issue, dragging it out into the daylight where it could not be ignored any longer.

The House was in the Committee of the Whole, working over amendments to a civil service bill, when Smith proposed a flat ban on the employment of close relatives by federal officials, including members of Congress. It was one of those magic moments when Congress, having dodged an embarrassing issue for years— 178, in this case—is shamed into casting a record vote for decency over iniquity. On a standing division, the Smith amendment was adopted 49–33; no one was even bold enough to object that a quorum had not been present, so the action went through unchallenged.

When the bill came up in the full House, no member had the nerve to propose striking the ban on nepotism. Nor was the Senate prepared to defend the odious practice when the bill got there; in fact, it extended the ban to sons-in-law as well as blood relatives. The resulting law, needless to say, did not dislodge relatives already on the payroll but righteously turned away those who might apply in the future.

Another area where ethics complicate congressional housekeeping is the "office fund," money collected from concerned constituents to help a senator or representative function, mechanically rather than politically, above the minimum level afforded by the government allowances. It was the discovery of such a fund that proved so embarrassing to Senator Richard Nixon in 1952 when he was running for Vice President, and most congressmen who use the system have since gone to some lengths to keep it quiet.

Not Charles Percy. The wealthy young corporation executive was elected to the Senate in 1966 by defeating the aging Senator Paul Douglas, probably the most scrupulous man in the institution's history (he sent back all gifts worth more than $2.50). Percy soon learned that an ambitious freshman representing a big state needed far more operating money than the staff and travel allowances provided, but he was determined to keep everything above board. So the Illinois Republican let it be known to his constituents that he was raising $100,000 to underwrite the cost of a really modern and efficient Senate office and that anyone who gave $500 or more was to become an "unofficial adviser." His letters would be routed directly to the senator, and he would receive periodic special briefings on the inside news from Capitol Hill. After a few months of comments from people with $500 who thought they were being black-jacked and people without $500 who thought they were being discriminated against, the scheme was quietly dropped.

After much soul-searching, the Senate decided in its 1968 ethics code to permit members to accept contributions to help meet the cost of travel, printing, radio and television reports to constituents, telephone, telegraph, postage, and stationery as they exceed the regular allowances. The bar association study concluded that members should "avoid" such funds but, if they could not, should disclose all contributions and expenditures, which seems like a minimum requirement.

Gifts to members of Congress are very little discussed, mostly because they are very little known. In the major scandal of the Eisenhower Administration, Bernard Goldfine was indicted for influence peddling and jailed for tax evasion, and Sherman Adams, the President's right-hand man, was dismissed from the White House for accepting favors. But not one thing happened to three Republican senators from New England who had accepted $1,200 worth of free hotel rooms from Goldfine. One regrettable interpretation was that the public did not find it out of the ordinary for members of Congress to be on the take.

The bar association study recommended that no member be permitted to receive "a substantial personal gift" from anyone other than a relative. To help enforce such a ban, members would be required to report all gifts worth more than $25 that they receive from nonrelatives, as part of a comprehensive disclosure system.

If nepotism, gifts and office expenses are minor-league problems, conflict of interest can raise major questions at a higher level. What, very simply, is to be done with a man like Senator Russell Long? Chairman of the Senate Finance Committee, which has jurisdiction over special tax treatment given the oil industry, he feels free to say, "Most of my income is from oil and gas. I don't regard it as any conflict of interest. My state produces more oil and gas per acre than any state in the union. If I didn't represent the oil and gas industry, I wouldn't represent the state of Louisiana."

Or what about Senator James Eastland of Mississippi, third-ranking Democrat on the Senate Agriculture Committee, which processes all farm subsidy legislation? In 1970, Eastland Plantation Inc., the family corporation, received $163,000 in cotton subsidies for its 5,200 acres of rich delta farmland. Later the same year, Congress enacted a ceiling of $55,000 on the amount of subsidy any "person" could receive. Eastland resourcefully split his corporation into six new units—one each for himself and his four children and a new family corporation—and in 1971 their total cotton subsidy was $160,000. (There was another minor change in the law that the artful Mississippian was unable to find his way around.)

And there is Representative Seymour Halpern, then third-ranking Republican on the House Banking Committee, who was revealed by the *Wall Street Journal* in 1969 to have borrowed $40,000 from the First National City Bank of New York. This friendly loan was made without any security at the lowest available interest rate at a time when bank-holding-company legislation, in which First National City had a specific interest, was before the committee. In a sterling piece of investigative reporting, Jerry Landauer discovered that at the time of the loan Halpern was already in debt for over $75,000 to thirteen other banks. The next year, in an unusually direct response, the House voted to require its members to disclose the name of any creditor from whom they had borrowed $10,000 or more for ninety days or more without collateral—but not the size of the loan. What happened to Halpern himself? Well, in the 1970 election, the Queens County Democratic organization did not even bother to run a candidate against him, a courtesy he had never been extended before. Re-elected, he was transferred in 1971 to the bottom of the seniority ladder on the House Foreign Affairs Committee, a position unlikely to provide as much support for his credit rating as his former assignment. That was the sum total of his punishment.

It is this sort of situation, multiplied many times over, that led the bar association to recommend, rather modestly it would seem, that every senator and representative "should, if reasonably possible, avoid all economic interests which may be specially affected by legislation within the jurisdiction of his committee." To reinforce this principle, the study also concluded that each committee should make mandatory rules about members' and employees' financial interests in matters coming before it, tailored in each case to the particular subject matter.

Realistically, it is not all that important how a member votes on the floor, where his individual influence is merged in the collective decision of 100 or 400 others. But in committee, where a relatively small number of votes can control, where personal influence is effective, where seniority is power, where virtually all the basic legislative decisions are made—there, the private interests of an oil baron or a corporate landowner can have tremendous impact, for the nation's good or for his own.

Very damned little would have been done about congressional ethics had it not been for three particularly offensive scandals that found their way to daylight during the 1960's. Speaking of the tentative self-regulation that resulted, the bar association report said:

> To a great extent, Congress embraced such codes and committees under the force of public opinion. They would not have arrived without the impetus of the Baker, Powell, and Dodd cases. The general reluctance to use self-discipline is still in the background

and could be a key factor in the effectiveness of the new codes and committees.

These three cases have been extensively explored in newspapers, magazines, and books. Suffice it here to indicate briefly what they showed the country about how the congressional process can be perverted and corrupted and how only a full-scale investigation, forced upon unwilling colleagues, can get at the shocking truth.

THE BAKER CASE. When Bobby Baker became secretary of the Senate majority in 1955 at the designation of Senator Lyndon Johnson, the twenty-six-year-old lawyer and former Senate page from Pickens, South Carolina, was worth $11,000. When he was forced to resign eight years later, he was worth $1.7 million, according to official government estimates. His peak salary during the period was $19,600, so something must have been going on.

Some of what was going on, it developed in the course of a Senate investigation, a civil suit, and a criminal action that finally sent Baker to jail in 1971, was the following:

• A newly chartered Washington bank of which he was a stockholder gave Baker a $125,000 mortgage for the full value of a home without down payment, any security, or any investigation. A bank officer reported: "Mr. Baker's position with the United States Government recommends our serious consideration to the transaction, as he is a gentleman with innumerable friendships and connections whose good office in behalf of our bank could be very valuable in our growth." Grammar about on a par with judgment.

• Baker was cornered on a tax, theft, fraud, and conspiracy charge that centered on his acceptance of $100,000 from California savings and loan officials to distribute as "campaign contributions" to members of both houses who might be helpful on a pending bill to increase savings and loan taxes. There was evidence that the Senate secretary kept $80,000 of this, but he said he had passed it over to Senator Robert Kerr. By that time, alas, the Oklahoma oil millionaire was dead and the truth had been obscured.

• A two-year investigation by the Senate Rules Committee found Baker guilty of "gross impropriety" and recommended that all senators and key employees disclose their sources of income. Instead of accepting this proposal, the Senate set up a new Committee on Standards and Conduct to study the idea some more; this group did nothing at all until Senator Thomas Dodd complained to it that he was being maligned in the press, of which more shortly.

• When the Baker scandal was in full bloom, President Johnson cut the errant young man adrift without the slightest compunction, telling a national television audience that Baker was merely "an employee of theirs [the senators], no protégé of anyone." Since Senator Johnson had placed Baker on the platform from which he operated and had, at the very least, fostered his career, this denial took "breathtaking audacity," according to Rowland Evans and Robert Novak in their estimable book *Lyndon B. Johnson: The Exercise of Power*. It took that, all right, and it was also a classic example of the law of the political jungle: he who gets caught cannot expect mercy or even notice, only to be left along the trail to die.

THE POWELL CASE. Adam Clayton Powell was not punished by the House for any gross breach of ethics, for any use of his position in Congress for private profit. Instead, his downfall stands for the proposition that the House, which will put up with almost anything in a member—and has—will ultimately reject a man who seems bent on destroying its reputation along with his own.

The trouble with the flamboyant Harlem minister was his exhibitionism: when Adam broke the rules, he wanted everyone to know about it, to see that a black man could do it, too. No one would have questioned his putting his wife on the congressional payroll for $20,500 if she were living in Washington or back in the district. But living year round in Puerto Rico? Few were in a position to protest his government-financed junkets, accompanied by a comely secretary. But *two* comely secretaries? Powell had been convicted of libel in the New York courts, and House members recognized that that could happen to any politician.

But when he refused to pay his judgment, had mounting contempt fines slapped on top of it, and made a circus of returning to New York to preach on Sunday, the only day when he was protected from process servers, it was just too much.

Like Joe McCarthy in the Senate a decade earlier, although in a very different social and political framework, Powell had seriously embarrassed the House. Like McCarthy, he refused to cooperate with a reluctantly ordered investigation, the final indignity to the institution. A special committee recommended censure of Powell for "gross misconduct," but early in 1967 the House, its anger no longer containable, voted instead to exclude him, to deny him the seat to which he had been elected the previous November.

Other than demonstrating that there is a limit to the House's tolerance for its members' misdeeds, the Powell case was important legally. After his exclusion, Powell went to court to claim his seat and, more than two years later, the Supreme Court held he had been entitled to it. (He had already gained political vindication by running again in 1968 and winning.) The Court decision was carefully hedged: it said the House could not exclude an elected member whose age, citizenship, and residency requirements were intact, as Powell's had been, but it did not rule on whether the House could expel an already-seated member for improper acts during his term. Most important for the future was the Court's decision that it could set aside an internal action by the House as long as an unconstitutional act was involved, thereby violating the doctrine of the separation of legislative and judicial powers. The Court gave a nod to the doctrine, however, by saying it lacked the power to order House leaders to reinstate Powell but was able to order House employees—the clerk, sergeant at arms, and doorkeeper—to pay him and admit him to the chamber and his office.

But Powell lost the last round after all. A year and seven days after his court victory, the voters of Harlem finally gave up on Adam and chose his Democratic primary opponent, a hardworkin black lawyer named Charles Rangel, to fill the House seat. Less than two years later in May of 1972, Powell died after an operation in a Miami hospital, where he had been flown from self-exile in the Bahamas.

THE DODD CASE. In 1966, a series of well-documented attacks on the behavior of Senator Thomas Dodd of Connecticut began to appear in the syndicated newspaper column of Drew Pearson and Jack Anderson. It soon became clear that the columnists had access to copies of revealing records in the Dodd files; it was less clear what motivated staff aides who leaked them. In any event, the reports charged that Dodd had held fund-raising dinners to finance his 1964 re-election campaign and then diverted a fair share of the money, at least $116,000 out of $450,000, to his personal use; that Dodd had repeatedly billed the Senate for airplane fares for which he was also reimbursed by groups that invited him to speak; that he had improperly used his position as a senator to assist a publicity agent for West Germany, Julius Klein.

The last charge stung Dodd, and he asked the new Senate Select Committee on Standards and Conduct, created in the wake of Bobby Baker, for an investigation. He got more than he bargained for. Reporting a year later, the committee dropped the Klein charge but recommended that the senator be censured on the other two. His colleagues had little choice, for Dodd had agreed to a bill of particulars that conceded most of the facts of his conduct, an action in which the purloined records left him little choice.

The Senate voted, 92–5, to censure Dodd on the charge of pocketing campaign funds, but it refused, by a 51–45 vote, to take the same stand on the double-billing count, which he insisted had been a matter of poor bookkeeping. Presumably some of his colleagues were familiar with this sort of problem. The question of whether Dodd owed back taxes on some or all of this shady income was referred to the Internal Revenue Service, but no charges ever resulted, despite the fact that a corporation that had given him an illegal $8,000 contribution was fined $5,000. When there is any other option, members of Congress rarely get prosecuted.

Dodd declined to seek the Democratic nomination for his seat in 1970, knowing the Connecticut party organization was prepared to dump him. Instead, he ran as an independent, finishing third with a quarter of the vote. He cannot be fully credited with electing the Republican candidate, Lowell Weicker, however, for many of the more conservative Dodd votes would probably have gone Republican, anyway, had he not insisted on running. Six months later, he was dead of a heart attack.

As a result of these cases, a suddenly self-conscious Congress created two watchdog groups: the Senate Select Committee on Standards and Conduct and the House Committee on Standards of Official Conduct. (Interhouse Rule: never use the same name when a different one can be thought up). The Senate moved first, in 1964, prodded by the matter of Bobby Baker, but its committee got involved in the Dodd case and did not produce an ethics code until 1968. The House named a study committee after the Powell exclusion in 1967, then created a permanent committee and adopted its own code, also in 1968.

The Senate ethics code danced around the edges of the Baker and Dodd cases. It prohibits officers or employees of the Senate from paid outside activity that is "inconsistent" with their duties on the Hill and requires them to report any such work. It bars Senate employees from receiving contributions, except for one or more staff aides publicly designated by each senator. Proceeds of a fund-raising event can only be accepted if the senator approves it in advance and gives a complete accounting.

The disclosure system for senators is really not disclosure at all, although it could have some inhibitory effect on misconduct. It requires each member to put in a sealed envelope each year: a copy of his income tax return and a list of all businesses with which he has a connection, all real or personal property worth more than $10,000, any interest in a trust of $10,000 or more, any debt of $5,000 or more, and all gifts worth $50 or more.

These envelopes are filed with the comptroller general, the chief auditor of Congress, but nothing at all happens to them unless the senator gets into trouble. Then the Conduct Committee, by majority vote, can open the envelope and use its contents as the basis for an investigation. There is nothing, of course, to prevent any senator from leaving some facts out of his envelope, doctoring those he does file, or, for that matter, filing blank sheets of paper. If his situation gets hot enough so that a Senate investigation is on the way, a careless disclosure file is unlikely to add much to his problems.

The only public filing required by the Senate code covers honorariums of $300 or more from speeches, magazine articles, or books, gifts of more than $50, and all contributions from fund-raising events, both those devoted to the campaign and those applied to office expenses. So far, the honorarium figures have been the most enlightening, showing that a prominent senator can double his income on the lecture circuit. In 1970, for example, Senator Birch Bayh of Indiana earned $44,300, and Senator Mark Hatfield of Oregon $41,900. Most senators charge from $1,000 to $1,200 for a commercial appearance.

The House Conduct Committee has its powers spelled out more explicitly. It may give advisory opinions at the request of a member. Equally divided between the two political parties as the Senate committee is, it cannot take any action without seven of the twelve votes. It may take up a case on its own initiative, on a written complaint from a member, or on a complaint from an outsider after three members have refused to transmit it to the committee.

The ethics committee has proved less than bold in initiating clean-up activity. Representative John Dowdy of Texas was convicted of bribery and perjury in December, 1971, and sentenced two months later to eighteen months in federal prison and a $25,000 fine. Three months after that, the committee was still waiting for someone to complain that Dowdy should not continue to serve in the House, because he was a convicted criminal.

The Texan felt secure. He told a news conference that any House action against him would be "going against two hundred years of history." He appeared not to be embarrassed by the fact that his wife, J. D. Dowdy, was campaigning to suceeed him while holding a $22,000 job as a clerk in his office or by charges that he had franked her political literature. The whole thing, he insisted, was a plot by homosexuals, urban renewal interests, and the Eastern liberal establishment. (Mrs. Dowdy lost.)

The House code roughly parallels that of the Senate, but its disclosure system is more informative and thus, presumably, more effective. The code prohibits members from accepting compensation "by virtue of influence improperly exerted," accepting any gift from anyone interested directly in legislation, receiving excessive honorariums, converting campaign funds to personal use, or putting people who do not work on the payroll.

Under the House disclosure system, all sources of income are a public record, but the amounts are kept secret. A representative must list any business in which he has an interest of $5,000 or more, or from which he derives income of $1,000 or more, but only if it does "substantial business" with the federal government or is federally regulated. It will presumably take a good many case-by-case decisions by the committee, the House, or the courts—if, indeed, any such are forthcoming—before we know precisely what that means.

A representative must also list publicly the name of any professional organization, such as a law firm, in which he is an officer, director, partner, or consultant and from which he gets $1,000 a year or more. Also the source of any income or capital gain exceeding $5,000 a year and any reimbursement for expenses over $1,000 a year.

The bar association study is summed up in a model code of conduct and a set of model disclosure rules for all of Congress, both of them more comprehensive than either house has yet enacted. These are the major conduct rules:

- A member shall conduct himself at all times so as to reflect credit upon the Congress.
- He shall not use official power for personal economic benefit and shall try to avoid situations where he might seem to be doing so.
- He shall avoid personal economic interests in areas within the jurisdiction of any committee on which he serves.
- When he must vote or otherwise act in an area of personal economic interest, a member shall consider either eliminating

his interest or abstaining from action, but he need not do so if, in effect, he plans to vote against his own interest.

Under the bar association's disclosure rules, a member or any congressional employee earning $18,000 a year or more would identify yearly to the ethics committee of his house any real or personal property he owned worth more than $5,000 except for his home and furnishings, personal effects, bank balance, and insurance. He would also identify the source of any income over $1,000 a year, debts of over $5,000 except his home mortgage, honorariums over $300, and gifts over $25 from other than family members. In all instances, the sources would be public but the figures sealed.

A member's property would be considered as including that of his wife or husband and their minor children, assets of any corporation controlled by him or his family, assets of any partnership of which he is a member, and assets of trusts of which he is a beneficiary unless it is an irrevocable "blind" trust under which he had no knowledge of the assets. The model code would permit the "office fund" but require full public reporting of all contributions and expenditures.

These recommendations probably represent as balanced an approach as is possible to minimize the opportunity for congressional misdeed while preserving some legitimate personal privacy for the members. At the very least, filing of annual reports by members would be a regular reminder of potential conflict situations; at best, an alert press would be able to report, for each major vote, which members participating had direct financial interests in the outcome.

But we are still a long way from such a "model" Congress. The House disclosure system, while a major step forward, is too vague as to what private interests must be publicly reported. In the Senate, where nothing consequential is made public, Birch Bayh put the bar association's disclosure rules in bill form and introduced them in 1970 and again in 1971. Not until late in the second year was enough interest generated among the members and their leaders even to call a hearing.

And it is not hard to see why. To demonstrate the need for

such rules, it would be necessary to rake over some of the old examples of members who abused their trust, perhaps even discover a few new ones. And that is simply never, never done. Congress, on the whole, would rather run the chance of remaining privately corrupt than submit to public embarrassment.

# 15 · You Wouldn't Believe the Way They Keep the Books

Imagine, if you will, the UniStuff Corporation, a huge multibillion-dollar national complex, which lets each of its thirteen divisions decide how much to spend each year, completely independent of the others and, just incidentally, of total corporate income.

To make sure these spending decisions are sound, each UniStuff division has not one Expenditure Board but two. First, one board devotes months to the secret drafting of a spending list; then the second, without consulting the first, rewrites the list any way it sees fit. Finally, top officers of both boards meet and try to fit together the two spending lists into one. Not surprisingly, there is often considerable disagreement.

None of UniStuff's freewheeling thirteen divisions pays the least attention to what the others are planning to spend or to any total figure for the corporation. Nor are they concerned with how much income the corporation may take in to cover all their spending. That is up to an Income Commission (also with two separate boards), which recommends its own figure to the corporation's directors, without any consultation with the Expenditure boards. Then they all sit back and hope the corporation will remain solvent.

From time to time, some of the UniStuff's directors get a

feeling that the Jet Engine Division ought to be spending a little more and the Buggy Whip Division a little less, what with the way transportation is going, but there isn't a damned thing they can do about it. From time immemorial, the board has taken up each division's spending plans one at a time, without any reference to the others, and UniStuff isn't about to change that orderly system. Every year, the chairman of the board does mail the corporation a set of financial guidelines, hoping the Income Commission and the Expenditure boards will pay some attention to them. Sometimes they do, and sometimes they don't. Mostly, they go on as they have for years, free, independent, and almost totally without order or restraint. It's a good thing UniStuff has a monopoly in its field, or the corporation just might go bankrupt.

With very few liberties, that is precisely the way Congress raises money for the \$200-billion-a-year U.S. Government and determines how it should be spent. The system is antiquated, slipshod, cumbersome, and almost totally without organization or defensible rationale. It presents an open invitation, concurrently, to petty politicking and the grossest kind of irresponsible fiscal mismanagement. The operation is nothing short of a national disgrace. Congress likes it.

Congress feels that way because the present appropriation and tax system provides its members with power. Not power of real scope and dimension that could reshape the executive structure and strengthen the legislative function, but power in small manageable units. The power of a member of the House Defense Appropriations Subcommittee to influence the location of a new army base in his district. The power of a Senate Finance Committee member to sponsor successfully an amendment providing special tax treatment for an industry whose profits affect his state's economy.

Although there have been sporadic attempts since World War II to introduce some order and unity into congressional fiscal planning, all have failed. As we shall see, the main obstacle has always been the members' preference for the present ante-bellum, counting-house system; they understand how it works, it fits (or can be made to seem to fit) into their work load, and they can turn it to modest political profit from time to time. The fact that this nonsystem is robbing Congress of great potential influence and failing the nation bothers few of them in the least.

Recently, some senators and representatives have begun to raise intermittent objections to their fiscal role, but, with a few exceptions, their concern has been directed at the fact that the manifestly imperfect system is not even meeting its own very limited goals rather than at the fact that it is manifestly imperfect to begin with.

Representative George Mahon, the House Appropriations chairman and a pillar of the congressional establishment, is probably as reluctant as any member to concede institutional failure. But one morning late in 1971, the Texan told the House Rules Committee, "Congress is not breaking down, but to some extent it has already broken down, in terms of the business we're trying to transact."

The occasion was revealing. Four months after the 1971–72 fiscal year had already begun on July 1, Mahon was seeking Rules clearance, not for four unpassed, long overdue appropriations bills to get to the floor, but for a temporary continuing resolution instead. It would provide emergency funding at the previous year's level, to keep these four major areas of the government running until the appropriation bills could be processed and passed, which was clearly going to take weeks, perhaps months, more. By the time they became law, the year they covered would be half over; in fact, one of them was not enacted until well into 1972.

This congressional inability to meet the constitutional deadline, this failure to let the government know what it is entitled to spend until the spending period is part over, is not the exception on Capitol Hill. It is the rule. In the last full term of Lyndon Johnson and the first two years of Richard Nixon, only six of some eighty regular appropriations bills were actually enacted before their fiscal year opened in July; eight did not become law until after the following January 1, more than six months late.

In the worst congressional showing yet, the 1970 fiscal year, the first appropriations bill that managed to clear both houses —it only covered 2 per cent of the budget—was not enacted until October 8, and two of the money bills were still unpassed at the late December adjournment. One of them did not finally make the grade until the next March.

So accustomed have Congress and its observers become to this slovenly practice that the signature by President Nixon on July 22, 1969, of a $4.4 billion supplemental appropriations bill for the fiscal year that had ended three weeks earlier aroused almost no public attention at all. Legal authorities believe it was almost certainly unconstitutional to appropriate money for a fiscal year already closed, but no one went to court so nothing happened.

As anyone who has ever operated on a budget can imagine, this failure to provide money for the government until long after it is due creates immense confusion and uncertainty. All the vast apparatus of one or more departments and agencies is plunged into fiscal darkness; bills pile up, as no one knows how much money is going to be forthcoming for any one of its functions. Bad programs that Congress intends to cut back proceed full force. Imaginative new programs, even those for which authorization bills have been enacted, cannot be begun. (Authorization is congressional approval to proceed with a government project or program; specifically, it involves passage of a bill that is the result of study by a regular standing committee. Appropriation is congressional approval of money to fund such a project or program; it involves passage of a second separate bill that comes from—and can only come from—the appropriations committee. Authorization without appropriation is merely a statement of intent. No action results.)

The impact of long postponed appropriations is felt far beyond the federal government. State and local governments depend heavily on the billions of dollars of assistance they get from Washington. When they have no assurance that the money is forthcoming, they cannot proceed with their schools and hospitals and highways. States can borrow from their reserves—if they have any—on the assumption the federal money will be along later, but they run a risk.

Even the President suffers a loss of power. Department heads find it necessary to by-pass the White House and make informal private deals with the appropriations committee and subcommittee chairmen so they can gain enough confidence to move forward in the fiscal vacuum. "The bureaucracy proceeds to conduct ongoing activities in default of policy determinations," the Committee for Economic Development observed. "The resulting stagnation and confusion are indefensible and, in our view, intolerable." (The Committee, a private research group of businessmen and educators, noted ominously that a device very like the continuing resolution—stopgap financing awaiting an overdue legislative decision—became common in France during nearly a century of the Third and Fourth republics. When the Fifth Republic under de Gaulle produced a new constitution in 1962, the powers of the national assembly were considerably curtailed.)

But Congress's inability to meet its financial deadlines is only a surface manifestation of a much deeper and more pervasive disorder. As it is now structured, the institution is totally incapable of making reasoned judgments on the relative merit of funding one project over another or the balance between overall income and expenditure, the two areas in which it presumably should be the most active.

Numerous books, too many of them dull, academic, and thus ignored, have been devoted to single aspects of this critically important and very complex problem. What follows here is a simplified layman's view of how the system evolved, what it does and does not do, and how it can, perhaps, be changed. Difficult as the entire problem may seem, there can be no responsive, authoritative Congress in the future without a rigorous revision of its vital money-management function now.

In the early days of Congress, the fledgling Republic's modest financial affairs were handled, like almost all matters of concern, by select committees, which were created individually to process a specific bill and were then disbanded. House Ways and Means, established in 1802, was one of the first of the standing or permanent committees that have since come to dominate virtually all activity off the floor. It was given the power both to levy taxes and to appropriate funds, which seemed logical enough. By 1865, this work load had become too heavy, however, and a separate Appropriations Committee was created and entrusted with all spending authority.

With that act, although probably no one recognized it at the time, Congress ceded a major part of its fiscal authority to the executive branch. As long as one committee controlled both taxing and spending, it could pretty much write its own budget, raising or lowering total income and outgo, or readjusting them to produce whatever surplus or deficit was desirable or tolerable. But when the two functions were separated, the real power to lay out the budget passed to the President. He set income and outgo figures, and each pair of committees tended thereafter to maneuver within his limits. There may have been some taxing-to-spending committee communication in the early years, but there is essentially none today, and Ways and Means and Appropriations go on their stubbornly separate paths with little choice but to accept the basic structure of the President's budget and tinker with the details.

This transfer of power to the executive did not take place fully until 1921 when Congress passed a sweeping new budget act designed to pull things together. Before that time, under a mind-boggling system that had evolved out of necessity and greed, each government department had applied directly to the appropriations committees for its funds, without any reference to each other or much to the President's desires.

Beginning with President Harding's appointment of the nation's first budget director, Charles Dawes (later Vice President), things changed. Every department had to pass its spending requests through the White House, where they were included in —or excluded from—the President's over-all financial plan. If they were excluded or reduced, department heads were forbidden to discuss the fact when summoned before the congressional spending committees.

The prohibition still exists, but Administration loyalty often wilts in the heat of an agency head's desire to get his hands on some more money. A typical exchange in a Senate appropriations subcommittee hearing:

*Senator Blunt:* Mr. Director, the budget shows you have only asked for $50 million for your new sludgepot program. I thought this was a much bigger proposition.

*Director:* That is our request, Senator.

*Senator Blunt:* I don't have to tell you that sludgepots are very big in my state's economy. Now, if you really wanted to get this exciting new program off the ground, how much would you need? How much could you really use?

*Director:* Well, Senator, if you put it that way, I don't think $75 million for the first year would be too much at all.

And there goes the old budget again.

In any event, for the past fifty years the system has been operating about the same way. Departments and agencies submit their requests for the next fiscal year to the White House—now to the Office of Budget and Management—where they are carefully analyzed, usually trimmed, and finally incorporated in an over-all spending plan. This may include a request for new taxes to bring the budget into balance or near balance, or it may rely solely on revenue produced by existing taxes.

The budget is sent to Congress with a lengthy explanation by the President, then dismembered into thirteen weighty pieces, each of which is entrusted to a House appropriations subcommittee. Action always starts in the House rather than Senate committee, out of a curious combination of custom, quasi-authority, and inertia. The Constitution provides that "all bills for raising revenue shall originate in the House of Representatives," and this has been extended in practice to cover all bills for spending revenue as well.

This rather liberal interpretation almost certainly goes back to the time when the same House committee handled both tax and appropriations bills, and it seemed logical to have them proceed together through Congress, rather than begin at opposite ends of the Capitol and cross at midsession. (If you can find anything logical in the congressional fiscal process, hang onto it.) The arrangement was also reasonable because the much larger House had more manpower to devote to examining the detailed appropriation bills; the present fifty-five Appropriations Committee members do not serve on any other committee.

But the custom also involved a very substantial grant of extra power to the House, one that the Constitution never clearly envisioned. (Exclusive power to originate tax bills was given to the House because, for the first 125 years of the nation, it was the only body whose members were elected directly by the people, who could thus turn them out if displeased.) For, as the system developed, it became clear that most of the major spending decisions were reached by the House and left intact by the Senate, where there was little time or inclination to rework them extensively. From time to time, the Senate has expressed official resentment or even resistance to this assumption of spending authority by the House, but never with any conspicuous success. In the Great Appropriations Impasse of 1962, a combination of interhouse hostility and leadership senility brought Congress to a halt for several months over the issues of where the appropriations conference should meet in the Capitol and who should head it. In the end, the Senate gave ground, sharing some of its conference control without any House concession of appropriating power in return.

Before any House appropriations bill can be brought to the floor, one or more authorization bills covering the same area of activity must have passed Congress and been signed by the President. It stands to reason that the House Appropriations Committee cannot draw up a complete spending plan until it knows all the projects and programs that the standing committees, the full Congress, and the President want put into operation. This requirement contributes substantially to Congress's perennial failure to meet the July 1 appropriations deadline. The standing committees are slow in passing the authorization bills, often delaying key measures into the summer and fall, and the appropriation bills get stacked up behind them, like a string of planes circling National Airport awaiting clearance to land.

Authorization bills are often far from flawless. The dollar figures they set do not guarantee any spending at all but merely fix a maximum figure for the program involved, and that figure is often deliberately misleading. An enthusiastic committee will push through an authorization bill with a popular $10 million plan in it, with full knowledge that the initial appropriation is unlikely to run more than $500,000. Alternatively, a committee fearful of public reaction to the ultimate cost of, say, the Rayburn House Office Building (over $100 million), will pass an authorization bill for $10 million worth of plans and foundation work. The members know this is only the beginning, that there will be further authorizations, year after year, to keep piling floors and rooms on top of that foundation. The members know, but many of the innocent taxpayers do not.

The power of the appropriators is considerable and, to a degree little realized outside the inner circle of Congress, highly concentrated. It resides primarily in the chairman and ranking minority member of each of the House appropriations subcommittees. (The House has thirteen of these, the Senate one more to process the late-session supplemental bill that covers all last-minute authorizations, a job the full committee handles in the House.) The chairman and ranking minority member on the Senate subcommittees are also very influential, but by the time the bills get over to the Senate their basic form has been largely resolved. The subcommittee leaders there make significant increases in some programs, add new ones, and occasionally even cut, but they do not usually reshape the House product to any meaningful degree. That House product is, to a very real extent, the work of the subcommittee chairman and his senior colleague of the minority party, superimposed on a background of staff recommendations. This is true because the subcommittees are small, from seven to eleven members, and their leaders, by dint of long years of service on the group, are the most familiar with the area of jurisdiction. In some subcommittees these two men—at this writing there is one woman on the fifty-five member House Appropriations Committee—meet informally before the official mark-up sessions and thrash out most of the controversial questions. And that is generally that.

Any appropriations subcommittee member can always challenge the leadership and force a vote on his amendment to raise spending here or cut it there, but it isn't done too often. These subcommittees are much like small private clubs, where the initiates do not overpresume. Party lines mean very little; any division is more likely to reflect liberal-conservative or urban-rural distinctions. The senior members lay out the plan. Adjustments are made to accommodate members of middle seniority, considerably fewer for their juniors.

Once this House subcommittee bill is prepared, something approaching 90 per cent of the basic decisions have been reached. The full House Appropriations Committee makes few changes as each subcommittee defers to the others' autonomy and expertise; indeed, it is almost regarded as bad manners to question subcommittee decisions. In general, the full House follows this policy of respect. Floor amendments to appropriations bills are voted, and occasionally there is a pitched battle over one or more items, but relatively few changes are made altogether.

Appropriations mark-up in the Senate subcommittee is often even more of a private, two-man process than in the House, with members shuttling in and out of the executive session as their schedules permit and the chairman and ranking minority members presiding over the real multimillion-dollar decisions. Here, in the current Democratic congresses, a Republican probably has more power than in almost any other situation. The chairman may not accept all the proposals of his senior colleague of the other party, but the minority member rarely fails to win those changes for which he is willing to press as important to him or his constituency.

There are often areas in which the chairman rules almost autocratically. When Senator Lister Hill of Alabama was chairman of the Labor-HEW Appropriations Subcommittee, his particular province was the National Institutes of Health, in which he reposed great confidence. He always inquired solicitously how much more money they needed than the House had allowed, wrote it into the bill, and then announced to the subcommittee that these were the new figures. It was understood that no one ever challenged Hill in this area, certainly not if he wanted consideration later for a pet project of his own.

A senator who has something special he wants to get into an appropriations bill as it goes through the Senate, even if he is a member of the subcommittee himself, would do well to approach the chairman or ranking minority member or both early, before they can hold any informal mark-up. If he waits to submit his amendment at the formal committee drafting session, it may be too late, with the decisions already made. A senator who does not play the game can lose a prized appropriation item, even though it cleared the subcommittee, the full committee, and the Senate floor. In 1963, just out of his freshman term, Senator William Proxmire of Wisconsin succeeded in persuading his committee colleagues to include in the Interior appropriations bill $3.8 million for a new forest products laboratory in Madison. But, while the bill was on the floor, Proxmire voted against the Democratic majority and for two broad economizing cuts. In conference, the House managers immediately proposed that if Proxmire was so ardent an economizer, he could hardly object to the elimination of his own increase in the budget. No senator objected, and the laboratory died on the spot.

With this sort of final control over all government spending, the Appropriations committees in both houses have traditionally been among the most politically powerful and prestigious, with several members scrambling for appointment to any vacancy. (The other contenders for such ranking are Armed Services in both houses, Foreign Relations and Finance in the Senate, and Ways and Means in the House, with some gradual shifting as events and issues change.) Members like to serve on Appropriations because they can make visible contributions, like public buildings, to their state and district and, at the same time, have influence over a broad range of the affairs of government. In some states, not just the voters but the movers and shakers are impressed by Appropriations members. Stephen Horn, in his illuminating study of the Senate Finance Committee, *Unused Power*, quotes one senator as saying, "The money power structure in my state has its hands in the federal treasury up to its armpits, and I want them to think that I might be able to turn off the faucet."

Other members argue that those who benefit from public spending, with the exception of some construction contractors, are more likely to be garden-variety voters than big campaign contributors. They say that a senator or representative can more readily excite gratitude from the real sources of wealth back home by service on the committees that raise and lower taxes or that regulate business.

Deeply involved in the appropriation process is one of the great unresolved problems of congressional responsibility: governmental oversight. Almost everyone agrees that the Senate and House should devote considerable energy to overseeing the consequences of their legislating. How has the new program worked out? Did the higher research appropriation really achieve something? Is the department carrying out the clear mandate of the new legislation or not?

These questions should be asked and answered, but few members are ready to take on the onerous, unglamorous, unending responsibility. Committee hearings, particularly on appropriations, provide the nearest thing to some kind of continuous oversight that Congress offers today, but most members believe that not enough searching scrutiny is applied. The Government Operations Committees of both houses are normally only aroused to make spot checks, and then most often when a brewing scandal promises publicity.

Congress has an investigatory arm, the General Accounting Office, which was created along with the Budget Bureau in 1921. The idea was that the GAO would help Congress examine the President's budget before it was approved, providing continuing professional and technical expertise. It has never worked out that way. The comptroller general, who presides over GAO, has deployed his investigators and accountants in response to specific congressional inquiries about irregularities and abuses in the executive branch, but very little general oversight has ever resulted.

The process by which Congress parcels out the billions of dollars at its command is very largely a private one, only becoming public when it is too late for the common people to influence most of the basic decisions. House appropriations subcommittee hearings are almost always closed, with the press and public excluded and the only witnesses the heads of agencies and departments who try to justify their budgets. Citizens' groups in areas like conservation and education have no direct access to the proceedings and can only make their views felt if they can find a sympathetic subcommittee member willing to speak up in the closed sessions on their behalf. (The Legislative Reorganization Act of 1970 proclaimed the salutary principle that all committee hearings should be open, but it also provided that they could be closed at any time by a majority vote of the members. The House appropriations subcommittees opened their doors only one chink; all but 8 percent of their 1971 sessions remained closed.)

As a perfunctory nod toward public information, the House Appropriations Committee releases the record of its closed hearings a few days before each appropriations bill is scheduled to reach the floor. But these records are long and windy and only enable members to check on specific projects of interest to their districts. No one could be expected to read this entire record and prepare amendments of any scope or substance in the two or three days between its unveiling and final passage of the bill. Which is precisely the way the committee wants it.

On the Senate side, subcommittee hearings are open, but by this time the great majority of the basic decisions have already been made. A considerable share of the Senate's appropriating task involves deciding just how much of the money the House cut out of the President's budget should be restored. The roles have become fixed and traditional; the House, closer to the people, economizes, while the Senate, more secure and sympathetic to the executive branch, puts money back and adds a few items of its own. Then the conference splits the difference.

But at no point in the entire cycle is there really much opportunity for public participation in the process. It is true that closed hearings and meetings protect the spending subcommittees from a wide variety of fierce pressures from interest groups, public and private. But the appropriation process is so central to the entire operation of the government that it cannot continue as the private preserve of a small group of secretive old men.

Tax legislation, an infinitely complicated and delicate field, can only be considered here in its broad functional role in the congressional financing process. And, despite considerable technical insight into how much a tax will raise, the legislative branch makes only the most diffident attempt to relate the money it raises to the money it spends. Congress has simply never bothered, in the 100 years that these functions have been separate, to set up a system under which taxing and spending can be reconciled.

Part of the problem is related to proven congressional inability to keep up with the fiscal calendar. The standing committees move so slowly that the authorization bills are not approved until well into the year. The delay in turn holds up the appropriation bills, which cannot begin their transcongressional course from the House until the enabling authorization is enacted. And without knowing what the appropriations bill will total, how can the House Ways and Means and Senate Finance committees know whether taxes should be raised or lowered and how much?

The answer is that they can't and they don't. All they can do, under the circumstances, is follow the rough outlines of the President's budget, on the assumption that the appropriations committees will keep within the budget limits, a chancy assumption at best. Or, more accurately, the fiscal committees follow as much of the President's plan as they see fit; they may feel some responsibility to provide about the same level of financing, or they may not. Since the actual spending level determined by Congress remains a mystery until late in the year, they can feel free to raise or lower proposed taxes or replace one with another, more or less at will.

Although individual members have been blaming the Administration since time immemorial for failure to balance the budget, Congress has never felt called upon collectively to shoulder any share of this responsibility, to face up to the problem of raising the money to assure a surplus, or recognizing the utility of a deficit when the state of the economy makes it advisable. (Deficits are nothing new in Washington. In 1792, government income ran $1.4 million below expenditures, which must have been a somewhat unnerving amount when expenditures were only $5 million.)

For several decades now, Congress has been largely content to let the Administration take the initiative on tax legislation, for obvious political reasons. Congress is never happy raising taxes, but to do so at the request of the chief executive is a good deal easier. Particularly if you refuse to give the White House all it asked for or readjust the package and claim improvement. But this is not always the case. In 1969, President Nixon sought no tax changes, but Representative Wilbur Mills, the Ways and Means chairman, decided Congress should take the lead. The result was a massive reshaping of the tax law that increased all exemptions and some deductions under the income tax, raised social security benefits, created a new "minimum tax" on millionaires who had escaped paying, and reduced the special advantage given the oil industry.

When tax revenue begins to fall seriously behind spending, the present congressional machinery is too slow and clumsy to respond, with political reluctance often another inhibiting factor. When the White House is similarly unwilling to face the political consequences of higher taxes, the rickety system, such as it is, comes close to collapsing altogether.

Military activity in Vietnam began to expand rapidly in 1965, but President Johnson did not choose to recognize the financial implications of this decision by seeking higher taxes until 1967, and it took another year for Congress to enact the 10 per cent income tax surcharge. When that tax was heading toward a mid-1969 expiration date, candidate and then President Nixon proved no bolder. He ducked the issue of extending the surcharge during his 1968 campaign and did not request such action until the April after his election. An undereager Congress, unable to comply in two months, improvised a few temporary extensions and finally wrote the surcharge continuation into the tax reform bill signed the last day of the year.

Revenue legislation proceeds through Congress in much the same way that appropriations bills do, but with the Senate generally somewhat more active. By constitutional mandate, tax bills must originate in the House, where they are considered at public hearings, and then drafted in long, closed Ways and Means Committee sessions. When they emerge, the chairman, Representative Mills, traditionally asks the Rules Committee for a closed rule, a ticket to the floor that prohibits any amendment there.

This prohibition is not absolute. The minority always retains the right, under House rules, to make one motion to send any bill back to committee with instructions to change a specific provision, a section, or the entire measure. Aside from that, changes are not permitted in any bill granted a closed rule. That rule is a tacit acknowledgment that revenue legislation is so complex, so technical, and—most important of all—so interwoven with the profit margins of business and industry that it cannot be exposed to the political free-for-all of the House.

The same consideration, operating in reverse, has resulted in the two taxing committees, Ways and Means and Finance, not using subcommittees but always meeting in full. Where the House is too big and unmanageable to handle this delicate work, subcommittees would be too small. Bluntly, if subcommittees operated, a given industry could get a beneficial tax bill past the first round and into the full committee by commanding the loyalty of only a handful of men. Reversing a subcommittee in full committee is unpleasant and uncongressional activity. The risk posed by small, manipulatable revenue subcommittees is too great.

The closed rule does not prevent individual representatives from offering amendments of incalculable value to private interests. It merely restricts that privilege to members of Ways and Means in committee, and this ability to confer vast financial advantage under the guise of correcting inequity puts these twenty-four men and one woman at the power center of Congress. Correspondingly, their chairman, if he is alert to the potential of his role—and Wilbur Mills most certainly is—can be more powerful on occasion than anyone else in the federal establishment except the President. And there have been days when Nixon would argue that point.

In much the same way that departments and agencies whose budgets are cut by the House appeal to the Senate Appropriations Committee, lobbyists whose clients' tax problems have failed to arouse sympathy in the Ways and Means Committee converge upon Senate Finance. The widespread belief that the Senate is overly susceptible to such special interest pressure may be somewhat unfair. The House situation—a tightly controlled committee meeting in closed session, with its bill exempt from change on the floor—leaves most lobbyists little choice but to turn to the Senate.

The Senate Finance Committee has rarely played the role

of innovator, doomed by the Constitution to serving as a review board. But the Senate does rewrite tax bills, and, unlike the House, amendments that are rejected in committee will almost certainly reappear on the floor if the interests behind them are interested enough. For the Senate does not merely reject the authoritarian concept of the House's closed rule but glories in the libertine abandon with which amendments, score upon score, can be proposed on the floor, with no limit on debate or even any requirement that they be germane.

Tax bills are favorite vehicles for unrelated riders. Almost any tax bill of any consequence has a hard nugget of economic necessity at its core; the President cannot veto it without losing the economic stimulus and political popularity of a cut or badly needed revenue from an increase. And nothing draws amendments like a presumably veto-proof bill. In 1966, the relatively modest Foreign Investors Tax Act, designed to curb the flow of dollars abroad, acquired in the Senate a whole host of special interest provisions, even including the first Democratic scheme for public financing of Presidential campaigns.

If some Senate amendments to tax bills are sinister, more are relatively innocent, representing ideas that senators know are unlikely to survive in the conference, even though adopted on the floor. Members press for this sort of unpromising amendment for two reasons: to earn political credit for having labored in a good cause and damned near won, or to set a constructive precedent so that the same proposal will not seem so revolutionary to the conferees and the House the second or third time it appears.

Senate conferees on tax legislation have not competed very successfully with the House managers for some time now. Ways and Means members, led by the resolute Mills who usually has bipartisan backing, wrote the bill in the first place. They are unlikely to accept more than half of any Senate amendments, partly because they fear special interests have been at work, partly out of pride of authorship, and partly because they bloody well intend to demonstrate that the Senate isn't running Congress. On that day.

There is an observers' rule of thumb on the tax, trade, and

social security legislation that comes out of Ways and Means. The House writes 100 per cent of the bill; the Senate, in committee and on the floor, revises about 20 per cent of it; then the conference eliminates about half the Senate amendments. This means, give or take special circumstances, that the Ways and Means Committee writes about 90 per cent of every tax bill that goes to the President, whatever the intervening parliamentary activity. Which goes a long way toward explaining why Chairman Mills, who writes about 90 per cent of what the committee approves, is such a pivotal figure.

Occasionally, the Senate may bend the Constitution a little and originate a tax proposal as an amendment to some House-passed revenue measure. The 10 per cent income tax surcharge of 1968 first appeared as a Senate rider on an innocuous excise tax bill, but it took considerable negotiation to get it back through Mills, his loyal conferees, and the House. This sort of role reversal doesn't happen very often.

Aware that its financial grasp on the government is less than firm, Congress has tried from time to time to use special devices to curb spending and somehow relate it to revenue. One of these is the debt ceiling, first set at $11.5 billion in 1917 as part of a Liberty Bond issue and last seen passing $370 billion, still heading up. The theory is that if Congress refuses to raise this ceiling, the executive branch will have to stop borrowing and start economizing. Former Representative Thomas Curtis of Missouri called this idea about as practical as trying to keep an elevator from going up by holding down the floor indicator arrow, and so it has proved. For one thing, the debt ceiling question has been largely rhetorical; bills to raise the ceiling always pass. Critics fiercely debate and vote against them, but Congress as a whole has never been willing to bring the entire government to a halt by refusing it just a little more borrowing authority.

(The national debt got as low as $37,500—can you believe it? —in 1835 and did not make its real quantum jump until World War II, from $43 billion in 1940 to $259 billion in 1945. If it makes you feel any better, the per capita share of the national debt in 1970, just over $1,800, was $43 lower than the comparable figure for 1945.)

Another device, more recent but little more effective, is the expenditure ceiling. In 1967, the first one was written into a continuing resolution, the stopgap financing move that keeps part of the government running between the opening of a new fiscal year and tardy enactment of appropriations bills to cover it. But, by the end of the session, noncontrollable expenditures such as interest on the national debt had risen more than the ceiling's theoretical reduction in controllable items.

In 1968, Congress added a mandatory $6 billion reduction in expenditures to the income tax surcharge, over agonized protests by the appropriations chairmen, who could feel their hands being ever so gently tied. In 1969, Congress officially called on the President to hold spending to $191.9 billion, or about $1 billion less than he had planned, but both the lawmakers and the chief executive were given ways to get around the figure. The expenditure ceiling is at best an imperfect mechanism; the Committee for Economic Development maintains that both spending and debt ceilings "constitute an evasion of the fundamental responsibility of Congress to set national priorities and to impose limits on specific programs."

It is not difficult to trace Congress's efforts to coordinate and rationalize its taxing and spending work. The tries have been few, and success almost negligible. In 1926, the Joint Committee on Internal Revenue Taxation was created, consisting of the ten senior members of Senate Finance and House Ways and Means and aimed at substituting a unified approach toward tax legislation for the two houses' separate and often conflicting efforts.

On the staff level, the committee has been a resounding success, producing a highly skilled corps of professionals who provide identical technical information and advice to both committees. Its chief of staff, Laurence Woodworth, is the only man on any congressional staff who sits beside the floor manager of legislation in *both* the House and Senate, for guidance on all tax measures. No other adviser is permitted to furnish this kind of continuity and coordination, which says something about congressional separatism. But the committee itself is only a vehicle to justify this single staff for drafting tax legislation. It never meets and makes no attempt at unified planning. Only the constitutional requirement that both House and Senate pass an identical bill, carried out by the conference committee, results in their ultimate agreement on the same changes in the tax structure.

There is also a Joint Committee on the Reduction of Nonessential Federal Expenditures, which makes a contribution in inverse proportion to the length of its name. Created in 1941, it was the private preserve for twenty-five years of the late Senator Harry Byrd of Virginia, the great economizer. Potentially, it could be a strong force for coordinating fiscal planning, for it consists of the dozen senior members on the spending and tax-writing committees of both houses, plus the Secretary of the Treasury and the Director of the Office of Management and Budget. But, alas, this is another committee that never meets. Its staff produces periodic booklets showing how the government spent less or more in a variety of categories during a certain time period, and that is about the size of it. Senator Byrd used his chairmanship in his later years to enlarge his personal staff by putting added starters on the committee payroll not an uncommon practice for chairmen. When he was succeeded by Representative George Mahon in 1966, there was some hope that new activity would result. It hasn't.

The Joint Economic Committee, particularly under the current aggressive leadership of Senators William Proxmire and Jacob Javits, would dearly love to play a stronger role in pulling together the disparate economic activities of Congress, but the rules do not permit. The economic committee was deliberately conceived as sterile: it cannot originate legislation of any kind, for that, of course, would impinge on existing committees. It can only report to Congress on the President's budget and economic report and offer some general recommendations of its own on priorities and financial sanity. This is a lot better than having no Joint Economic Committee at all, but it falls far short of real effectiveness. The taxing and spending committees pay little attention. Why should they? The joint committee is only a forum, in which no real power resides.

There have been two more ambitious attempts in the past twenty-five years to introduce some order into the fiscal chaos that Congress seems to prefer. Both failed, with the self-interest of small power brokers sharing responsibility with inadequacy of the new mechanisms themselves. In 1946, as part of a major post-war reorganization, a new Joint Budget Committee was established, consisting of all the members of the Appropriations, Ways and Means, and Finance committees. This group was to draft each year by February 15 a budget resolution, a congressional outline of revenue estimates, maximum spending figures, and an over-all appropriation ceiling, to be passed by both houses and then observed. The 1947 resolution went through on time, but the Senate added spending later, and a deadlock developed over how to apply an anticipated surplus. In 1948, the resolution was passed again, but Congress calmly exceeded the spending ceiling by $6 billion.

In 1949, a faltering Congress postponed the deadline for the budget resolution until May 15, but by that time several appropriations bills had already been enacted in the absence of any guidelines, and the whole project was finally abandoned. The problems were manifest: there was too little time to prepare the congressional budget outline, not enough staff, and a thoroughly unwieldy joint committee of some 100 members. But, most important, the new system cost House appropriations subcommittee chairmen some of their power, and that they did not care for.

Predictably anxious to strengthen its own fiscal role, the Senate continued to regard the Joint Budget Committee as a good idea and passed resolutions for its revival seven times between 1952 and 1965. None of them, however, got past the petty fiscal barons of the House, who also managed to derail the only other real try at financial reorganization, made in 1950, when Congress decided to put together a single omnibus appropriation bill.

This move enabled the two full committees to balance out spending among their subcommittees with some view to priority and to produce a single, over-all expenditure figure against which the revenue committees could operate. The first trial was widely judged a success. The 1950 omnibus bill was approved two months earlier than the last of the 1949 appropriation bills, and the total spending figure was $2.3 billion under the Truman budget, which should have satisfied the loudly proclaimed House craving for economy. But another hunger, to retain power, proved stronger than the delight of saving. The next year, a resolution to continue the omnibus system was defeated by the House Appropriations Committee 32–18, despite strong support from the chairman, Representative Clarence Cannon, a staunch conservative. He observed bitterly that the opposition had consisted of "every predatory lobbyist, every pressure group seeking to get its hands into the U.S. Treasury, every bureaucrat seeking to extend his empire."

Obviously, the opposition also included some of the subcommittee chairmen, who could see their autonomy ebbing as the full committee began judging the relative merit of their bills, plus senior members of both parties who thought they could see subcommittee chairmanships only a few years away. The Senate voted in 1953 to try the system again, but the House refused and there has been no effort since.

The 1970 Legislative Reorganization Act made a pass at introducing some coordination into the appropriations process. It specifically required the full House Appropriations Committee to hold broad open hearings on the President's budget as a whole, calling in top Administration officials. More or less perfunctory hearings have been held yearly as a result, lacking effectiveness because they were followed by the same old independent, uncoordinated drafting of thirteen subcommittee spending bills.

What can be done about this intolerable disorder? There must be some system that will permit Congress to exercise a proper constructive role efficiently and, at the same time, be acceptable to Congress. Something has to happen if the government is ever to be effectively and rationally financed, a not unreasonable notion. There have been a lot of suggestions over the years, all well-intentioned, some totally impractical, others aimed squarely at the problem but very difficult to achieve politically. The following proposals are offered with full realization that some may be regarded as beyond the willingness of Congress to work out its own salvation:

1. The fiscal year should be shifted to coincide with the calendar year, giving Congress almost eleven months instead of five in which to process and pass timely appropriation bills for the next

year. This simple change should successfully eliminate the need for stopgap continuing resolutions. It would give federal, state, and local government a clear picture of what assistance Congress is going to provide for a given year well before that year opens. At least, it cannot help but function better than the present jury-rigged system. The idea is supported by the Nixon Administration, which ought to give it a boost in Congress, but has not succeeded yet.

With this much time at hand, Congress could concentrate on authorization bills from March through June, clearing the way for regular appropriations bills from June through October and the supplemental clean-up in November. The Committee for Economic Development suggests that this timetable could be enforced by a pair of deadlines: If an authorizing committee failed to act on an item in the President's budget by, say, August 1, the appropriations committee could fund it, anyway; if the appropriations committee failed to act on a budget item by January 1, it would go into effect automatically for the fiscal year then beginning. This is fairly strong medicine, a substantial grant of further fiscal authority to the executive, and should probably be held in abeyance until Congress is given a fair trial at meeting the new timetable without such sharp prodding.

2. Congress must assume an active role in shaping the budget as a whole if the legislative branch is ever to be more than a dog's tail to the entire governmental process. This can only be done by a group that represents both houses and both the taxing and spending functions. Say, a Joint Fiscal Committee that consisted of the top five members, three majority and two minority, of the appropriations committees, Ways and Means, Finance, and the Joint Economic Committee, for a manageable total of twenty-five.

This committee, backed by a professional staff and an information system that could maintain year-round oversight, would review the President's budget and hold early hearings at which the Secretary of the Treasury, the director of the Office of Management and Budget, and the chairman of the Council of Economic Advisers would testify. The objective would be a broad, over-all look at government spending, an effort to establish relative priorities and to balance income against outgo.

This fiscal committee would then draft its own budget resolution, not a detailed document but an outline consisting of spending limits for each appropriations subcommittee and a revenue total deliberately set to create a specific surplus or deficit. Many of these committee figures would probably be fairly close to the President's, but this process could enable Congress, in its own right, to take, say, $5 billion out of the Administration's defense budget and divide it between education and the environment. Under present procedures, Congress can talk about such a move but is virtually powerless to achieve it in any organized way.

The budget resolution would be submitted to both houses, where it could be amended on the floor, and a final compromise would be worked out in conference by a deadline of June 1 or earlier. From that time on, both appropriating and revenue committees would operate within this outline. It would probably be necessary to make the spending limits and funding requirements binding upon Congress, at least until the system had demonstrated its value. But within the new mandatory ceiling, each appropriations subcommittee would be free to allocate money essentially as it does now. The revenue committees would be comparably free to devise whatever tax increases, decreases, or readjustments they chose, as long as they produced the over-all income figure in the congressional budget resolution. Working in this fashion, Congress could place its own imprint on the financing of the government, making reasoned rather than haphazard judgments and sharing responsibility for the outcome.

Such an arrangement would not materially reduce the political power of the committees and subcommittees involved, only subject them to maximums and minimums that were part of a rational, over-all fiscal plan. Congress as a whole would gain great political influence in terms of taking a stronger hand in the operation of the government. When Congress and the White House were in different political hands, the issue of which branch had been more fiscally responsible or imaginative would become, properly, much clearer to the voters than it is now.

3. Expanding a trend already under way, authorization bills

should cover more than one year, except for new special projects, giving the appropriations committees more time for their annual survey. The Committee for Economic Development has proposed a system of rotating four-year authorizations under which a standing committee would have to review only a quarter of its jurisdiction in detail every year, but this might not be frequent and responsive enough for some members. At the least, Congress could shift to two-year authorizations, passing the authorizing bills in nonelection years so that, when the members wanted time off for the campaign, the appropriation process could be accelerated and the session shortened.

4. Every authorization should carry a full-cost figure where a construction project, a weapons system, or the like is involved, or a five-year projection where services rather than goods are to be provided. Subsequent authorizations would keep this figure up to date, and neither the spending committees nor the public would be deceived as to the size of programs the government was entering into.

5. House appropriations subcommittee hearings should be open to the public and press. The decision-making power exercised there is so strong and pervasive that some reasonable public access to the process is essential. Surely, it would put no undue stress on the legislative machinery to let people learn how much money heads of agencies and departments want and how they intend to spend it, as long as the committee mark-up of each bill, with its unavoidable bargaining and compromises, remained closed.

6. The General Accounting Office should become a major participant in the revival of congressional fiscal activity and responsibility. It already has the authority to conduct broad management analyses of agency performance, but the House Appropriations Committee, which attends to the function, has never been willing to provide the necessary money. This office, which is, after all, an arm of Congress, could be invaluable to the Joint Fiscal Committee in preparing the annual budget resolution and to the appropriation subcommittees during their more detailed examination later. The Legislative Reorganization Act of 1970

made a hesitant move in this direction, but no results have yet been discernible.

Achieving something resembling the above changes is not going to be easy. The members of the appropriations committees make up more than a tenth of the House and nearly a quarter of the Senate, and they are among the most senior and thus most powerful, the most conservative, the most political, and the least intellectual men in Congress. That's saying something. Unless there is substantial support for modernization among this stubborn group, it is going to require an unprecedented wave of public indignation and protest to make any headway toward a rational new system.

When the two octogenarian chairmen of the appropriations committees, Senator Carl Hayden and Representative Clarence Cannon, were locked in bitter dispute in 1962, Cannon argued that the right of the House to originate spending bills "is buttressed by the strongest and most compelling of all rules, the rule of immemorial usage." So are most of the other half-operative mechanisms of the feeble, ineffective congressional fiscal system. Unless they are changed, there is nothing but confusion, impotence, and frustration ahead for Congress in this, its single most basic function.

# 16 · It Took a Really Rotten War

It is very easy to scoff at the protest march-ers who climb the Hill almost daily, convinced that their office calls on senators and vigils on the Capitol steps will sway the national assembly, bringing it to reason. Few members give them any more than a courteous hearing, and even that duty is more likely to be passed down to a staff member. The congressional institution tends to regard protesters with the same suspicion it bestows on those few members in its own ranks who become passionate advocates for a cause, any cause.

But there are times. During the first two years of the Nixon Administration, squadrons of youthful Vietnam protesters flocked to Washington, and one of their folk heroes was Senator Charles Goodell of New York, a once conservative Republican who had lately donned the plumage of a superdove, decrying the war with increasing bitterness as his re-election campaign approached.

The same flying squads regularly descended on the office of Goodell's senior colleague, Senator Jacob Javits, demanding to know why the veteran Republican liberal was not as active in the peace movement. The Javits staff became desperate for some honorable reply, and a group, gathered one evening in a Hill restaurant, scribbled the outline of a new legislative proposal on the back of a menu. The Senator bought the idea, refined the language, and introduced it.

Thus was born the Javits war powers bill, probably the most enterprising attempt in generations to reassert congressional influence over the military decision-making of the White House, possibly even a future milestone in American foreign policy. Congressmen had belittled the war protesters and called Goodell a political gadfly, but together they helped produce a notable advance in a positive new area of congressional activity.

It should surprise no one today to learn that the birth of the Republic was directly followed by a clash between the first President and the first Congress over who was to conduct the foreign affairs of the nation. Then, with the Union only strong enough to take its first hesitant steps, the issue was not making war but avoiding it.

In 1793, Washington issued a proclamation of neutrality in the war between Britain and France. Almost at once, Jeffersonian Republicans protested that this exceeded his authority under the Constitution, that since Congress had specifically been given the power to declare war, only Congress could declare peace. But Hamilton and the Federalists insisted that foreign relations were inescapably an executive responsibility, with the President's powers to be construed broadly and those of Congress strictly.

The Federalist view generally prevailed for more than a century, with the emerging nation so concerned with its domestic affairs that Congress gave little thought to challenging the relatively limited international activities of the President. Not until 1898, when Congress attempted unsuccessfully to prod Grover Cleveland into the Spanish-American war and then helped elect the eminently proddable William McKinley, did the lawmakers assert themselves in the area to any extent.

With Theodore Roosevelt and Woodrow Wilson, the era of strong Presidential leadership in international affairs opened and was interrupted during the next sixty years only by the Senate's 1920 rejection of the Treaty of Versailles and the League of Nations. As the nation moved away from the first world war toward the second, public conviction mounted that this had been a harmful congressional repudiation of sound Presidential judgment. This belief, in turn, contributed to creation of the bipartisan congressional foreign policy that sustained Franklin Roosevelt before and during World War II.

That war was followed by an extraordinary period of foreign policy cooperation, between Congress and the White House and between the political parties within Congress. It produced the United Nations charter ratification, peace treaties, regional security alliances, the Marshall Plan, the Truman Doctrine, and, finally, even united support for the intervention in Korea. Harmony was pervasive, almost institutional. As an instance, the Eightieth Congress (1947–48), with the Republicans in the majority and Truman's popularity on the decline, was tumultuous and bitterly political in most respects. But the Senate Foreign Relations Committee, according to its then chief of staff, Francis Wilcox, took only one vote in the entire two-year period that was not unanimous.

But today, with the nation retreating from a disastrous foreign war and determined to avoid the path to retreat again, congressmen and historians have turned to flyspecking the Constitution and the skimpy record of its drafting in search of clues that may strengthen the international hand of Congress and provide an operative check on the President when blood threatens to be spilled abroad.

This is as real and portentous a matter as Congress faces today. Some of its leaders are convinced that only the legislative representatives of the people now stand across the path to costly, rash, and futile conflict ahead. They believe that Presidential acts of the last two decades confirm this danger, and they are determined to hold in check as much of that presidential power as is required to keep the peace whenever justified and feasible.

There are all kinds of fundamental questions involved. How big a share of the war-making power did the Constitution give Congress? Is Congress wise and experienced enough to share this responsibility now? How could the Founding Fathers ever have anticipated a situation like Vietnam, anyway? Should Congress be limited to making its influence felt on foreign affairs by its presumably unquestioned power to cut off funds for wars and alliances of which it disapproves?

The answers, though elusive, are far from academic. Highly

charged emotionally and politically, they form today's headline and program-interrupting news bulletins. Such answers as can be produced by Congress, negotiated and proclaimed by the President, and survive the courts' testing will direct the course of the nation, domestic as well as foreign, into any future we can now perceive and will correspondingly affect the rest of the world.

The Constitution and its cloud of interpreting historians have woven an intriguing background for this critically important controversy over foreign policy, but it is more realistic to face present facts than to explore past theories. For Congress today, this is the indisputable picture: first, the direct, explicit powers granted by the Constitution, declaring war and ratifying treaties, are no longer of any real consequence, having been commandeered by the President for all practical purposes. Second, the indirect powers given Congress, providing money for the armed forces and making laws to regulate peacetime international activity, have rarely been used in the past to assert effective legislative control over executive decisions. They are being tested now, with growing but still modest success, on what amounts to an emergency basis, filling the need for some sort of countervailing congressional authority until a new balance of power can be struck between the Hill and the White House over international commitments.

The Constitution's declaration that a two-thirds majority of the Senate must "advise and consent" to the ratification of a treaty before it can take effect is no longer a functional grant of power, if it ever really was. For one thing, Presidents do not declare wars any more, and therefore there is no need for treaties to pronounce their formal end. The Korean War ended with agreement on a permanent ceasefire in 1953; the Senate talked about the United States's entry into Korea a good deal thereafter, but did not seem much concerned that it had not officially blessed the terms of exit.

Besides, treaty ratification was almost always a lame sort of after-the-fact power. Only eleven times out of several thousand in the nation's history did the Senate ever reject a treaty that the President had negotiated and submitted. The single signal rejection, the Treaty of Versailles after World War I, was such a thunderous assertion of congressional influence that the executive branch thereafter developed a system of avoiding the fearful trip to Capitol Hill with each new international agreement. Since the Senate fell six votes short of authorizing American participation in the World Court of 1935, only one treaty has been defeated, a minor agreement on settlement of international maritime disputes that went down in 1960. Historically, the treaty power was given more substance by early Presidents, who sent their negotiators' names to the Senate for approval or even submitted tentative treaty terms to test reaction, but nothing like that has happened in the last 100 years.

What has come close to neutralizing the treaty power during the past thirty years is increasing White House reliance on the executive agreement, a piece of paper that looks very much like a treaty, has the same effect as a treaty, but is not called a treaty and thus escapes the requirement for Senate scrutiny and approval. Some are routinely published; the more sensitive are kept secret. Nominally, executive agreements deal with minor ministerial matters, like postal rates, that are deemed beneath congressional interest. In fact, a lot of them do, but some of them don't. For example, the 1953 arrangement under which the United States acquired air bases in Spain in exchange for providing certain protection for that country was an executive agreement. So were the wartime Presidential commitments made at Yalta and Potsdam. So were the agreements, made pursuant to the Senate-approved North Atlantic Treaty Organization treaty, under which our nuclear weapons are deployed abroad. So was the agreement under which Korea agreed to send two divisions to fight in Vietnam in exchange for about $1 billion worth of assistance.

Presidents of both parties, it can be seen, have used the executive agreement freely on matters of major importance when they wanted to keep them secret, when they feared that the Senate would not approve, or both. The numerical trend is revealing. In 1930, the nation concluded 25 treaties and 9 executive agreements; in 1968, the mix had shifted to 16 treaties and 266 executive agreements. Even allowing for the considerable discrepancy between the times and inclinations of Herbert Hoover and Lyndon Johnson, that is quite a shift. When President Nixon took office, the State Department records showed 909 treaties in effect between the United States and other nations, but 3,973 executive agreements. The Senate Foreign Relations Committee failed to persuade Nixon to submit the expiring Spanish bases agreement as a treaty, but its protest won a statement from the Administration that the nation was not committed to defend Spain. (The rising popularity among Presidents of the executive agreement has cost the House very little authority indeed. The only time that representatives have occasion to vote on a treaty is when the Administration fears it cannot command a two-thirds Senate majority and chooses to substitute ratification by a joint resolution, requiring only a simple majority but a vote in both houses instead of one. This technique was used for the annexation of Texas and Hawaii but, along with congressional consultation in general, has fallen into disuse.)

A bold campaign to put Congress into the picture on executive agreements got off to a flying start early in 1972 when the Senate approved unanimously a bill requiring that all such compacts be submitted to Congress for its information. Secret agreements would be forwarded to the two foreign policy committees on the Hill but not otherwise made public. Sponsored by Senator Clifford Case of New Jersey, the legislation would give the President sixty days in which to send executive agreements to Congress. The White House did not oppose the bill in the Senate, but few thought that such a considerable invasion of current Presidential privacy would be written into law without subsequent struggle and compromise. (Curiously, a similar bill under the orthodox Republican sponsorship of Senator William Knowland of California passed the Senate in 1955 as part of an effort to deflate support for more serious restrictions on Presidential treaty-making power proposed by Senator John Bricker of Ohio. The Knowland bill, however, would have required the White House to notify only the Senate of executive agreements and got a predictably cold and terminal reception in the House.)

"We have already given, in example, one effectual check to the Dog of war," Jefferson wrote to Madison in 1789, "by transferring the power of letting him loose from the Executive to the Legislative body, from those who are to spend to those who are to pay."

For, in a startling break with virtually all tradition, the Con stitution specifically granted Congress the power "to declare war." Nowhere else in the world did a legislative body even share in this responsibility. Blackstone had solemnly concluded in his *Commentaries* that monarchs enjoyed "the sole prerogative of making peace and war." The Founding Fathers bravely decided otherwise. But it just hasn't worked out that way.

For the Constitution also pronounces the President the com mander in chief of the armed forces, and the fact that Congress raises, finances, and regulates those forces has never seemed to count for a good deal when it came right down to starting a war. Of the nine generally recognized wars that the nation fought from its birth through 1945, only five were declared by Congress at the request of the President. The precedent set by ignoring authorization for the French naval war of 1798–1800, the Barbary wars of 1801–5 and 1815, and the Mexican border war of 1914–17 probably seemed innocent enough at the time. Today it does not.

Since 1945, the military record of the nation has been littered with undeclared conflicts. Obviously, there are Korea and Viet nam, incredibly costly in lives and money and fought, for all practical purposes, on the decision of one man alone. But there are many other cases in the file. Eisenhower sent troops into Lebanon in 1958 on his own authority. In 1961, Kennedy sanc tioned the Bay of Pigs invasion with the support of American forces. Then, later that same year, he dispatched 100 jungle fighters to South Vietnam as "advisers," again without consulting Congress. Johnson sent thousands more men to Southeast Asia before he felt insecure enough to pressure Congress into the Tonkin Gulf Resolution. He sent troops to the Dominican Repub lic in 1965 and transport planes to the Congo in 1964 and 1967 without any authorization from Congress. In the face of rising congressional hostility, Nixon sent troops into Cambodia in 1970 without authorization or even consultation on Capitol Hill.

Professor Henry Steele Commager of Amherst College told the Senate Foreign Relations Committee in 1971 that the nation was concluding "twenty years marked by repeated. and almost routine, invasions by the executive of the war-making powers assigned by the Constitution to Congress." Looking back over the nation's history, Commager concluded, Presidential decisions to make war without a declaration, except for the Civil War and Korea, were unnecessary and "on the contrary, in almost every instance, the long-run interests of the nation would have been better promoted by consultation and delay."

Recognizing slowly but with increasing certainty that the power to declare war is no longer any kind of power, Congress has taken a series of halting steps toward asserting some new measure of control in this perilous area. It has been a matter of building a constituency, first in the Senate and then even more slowly in the House, for the proposition that Congress should legitimately share in the momentous decisions of war and peace, that it *must* share if reckless ventures like Vietnam are not to tear apart the fabric of the nation again.

The two strongest rallying points for this movement have been Senator Mike Mansfield, the majority leader, and Senator William Fulbright, the Foreign Relations chairman. Freed by the 1968 Republican victory from any lingering vestiges of Johnson Administration loyalty, they began to explore a series of steps to confine and dampen the war in being and to lessen the prospect of future ones, turning existing congressional mechanisms to new uses. There was much talk before and since; this is the record of action:

In June, 1969, the Senate approved the Fulbright-sponsored National Commitments Resolution, an assertion that no use or promise of military action abroad could take place without "affirmative action by Congress specifically intended to give rise to such commitment." The last clause was an undisguised protest that Johnson, now safely in retirement, had stretched the Tonkin Gulf Resolution to cover war activity that Congress had not envisioned as within its scope—or, at least, came later to disapprove.

The National Commitments Resolution, although it passed 70–16, was not exactly a ringing cavalry charge. Fulbright had introduced it eighteen months earlier, then judiciously put it on the back burner during the bitter and confusing election year.

The resolution only expressed "the sense of the Senate," a force members tend to regard with more awe than does the rest of the world. Witness President Nixon, who ordered the Cambodian invasion nine months later as though he had never heard of the resolution at all.

Six months later, Congress took the unprecedented step of attaching to the Defense Appropriations bill an amendment prohibiting any funds to support combat troops in Laos or Thailand. The move resulted directly from hearings held by Senator Stuart Symington that had revealed a considerable, previously secret, United States military involvement in Laos. Rather than challenge, the Nixon Administration accepted the congressional limitation, insisting that it had no intention to move in that direction anyway.

In the wake of the Cambodian adventure of April, 1970, congressional response accelerated. The Senate voted 58–37 to cut off any spending for troops in Cambodia after July 1; the House later agreed to accept this amendment by Senators John Sherman Cooper of Kentucky and Frank Church of Idaho, but by the time it had become law, the Cambodian invaders had withdrawn into South Vietnam, so it did not have any immediate effect. Then the Senate spent two months debating a resolution cosponsored by Senators George McGovern of South Dakota and Mark Hatfield of Oregon that would have prohibited funds for troops in Vietnam after December 31, 1971, finally defeating it 55–39.

Even the House was galvanized into action of a sort. Disturbed by Cambodia, a Foreign Affairs subcommittee headed by Representative Clement Zablocki of Wisconsin held hearings on the President's war powers that resulted in a resolution requiring the President to report to Congress in detail when he committed combat troops overseas. Approved by the House in September, 1970, the measure was hardly a radical step in terms of the direction in which the Senate was moving, but it represented considerable progress for the House, which had not challenged the President on military matters for some three decades.

At the end of the 1970 session, Congress took symbolic revenge on Lyndon Johnson, repealing the Tonkin Gulf Resolution, which he had pushed through in three days in 1964. In the intervening years, some doubt had been cast on the seriousness of the PT-boat attack on U.S. destroyers off Vietnam, an action the President had used to arouse Congress to a pledge of continuing support for the war. But, more important, many members had come to regret their vote to authorize the President "to take all necessary measures to repel any armed attack against the forces of the United States and to prevent further aggression." It was not so much this language they regretted as the broadened purpose that Johnson had made it serve: an open-ended commitment to pour lives and money into one side of a foreign insurrection.

For good or evil, Johnson probably killed the emergency resolution as a means of obtaining congressional approval for military action, a sort of declaration of war, junior grade. Once he had frightened Congress into condoning "all necessary measures," the President took to rebutting his Vietnam critics on the Hill by quoting the resolution and citing the overwhelming vote: only two senators, Ernest Gruening of Alaska and Wayne Morse of Oregon, in the negative, and no representatives at all. Anyone who disagreed with his conduct of the war, Johnson suggested, should move to repeal the resolution.

The Senate came to resent these tactics and was so anxious to run from complicity in the Vietnam War that, when it finally summoned up the courage six years later, the world's greatest deliberative body repealed the Tonkin Gulf Resolution twice—once by a separate resolution that the House ignored and once as a rider on a military sales bill that became law.

By 1971, Congress was ready for still more aggressive action on the war powers issue. The McGovern-Hatfield amendment was strengthened to cover withdrawal of troops by the end of the year from all of Southeast Asia instead of merely Vietnam, withdrawal to be conditional on Hanoi's release of American prisoners of war. The new version was voted down 55–42, with only three more supporters than the year before; earlier, a compromise setting the withdrawal date at June 1, 1972, had been defeated 52–44.

If a Senate majority for Vietnam withdrawal was building very slowly, the House had an even longer distance to go. The day

after the McGovern-Hatfield defeat, an essentially similar amendment to cut off military funds in Southeast Asia at the end of
1971 was beaten there 254–158. The result was not quite as one-
sided as it seemed. For one thing, it was the first time that House
activists had managed to obtain a floor vote on the issue at all;
previously the unsympathetic Democratic leadership had blocked
any clear-cut expression of opinion by the members on Vietnam.
And 158 votes was by no means inconsiderable—60 less than an
absolute majority of the 435 members, but a respectable showing
for the first time out, considering the number of confirmed
jingoist representatives in both parties.

The Senate had not given up. A week later, in June, 1971, a
new amendment sponsored by Senator Mansfield, calling for
troop withdrawal from Southeast Asia in nine months, if the
prisoners of war were released, was approved, 57–42. For the first
time, the Senate peace forces had been able to put together a
majority, although the proposal had been softened to eliminate
any cutoff of funds.

The defeated White House maintained that the Mansfield
amendment would not bind the President, even if it cleared the
House. But when the House voted on a similar proposal, Nixon
personally persuaded Speaker Carl Albert of the virtue of keeping
the President's war-making power unfettered. Albert, to nobody's
particular surprise, did not control his party, but more than
a third of the Democrats voted against the amendment, which
lost, 219–176. The House minority was growing. Late in 1971,
the House finally reached a vote of sorts on the Mansfield amendment itself. In a rarely used parliamentary maneuver, Representative William Fitts Ryan of New York moved to instruct deadlocked conferees to report the foreign aid bill with the Mansfield
proposal intact. The motion, which caught the House leadership
off balance, came within a whisker of passing but lost, 103–101.

A new version of the Cooper-Church amendment, limiting the
use of military assistance funds in Southeast Asia to troop withdrawal, was attached to the foreign aid bill by the Senate Foreign
Relations Committee but stricken on the floor in late October
by a 47–44 vote. The narrow margin was a warning. The next
day the Senate stunned official Washington, and to some extent

itself, by voting to kill the entire foreign aid program, 41–27. Joining forces in this unexpected move were conservatives, who had long been suspicious of foreign aid and jealous of the spending involved, and liberals, who had finally concluded the program was more military than economic—what Senator Church called "arsenal diplomacy." Among facts reinforcing the liberal position was a three-year increase in assistance to Cambodia from nothing to $341 million.

It was clear as soon as the dust settled that the action had been symbolic, that the foreign aid program would continue, scaled down still further and with a greater economic emphasis. But it was also clear that a new chapter had been written in the continuing narrative of White House–Hill relations on foreign policy. Even though the unusual majority that temporarily derailed foreign aid might not be readily reassembled, Congress had demonstrated its independence, its insistence that its voice be heard on the nation's affairs abroad.

Just before 1971 closed, the Foreign Relations Committee set the stage for renewed assaults on the President's powers by unanimously sending two bills to the floor for action during the election year. One was the Case bill on submitting executive agreements to Congress, which the Senate promptly approved in February, 1972. The other was our old friend, the Javits war powers bill, a fundamental attempt to restore congressional authority in an era of undeclared war and unsanctified peace. If enacted, it will permit the President to order the armed forces into action to repel an attack on this country or to protect its citizens abroad but will require congressional approval to continue such military action for more than thirty days. The bill would also specifically prohibit the President from sending military advisers to a foreign country engaged in hostilities without congressional approval.

Senator Javits has enlisted a formidable range of cosponsors, among them the redoubtable Senator John Stennis of Mississippi, chairman of the Armed Services Committee and a fully credentialed hawk. Other original sponsors included conservative Republicans like Senator Robert Dole of Kansas, the party's national chairman, and liberal Democrats like Senator Thomas Eagleton of Missouri.

Among the many historical arguments on which backers of the Javits bill rely is one that tends to limit the constitutional independence of the President as commander in chief. For the commission that Washington held as the first commander in chief ordered him "to observe and follow such orders and directions from time to time as you shall receive from this or a future Congress of the said United Colonies or a committee of Congress for that purpose appointed." The counterargument is that these instructions, covering the general's military leadership from 1775–83, predate both the drafting of the Constitution and Washington's concurrent service as President and commander in chief under its authority. It still makes a nice-sounding precedent.

Arguing more currently, Javits maintained that the nation must be protected against "the Presidential war," of which Vietnam has become the archetype, the war prosecuted with only belated and inadequate congressional sanction. A convert from hawk to dove himself, the New York senator noted that "over the past five years it has been the Congress and not the President which has demonstrated an awareness and a responsiveness to the national will and the national mood respecting Vietnam."

In the same context, Professor Richard Morris of Columbia University told the Foreign Relations Committee that adoption of the Javits plan would restore to the U.S. Government "safeguards prudently inserted into the Constitution by men who were generally agreed that going to war and continuing at war were too serious and awesome responsibilities to be left to the decision of one man alone."

Underlying the case for requiring this kind of early congressional sanction is the fact that writing fund limitations later into bills that finance a flourishing although unpopular war is a very ineffective way to deal with the problem. As witness the refusal of the Senate, much less the House, to take such drastic action in Vietnam itself. It is simply asking a good deal of a congressman to refuse financial support for American combat troops that are following orders on a dangerous foreign engagement, however questionable it may be legally, morally, or politically.

In April of 1972, more promptly than anyone had anticipated, the Senate passed the war powers bill by a thumping 68 to 16 vote. The Nixon Administration opposed the measure as unduly restrictive, but all four Republican Senate leaders voted for it. Whether the House, still slow to reassert congressional prerogative in the foreign policy area, would follow suit remained unclear, as did the prospect of a Presidential veto. But, if the bill becomes law and Congress is returned to a position of sharing the decision to make war—or whatever the contemporary euphemism may be—all the troublesome amendments attempting to impose withdrawal deadlines or cut off funds will presumably become unnecessary. And, if Congress, or at least the senior members of its foreign policy committees, can be informed of the executive agreements that form much of the over-all national commitment abroad, there will be less likelihood of a President's moving militarily without congressional approval or of Congress refusing such approval where the full facts support it.

Is Congress really equipped to handle this imposing responsibility as things stand today? In spirit, but probably not in truth. Firm judgments are difficult because the Senate has only been trying to assume a significant role for a half-dozen years now, and in the House the desire to get in on the action has been less perceptible and even more recent. But there remains serious doubt that the rusty, ante-bellum machinery of Congress is adequate to handle the task and that there is enough information available on the Hill to ensure that sounder judgments are reached.

The Senate Foreign Relations Committee has been in continuous existence since 1816, often understaffed, ill informed, and pig-headed—but rarely inactive. (Even in a period of such international withdrawal as the Grant Administration, its chairman, Senator Charles Sumner, was forced out by the President for his refusal to cooperate in the annexation of Santo Domingo.) In the view of some—but not all—of those who believe in the reassertion of congressional authority, the committee reached its finest hour under Chairman Fulbright and his assembly of like-minded activists.

The House Foreign Affairs Committee—you cannot escape the hoary distinction: Senators have relations but representatives only affairs—came along in 1822 and spent the next 125 years looking for something significant to do. The Senate had the war-declaring and treaty-making power, so the Constitution said, and the House had to content itself with authorizing State Department funds and processing bills on international affairs in an era when there weren't any international affairs to speak of. It only began to take on some importance after World War II, as foreign aid and an expanding variety of foreign policy legislation grew out of vastly expanded American commitments abroad.

Representative Thomas Morgan, the Foreign Affairs chairman, is a sixty-five-year-old small-town doctor from the hills of southwestern Pennsylvania who has conceived of his role as "the quarterback, not the coach," and the second-string quarterback at that. Beginning to sense House potential in an assertive Congress, he reshaped his committee in 1971 by giving important subcommittee chairmanships to four of the young, more active members, none of them higher than tenth in seniority among his twenty Democrats.

There is some feeling among members that Congress could have a greater impact on foreign policy if the two joint subcommittees of the armed services and appropriations committees that deal with the Central Intelligence Agency were more active. It remains largely a feeling, however, because of the heavy cloak of security involved; until relatively recently, there was no official admission that this very secret and tentative oversight existed at all.

Going beyond the thirty-day deadline of the Javits bill, Professor Commager would establish two new Senate committees: one with a quorum always present in Washington that the President would be required to consult before any action "that might involve the nation in armed conflict," the other to consult with the President on all executive agreements and designate those it chose to as treaties. Such proposals probably serve their purpose if they press the Administration into accepting the less drastic Javits plan.

The most sensible suggestion for coordinating the congressional foreign policy function would create a new Joint National Security Committee of the senior members of the foreign policy, armed services, and appropriations committees in each house, including the appropriations subcommittee chairmen directly involved. Initially, the most that could be expected would be a single forum in which the diplomatic, military, and fiscal aspects of a problem such as the Middle East could be aired and even conceivably harmonized.

Although it may seem unlikely today, it is possible that such a national security group could evolve and then update a set of congressional foreign policy guidelines, not unlike the fiscal guidelines proposed in the last chapter to introduce some order and reason into congressional financial control. Such guidelines, admittedly less binding, might constitute a congressional policy to reinforce or set against that of the President; often they might divide along party lines into majority and minority congressional positions.

Under any circumstances, a Joint National Security Committee that met monthly could not help but improve the lines of congressional communication between the powerful but independent men on the Hill who seem certain to be playing a larger role in international affairs, even if only a closed debate were involved. For today, with the exception of the enlightened Senate Appropriations Committee policy of bringing into its meetings, ex officio, members from Armed Services and Foreign Relations, there is no coordination in the area worth mentioning.

Reorganized structurally or not, Congress is going to have to get better information about world affairs on which to base its decisions. There is simply no blinking the fact that the elected legislators will have more and more to say about such matters. They are likely to be more reflective of public opinion, as opposed to diplomatic expertise, than the State Department; if the present trend continues, it is also likely the public will know more and more about congressional foreign policy positions, as they conflict with the President's views and react to them.

Augmented committee staff resources plus the advent of a computer-based information system could achieve an essential increase in foreign policy data from outside the government, but the White

House and the State Department are going to have to share more and withhold less—if only for the selfish reason that additional facts may lead Congress to the same conclusion that the career foreign service men have already reached. For a simple example, two of the three men responsible for American foreign policy at the highest level are now outside the reach of Congress. The President, with full propriety, does not respond to any summons from the legislative branch. His chief lieutenant in the area, Henry Kissinger, declines to exchange views with congressional leaders except on his own terms, at semisocial, off-the-record gatherings held irregularly at his invitation. This leaves Secretary of State Willam Rogers, who is by far the most communicative of the three but, regrettably, the least influential. His reputation on Capitol Hill has never been the same since his testimony three days before the Cambodian incursion indicated, after the fact, that he had either been unaware of the impending move or had deliberately deceived the senators—equally disturbing alternatives.

White House reluctance to keep Congress up to date on foreign policy may be best symbolized by the fact that, for many months of the Nixon Administration, Tass, the Soviet news agency, was provided with a transcript of Kissinger's background press briefings, designed as the basis for anonymous newspaper articles, but Senator Fulbright could not get the same copy, except through unofficial channels. Better information for Congress could help moderate the historic adversary relationship that has developed between the legislative and executive branches. To preserve the image if not the fact of unity, the White House and the State Department like to conduct their foreign policy debates internally, shutting out Congress until the issues have been resolved. Then the press tends to focus on any congressional disagreement, and publicity-conscious members are often anxious to get into the picture, televised or otherwise.

Better information, particularly intelligence in advance of a real or threatened international crisis, can only serve to improve relations between executive and legislative leaders. Congressional investigations, like those undertaken in the wake of the Dominican intervention and the Tonkin Gulf Resolution, will recur and should, to keep the Administration honest. But they would be likely to be less frequent and far less embarrassing for both the President and the nation if Congress were not as shocked as the public by the events in the first place.

In his informative book *Congress, the Executive, and Foreign Policy*, Francis O. Wilcox, who served uniquely as both chief of staff of the Senate Foreign Relations Committee and then Assistant Secretary of State, suggests that the information gap, at least, could be bridged by the creation of a legislative-executive national security commission.

Imposing and surely unwieldy as an action group, it would include the President, the Vice President, the secretaries of State and Defense, the chairmen of the Joint Chiefs of Staff and the Atomic Energy Commission, the director of the Central Intelligence Agency, the President's national security adviser, and, besides, the congressional leaders and the senior members of the foreign policy, military, and appropriations committees. It would discuss but not decide issues, preserving the Hill representatives' right to dissent from policy later. At a minimum, it would certainly promote better understanding of the congressional viewpoint by the President and of the Administration's developing policies by the congressional leadership.

Whether transmission of information from the White House and State Department to Congress can lead the way to actual consultation with the lawmakers before policy is frozen remains to be seen. From the Administration's point of view, consultation is constructive when it produces agreement, bad when it produces opposition. But Congress—certainly much of the present one— is not going to be co-opted into merely reflecting Administration policy when it feels there is an important adversary role to be played.

Wilcox, who has seen the problem from both ends of Pennsylvania Avenue, says that Congress would be better equipped and more willing to cooperate with the Administration in an international crisis (fire-fighting) if it has been consulted on the most important issues as they developed (fire prevention). He also argues cogently that a foreign policy to which Congress has contributed materially is likely to be more stable and broadly based, reflecting a real national consensus.

"Call it intuition, call it horse sense, call it sound political judgement," the career official wrote, "legislators are invaluable in helping to strike a tolerable balance between the views of the expert and those of the general public. They help bridge an otherwise unbridgeable gap in the formation of our foreign policy."

# 17 · Life or Death

"To get the bad customs of a country chang'd, and new ones, though better, introduc'd," Benjamin Franklin wrote in 1787, "it is necessary first to remove the Prejudices of the People, enlighten their ignorance, and convince them that their Interest will be promoted by the propos'd; and this is not the work of a Day." But it need not take centuries, either.

In 1976, the United States will celebrate its two hundredth birthday, surely an occasion for stocktaking. The offical observance will be held in Philadelphia, at the scene of the nativity. But Washington is certain to attract more than its usual seasonal flood of thousands upon thousands of visitors, curious for a glimpse of how their government looks and what it does.

Many of these people will make the pilgrimage to Capitol Hill, to watch the legislative branch at work and judge whether anything constructive can be found under way in the halls of Congress. I can see two visions of what they may find. Both these views of 1976 may seem highly—and equally—improbable to you. But they are not. The compromise area between them becomes thinner and narrower with each passing day. More and more, as Congress continues to demonstrate its incapacity to adapt a great but imperfectly realized concept to the times it must serve, the people have less and less choice. If Congress can make the arduous and humbling decision to face reality and find effectiveness, there can be great hope, stability, and even inspiration in the institution. If it cannot, there is nothing but trouble ahead, like it or not.

There is less time left to avert disaster than almost anyone in Congress suspects, although there can be opportunity, money, and knowledge enough to do the job if the people recognize that today's Congress is basically inadequate and unresponsive—and demand change. Only this realization, broadly held and keenly pursued, can provoke the laggard members into reshaping an institution worthy of the Capitol and the people it was built to serve. If the job is done, the visitor to Washington in 1976 may find:

• A Congress directed by men and women chosen democratically for their intelligence, vigor, and effectiveness, rather than elevated automatically to power without any regard to their quality. (The new system would attract and hold better members, weeding out the inert and inept and promoting rather than discouraging diligence and imagination.)

• A Congress that is not afraid to operate in the open light of public attention, its sessions regularly televised, its committee hearings open, and its members fully informed, both as to the immediate questions before them and the increasingly complex long-range issues with which they must deal.

• A Senate in which majority rule has been restored with suitable guarantees for full but not endless discussion of the great issues, where a militant minority can no longer strangle the will of the House, where matters of moment are decided each on its own merits rather than coupled and interwoven for political advantage.

• A House that votes swiftly and identifiably, freed of the past tyranny of an uncontrollable Rules Committee, a body that surrenders its power to rewrite major legislation on the floor only if there has been genuine public access to its preparation.

• A Congress that sets exemplary standards of public behavior and personal honesty and demonstrably lives up to them, that requires fast and full reporting by lobbyists of every stripe and does not hesitate to expose any sort of illegitimate pressure, whatever the source.

• A Congress that makes independent, informed judgments in the areas of fiscal management and foreign policy, counterbalancing and supplementing those of the President and the executive branch, with a legislative budget and perhaps even a legislative foreign policy representing the collective judgment of the two houses, finally brought together.

It is easy to call such a picture visionary, to argue that the past record of Congress in recognizing its own shortcomings makes this sunny prospect dim indeed. But consider for a moment an alternative view that does not seem, taken squarely, any more unlikely:

It is the summer of the bicentennial year, 1976, and a protest encampment fills the Mall, just below the Capitol, and stretches west to the Washington Monument and beyond. Five years before, it had been the Vietnam War that drew thousands of disillusioned citizens to the same wide strip of public park land, in symbolic and peaceful protest. Now the issue is broader: It is the competence of the change-making arm of the government to effect change.

In the great marble monument on Jenkins Heights, very little is different from what it was 4—or 20 or 100—years before. The sitting Congress has managed to provide only a fragment of the money to run the government, although the fiscal year is already more than a month old. The Senate is mired in inaction while an unwieldy tax and trade bill is being filibustered from two sides, the liberals attacking one section and the conservatives another.

A conference committee has refused to accept any of a $10 billion reduction in defense spending voted by the Senate, because the senators in the conference, all of whom voted against the cut on the floor, collapsed under modest pressure early in the secret sessions and accepted the House version. A critically needed bill for intensive ghetto education is stalled in the House because the seventy-seven-year-old chairman of the appropriations subcommittee is both Southern and senile, and there is no way to deal with him. No way.

The House Appropriations Committee has authorized spending higher by some $5 billion than the most optimistic estimates of what the current tax structure will support, but the Ways and Means Committee has refused to hold hearings on any of the tax proposals introduced. A committee chairman named by a lobbyist at his bribery trial has been under private investigation for nearly a year by the Senate Ethics Committee, but no action has been taken.

Down on the Mall, in tents and sleeping bags, an army of the disaffected and disillusioned has gathered. Unlike the Vietnam veterans, they do not all have a single cause; there are housewives who feel cheated by lax consumer legislation, middle-income taxpayers who have broken under their growing share of the burden, blacks denied equal rights, young people who resent arbitrary rule by the aged, old people whose pensions are so inadequate as to be fraudulent.

But, most compelling of all, the protesters are bound together by their joint discovery that there is no hope for them in the change-making machinery of their government, as it exists. A majority of the Senate would spend less for war and more for education, but filibusters keep the bills from the floor. The House Judiciary Committee has approved a bold and innovative new civil rights bill, but the Rules Committee chairman will not call a meeting to consider it. In an election year, the senators and representatives are fearful, scrambling for campaign contributions and leery of any cause that might discourage them.

The protest encampment grows steadily day by day as more and more dissatisfied and frustrated Americans come to the nation's capital. Soon the mass of occupying citizens stretches back from the Washington Monument to the Lincoln Memorial and out into the parks of the Tidal Basin.

Finally, the marches, speeches, and symbolic gestures become inadequate in the face of stony congressional inaction. Late one night, a sympathetic official of the Smithsonian quietly opens a back door, and the museum's stock of muskets and rifles from the Revolution and the Civil War is passed out to a squadron of protest leaders. No ammunition, just the historic old weapons.

The next day at noon, as the Senate and House convene, the entire encampment begins to move in a body, led by men and women carrying the old guns. The Capitol guards fall back before an immense body of peaceful but determined citizens. Dimly within the Senate and House chambers, members begin to hear the sound of rifle butts pounding in unison against the ground, against the marble steps, on the tile floors of the Capitol corridors, then on the carpets of the lobby.

Into the two chambers the people stream—old, young, black, white, men, women, well-to-do, poor and poorer, to the cadenced thud of the weapons. As the members retreat, a protest leader takes the rostrum and says, "We occupy the Congress of the United States on behalf of the people of the United States."

# Bibliography

BOOKS

BOLLING, RICHARD. *House Out of Order*. New York: E. P. Dutton, 1965.

———. *Power in the House*. New York: E. P. Dutton, 1968.

BROWNSON, CHARLES B. *Congressional Staff Directory*. Washington: Congressional Staff Directory, annual.

CHARTRAND, ROBERT L., KENNETH JANDA, and MICHAEL HUGO, eds. *Information Support, Program Budgeting and the Congress*. New York: Macmillan Co., 1968.

CLAPP, CHARLES L. *The Congressman*. Washington, D.C.: The Brookings Institution, 1963.

CLARK, JOSEPH S. *Congress: The Sapless Branch*. New York: Harper & Row, 1964.

CLEVELAND, JAMES C., ed. *We Propose: A Modern Congress*. House Republican Task Force on Congressional Reform and Minority Staffing. New York: McGraw-Hill Book Co., 1966.

Committee for Economic Development. *Making Congress More Effective*. New York: Committee for Economic Development, 1970.

Congressional Quarterly. *Congress and the Nation 1945–64*. Washington, D.C.: Congressional Quarterly Service, 1965.

———. *Congress and the Nation 1965–68*. Washington, D.C.: Congressional Quarterly Service, 1969.

298   *Bibliography*

————. *Guide to the Congress of the United States.* Washington, D.C.: Congressional Quarterly Service, 1971.

DAVIDSON, ROGER H., DAVID KOVENOCK, and MICHAEL O'LEARY. *Congress in Crisis.* New York: Hawthorn Books, 1966.

DEGRAZIA, ALFRED, ed. *Congress: The First Branch of Government.* Garden City, N.Y.: Doubleday & Co., 1967.

DONHAM, PHILIP, and ROBERT J. FAHEY. *Congress Needs Help.* New York: Random House, 1966.

EVANS, ROWLAND, and ROBERT NOVAK. *Lyndon B. Johnson: The Exercise of Power.* New York: New American Library, 1966.

GALLOWAY, GEORGE B. *Congress at the Crossroads.* New York: Thomas Y. Crowell Co., 1946.

————. *History of the House of Representatives.* New York: Thomas Y. Crowell Co., 1969.

GRIFFITH, ERNEST S. *Congress: Its Contemporary Role.* New York: New York University Press, 1967.

HAYNES, GEORGE H. *The Senate of the United States.* Boston: Houghton Mifflin Co., 1938.

HORN, STEPHEN. *Unused Power: The Work of the Senate Committee on Appropriations.* Washington, D.C.: The Brookings Institution, 1970.

KIRBY, JAMES C., JR. *Congress and the Public Trust.* Report of the Association of the Bar of the City of New York Special Committee on Congressional Ethics. New York: Atheneum, 1970.

LAHR, RAYMOND M., and J. WILLIAM THEIS. *Congress: Power and Purpose on Capitol Hill.* Boston: Allyn and Bacon, 1969.

MCCLOSKEY, PAUL N., JR. *Truth and Untruth: Political Deceit in America.* New York: Simon & Schuster, 1972.

MACNEIL, NEIL. *Forge of Democracy: The House of Representatives.* New York: David McKay Co., 1963.

MILLER, CLEM. *Member of the House: Letters of a Congressman.* New York: Charles Scribner's Sons, 1962.

MORROW, WILLIAM L. *Congressional Committees.* New York: Charles Scribner's Sons, 1969.

PEARSON, DREW, and JACK ANDERSON. *The Case Against Congress.* New York: Simon & Schuster, 1968.

RIDDICK, FLOYD M. *The United States Congress: Organization and Procedure*. Manassas, Va.: National Capitol Publishers, 1949.

SALOMA, JOHN S., III. *Congress and the New Politics*. Boston: Little, Brown & Co., 1969.

SHUSTER, ALVIN, ed. *Washington: The New York Times Guide to the Nation's Capitol*. Washington, D.C.: Robert B. Luce, 1967.

TRUMAN, DAVID B. *The Governmental Process*. New York: Alfred A. Knopf, 1964.

Twentieth Century Fund. Task Force on Financing Congressional Campaigns. *Electing Congress: The Financial Dilemma*. New York: Twentieth Century Fund, 1970.

U.S. Capitol Historical Society. *We, the People: The Story of the United States Capitol*. Washington, D.C.: National Geographic Society, 1969.

WHITE, WILLIAM S. *Citadel: The Story of the U.S. Senate*. New York: Harper & Bros., 1956.

WILCOX, FRANCIS O. *Congress, the Executive, and Foreign Policy*. New York: Harper & Row, 1971.

WILSON, WOODROW. *Congressional Government*. New York: Meridian Books, 1956.

## GOVERNMENT DOCUMENTS

CANNON, CLARENCE. U.S. House. *Cannon's Procedure in the House of Representatives*. Washington, D.C.: Government Printing Office, 1963.

HARRISON, JAMES L. *Biographical Directory of the American Congress*. Washington, D.C.: Government Printing Office, 1950.

U.S. Congress. House of Representatives. *Jefferson's Manual and Rules of the House of Representatives*. Washington, D.C.: Government Printing Office, 1971.

U.S. Congress. Joint Committee on Printing. *Congressional Directory*. Washington, D.C.: Government Printing Office, annual.

U.S. Congress. Joint Committee on the Organization of the Congress. *Organization of Congress. Interim Report*. Washington, D.C.: Government Printing Office, 1965.

————. *Organization of Congress. Second Interim Report.* Washington, D.C.: Government Printing Office, 1965.

U.S. Senate. Appropriations Committee. *The Authority of the Senate to Originate Appropriations Bills.* Washington, D.C.: Government Printing Office, 1963.

U.S. Senate. Committee on Rules and Administration. *Standing Rules of the United States Senate.* Washington, D.C.: Government Printing Office, 1971.

WATKINS, CHARLES L., and FLOYD M. RIDDICK. *Senate Procedure, Precedents and Practices.* Washington, D.C.: Government Printing Office, 1958.

# Index